# A GUIDE TO
# AMERICAN ZOOS & AQUARIUMS

Other books from Willow Press:

A Birder's Guide to the Cincinnati Tristate, 1988
Hiking Ohio, Scenic Trails of the Buckeye State, 1990
Walking the Denver-Boulder Region, 1992
Walking Cincinnati (2nd Edition, November, 1993)

*About the Authors:*

*Darcy & Robert Folzenlogen are physicians, outdoor enthusiasts and certified zoo lovers. They have written and published a variety of regional guides, including those listed above. All of their books are dedicated to the themes of open space protection, wildlife conservation and historic preservation.*

# A Guide To
# AMERICAN ZOOS & AQUARIUMS

By Darcy & Robert Folzenlogen

## WILLOW PRESS
Littleton, Colorado
Glendale, Ohio

**ISBN 0-9620685-4-3**
**Library of Congress Catalog Card Number: 93-93806**


Published by    **Willow Press**
                6053 S. Platte Canyon Rd.
                Littleton, Colorado 80123

                1030 Willow Ave.
                Glendale, Ohio 45246

Printed by   Otto Zimmerman & Son Company Inc.
             Newport, Kentucky

Typesetting by  Debbie Metz
                Mass Marketing Inc.
                Cincinnati, Ohio


Cover illustration by   Jeff Folzenlogen
                        3441 Telford
                        Cincinnati, Ohio 45220
Maps by author
Photos courtesy of the Zoos & Aquariums

For Sarah, Zach and Ally

# ACKNOWLEDGEMENTS

This Guide could not have been produced without the assistance of the Zoo & Aquarium directors and their staffs. Public relations personnel were kind enough to send along background information and provided many of the photos that appear in this book. Special thanks to Beth Zebrowski, Public Affairs Director at the AAZPA, for her assistance.

We thank Jan Jolley, at Otto Zimmerman & Son Company, Debbie Metz, at Mass Marketing Inc., and Jeff Folzenlogen for their technical and creative assistance. Thanks also to the many photographers whose pictures grace the pages of this guide.

As always, our thanks to Sarah, Zach and Ally for their love and understanding.

*— Darcy & Robert Folzenlogen*

# CONTENTS

# INTRODUCTION

This book is a celebration of the modern zoo and aquarium. Designed to appeal to tourists, zoo lovers and conservationists, the guide places emphasis on the vital role that zoos and aquariums play in public education, research and wildlife conservation.

Those who monitor the lifestyle of Americans report that more of us visit zoos and aquariums each year than attend all paid sporting events combined. We hope that this trend reflects a growing interest in our natural heritage and feel certain that the evolution of the modern zoo is largely responsible for this social phenomenon.

## The Renaissance

Many of us who grew up before 1960 often had mixed emotions during a visit to the zoo. The excitement of seeing exotic animals from far-away lands was tempered by the spectacle of bored or neurotic creatures confined to small cells of concrete and steel.

During the 1930s, a number of zoos, including the Bronx, Detroit and St. Louis Zoos, introduced the concept of naturalized exhibits. Rock cliffs and moats replaced the steel bars and grassy, landscaped enclosures took the place of concrete paddocks. By the late 1960s this revolution was in full swing and newer zoos were designed to take full advantage of these more natural habitats. Today, "rain forests," "coral reefs" and "arctic wetlands" are found from both coasts to the Great Plains.

In concert with this trend toward spacious, mixed-species exhibits, zoos began to shift their emphasis from human entertainment to public education, research and conservation. Dwindling wildlife habitat, poaching, environmental pollution and other man-induced problems had begun to decimate wild animal populations and many species were on the verge of extinction. Rallying behind conservation organizations and led by the American Association of Zoological Parks & Aquariums, American zoos joined the worldwide effort to protect, breed and re-introduce endangered and threatened species of wildlife.

The naturalized exhibits fostered this effort, freeing the animals to assume their instinctive behaviors and greatly improving the science of captive propagation. The Arabian oryx, golden lion tamarin, black-footed ferret and Bali mynah are but a few species to benefit from these national and international breeding programs.

# The AAZPA

Formed in 1924, the American Association of Zoological Parks & Aquariums became a branch of the National Recreation & Park Association in 1966. Recognizing the need to gain more independence and to expand its commitment to conservation and education, the AAZPA split from the NRPA in September, 1971. A charter of incorporation was filed in November of that year and the organization opened its Executive Offices in Wheeling, West Virginia, on January 3, 1972.

Now headquartered in Bethesda, Maryland, the AAZPA represents the interests of North American zoos, wildlife parks and aquariums and ensures that its member institutions abide by the highest professional standards. Accreditation by the AAZPA is a lengthy process and, since 1980, has become mandatory for membership in the organization. Many of the newer zoos and aquariums in this guide are still in the process of gaining accreditation and are thus not yet members of this prestigious Association.

At its midyear meeting in 1980, the AAZPA's Board of Directors voted to make conservation the highest priority of the Association. A master plan for coordinated, captive breeding of threatened and endangered species was set in motion, eventually leading to the Species Survival Plans of the AAZPA. Member institutions take part in this program by loaning and/or trading animals to ensure genetic diversity of the offspring and by committing themselves to the propagation and eventual re-introduction of these endangered species.

The AAZPA's Conservation Endowment Fund was established in 1984 to solicit and coordinate funding of the Association's conservation programs. With the continued support of its member institutions, private corporations and a concerned public, the AAZPA is sure to remain a vital force in the preservation of our vanishing wildlife.

# A Guide to American Zoos & Aquariums

In the spirit of the modern zoo, this guide is designed to appeal to tourists, zoo lovers and wildlife conservationists. For the traveler, the book offers directions to the zoos and aquariums, hours of operation, admission fees, visitor programs and a schedule of seasonal festivals. Though information is current, as of early 1993, the reader should understand that fees and schedules are always subject to change.

Zoo lovers will enjoy perusing the list of special exhibits and are introduced to the future plans of their favorite zoos and aquariums. Most importantly, this guide emphasizes the vital role that modern zoos and aquariums play in public education and wildlife conservation. Captive breeding achievements and research activities are listed for each facility.

Although we have personally visited many of the zoos and aquariums included in this guide, we depended upon the cooperation of directors and public relations personnel to ensure that information in the guide is accurate and up-to-date. We are pleased to report that most institutions were very enthusiastic about our project and their generous contribution to our research was sincerely appreciated. Regretably, some facilities did not respond to our request for information or provided too little data to be included in this guide. The space committed to each zoo and aquarium in this book is directly proportional to the amount of information received.

No effort was made to "rank" the institutions in this guide and we hope that readers and visitors will judge American zoos and aquariums not by their size or age but by their level of commitment to education, research and conservation.

# How to get involved

You can become involved in the wildlife conservation movement in many ways. Here are but a few ideas:

- Become a member of your local zoo or aquarium. Membership support is crucial to the welfare of modern zoos and aquariums.
- Become a zoo/aquarium volunteer. Almost all of the institutions in this guide train volunteers and rely on their services.
- Provide financial and/or active support for local, state, national and international wildlife conservation organizations. Many of these groups are listed in the Appendix of this book.
- Participate in local cleanup and recycling programs. Loss of habitat remains the primary threat to our native wildlife species.
- Contact your elected representatives to show support for conservation initiatives.

In a perfect world there would be a sufficient quantity and diversity of untouched wilderness to ensure the well-being of all species on this planet. Unfortunately, human encroachment, agriculture, environmental pollution, poaching and "land development" have all taken a toll on the health of earth's ecosystems. Until the tide can be turned, zoos and aquariums will remain important refuges for threatened and endangered species of wildlife.

— Darcy & Robert Folzenlogen

# I. NORTHEAST REGION

1. **New England Aquarium** (Boston, Massachusetts)
2. **Franklin Park Zoo** (Boston, Massachusetts)
3. **Walter D. Stone Memorial Zoo** (Stoneham, Massachusetts)
4. **Roger Williams Park Zoo** (Providence, Rhode Island)
5. **Mystic Marinelife Aquarium** (Mystic, Connecticut)
6. **Beardsley Zoological Gardens** (Bridgeport, Connecticut)
7. **Aquarium of Niagara Falls** (Niagara Falls, New York)
8. **Buffalo Zoological Gardens** (Buffalo, New York)
9. **Seneca Park Zoo** (Rochester, New York)
10. **Burnet Park Zoo** (Syracuse, New York)
11. **Utica Zoo** (Utica, New York)
12. **Ross Park Zoo** (Binghamton, New York)
13. **Bronx Zoo/International Wildlife Conservation Park** (Bronx, New York)
14. **Central Park Wildlife Conservation Center** (New York, New York)
15. **Queens Wildlife Conservation Center** (Queens, New York)
16. **New York's Aquarium for Wildlife Conservation** (Brooklyn, New York)
17. **Staten Island Zoo** (Staten Island, New York)
18. **The Erie Zoo** (Erie, Pennsylvania)
19. **Pittsburgh Zoo** (Pittsburgh, Pennsylvania)
20. **The Aviary** (Pittsburgh, Pennsylvania)
21. **Clyde Peeling's Reptiland, Ltd.** (Allenwood, Pennsylvania)
22. **ZOOAMERICA® North American Wildlife Park** (Hershey, Pennsylvania)
23. **Philadelphia Zoological Garden** (Philadelphia, Pennsylvania)
24. **Bergen County Zoological Park** (Paramus, New Jersey)
25. **Thomas H. Kean New Jersey State Aquarium at Camden** (Camden, New Jersey)
26. **Cape May County Park Zoo** (Cape May Court House, New Jersey)
27. **Oglebay's Good Children's Zoo** (Wheeling, West Virginia)
28. **The Baltimore Zoo** (Baltimore, Maryland)
29. **The National Aquarium in Baltimore** (Baltimore, Maryland)
30. **Salisbury Zoological Park** (Salisbury, Maryland)
31. **Brandywine Zoo** (Wilmington, Delaware)
32. **National Zoological Park** (Washington, D.C.)

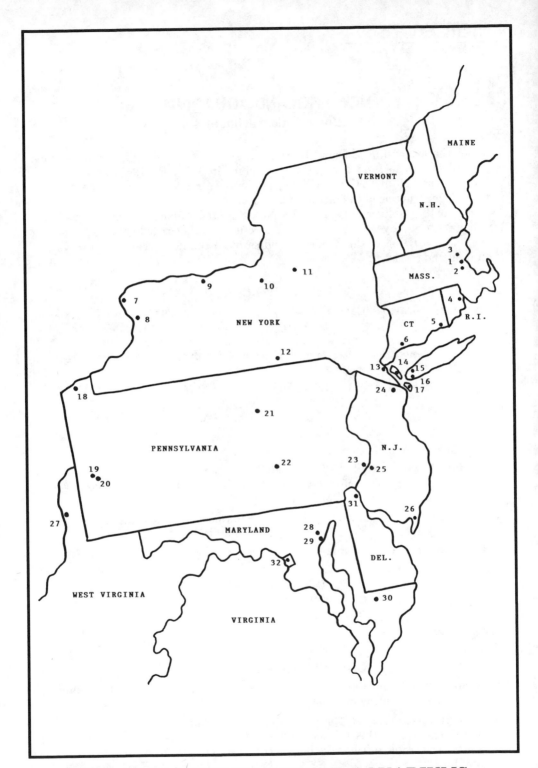

# NORTHEAST REGION ZOOS & AQUARIUMS

# 1

## NEW ENGLAND AQUARIUM
### Boston, Massachusetts

Under the leadership of David B. Stone, a group of New England businessmen organized efforts to fund a regional Aquarium in 1957. By 1965 the Aquarium Corporation had acquired Central Wharf, part of Boston's Waterfront Urban Renewal Plan, and construction of the facility was begun.

Opened to the public in June, 1969, the New England Aquarium has averaged over 1 million visitors per year. This private, nonprofit institution is dedicated to furthering man's understanding of the aquatic world through public education, conservation, exhibition and research.

## VISITOR INFORMATION

**Directions:** Located at Central Wharf on Boston's historic waterfront, three blocks from Faneuil Hall Marketplace. From the Southeast Expressway (Route 3), exit at Atlantic Avenue (if travelling north) or at Dock Square/Callahan Tunnel (if travelling south). Fish logo signs direct you to the Aquarium.

**Open to the Public:** July 1 to Labor Day: 9 AM-6 PM MTF, 9 AM-8 PM WTh, 9 AM-7 PM Sat., Sun. & Holidays; Remainder of year: 9 AM-5 PM MTWF, 9 AM-8 PM Thur., 9 AM-6 PM Sat., Sun. & Holidays

**Closed:** Thanksgiving & Christmas Day; opens at noon on New Years Day

**Admission (1993):** Adult: $7.50   Child: $3.50   Senior: $6.50
Discounted rates on Thursdays and Summer Wednesdays from 4 PM-8 PM

**Parking Fee:** No on-site parking; discount available at Rowes Wharf Hotel and at International Place (latter after 4:30 PM and weekends)

**Annual Membership:** Individual: $35   Couple: $45   Family: $55

**Programs & Tours:** The Aquarium sponsors a variety of educational programs including field trips and school outreach presentations. Also offers "Whale Watch" excursions (see Seasonal Festivals & Programs)

**AAZPA Member:** Yes

## COLLECTIONS & EXHIBITS

**Collection:** The Aquarium's current collection includes more than 9700 specimens, representing over 600 species of aquatic life.

**Special Exhibits** at the New England Aquarium include:
Giant Ocean Tank - this 187,000 gallon exhibit features sea turtles, moray eels, sharks and tropical fish; a Caribbean coral reef rises in the center of this 4-story habitat.

Edge of the Sea - this hands-on exhibit re-creates the tidal pool habitat of rocky coastlines.

The Ocean Tray - this 131,000 gallon pool is a playground for the Aquarium's black-footed and rockhopper penguins.

Rivers of the Americas Gallery - compares aquatic habitats in the Amazon and Connecticut River watersheds.

Special Exhibit Gallery - changing exhibits feature topics ranging from Whales to Rainforests.

Discovery - a floating Marine Mammal Pavilion; daily sea lion demonstrations highlight the natural talents of these mammals and their susceptibility to environmental pollution.

## CAPTIVE BREEDING & RESEARCH

The New England Aquarium has had special **breeding** success with the following species:

Black-footed penguins
Harbor seals

**Research projects** based at the Aquarium include:
- Edgerton Research Laboratory - this facility conducts basic and applied studies on Boston Harbor and Cape Cod Bay; also participates in research on the ecology of Lake Victoria in east Africa. Funded in part by the Maine Fisheries Service, National Science Foundation Department of Energy and the E.P.A.
- Marine Mammal Rescue and Rehabilitation: rehabilitation of and research on stranded and injured marine mammals.
- Red-bellied Turtle Head Start Program - joint project with the Massachusetts Department of Fisheries & Wildlife to preserve this endangered species.
- Black-footed Penguin Program - a Species Survival Plan administered by the AAZPA.

## SEASONAL FESTIVALS & PROGRAMS

Whale Watch - April to October; excursions on the Voyager II to observe humpback whales, finback whales, dolphins and other marine species; for schedule and rate information call 617-973-5277.

## FOR MORE INFORMATION

The New England Aquarium, Central Wharf, Boston, Massachusetts 02110; 617-973-5200; Director: John H. Prescott

# 2
# FRANKLIN PARK ZOO
## Boston, Massachusetts

Franklin Park, a 500-acre urban oasis on the south side of Boston, was designed and created by Frederick Law Olmstead in the late 1800s. Mr. Olmstead, who also designed New York's Central Park, created this Park as part of Boston's famed "Emerald Necklace."

The Franklin Park Zoo opened here in 1913 and is now operated by the Commonwealth Zoological Corporation. The Zoo's African Tropical Forest is the largest exhibit of its kind in North America.

## VISITOR INFORMATION

**Directions:** From the downtown area, head south on I-93 and take the Columbia Road Exit (Exit #15). Head west on Columbia, angling to the left at the third light; follow Columbia Road until it ends; cross Blue Hill Avenue and enter the Zoo.

**Open to the Public:** 9 AM-4 PM weekdays, 10 AM-5 PM weekends, April to October; 9 AM-3:30 PM the remainder of the year.

**Closed:** Thanksgiving, Christmas and New Years Day

**Admission (1993):** Adult: $5.00  Child: $2.50  Senior: $2.50

**Parking Fee:** None

**Children's Zoo:** Yes    **Separate Admission:** No

**Annual Membership** (includes membership to Stone Zoo):
    Individual: $25   Family: $35

**Programs & Tours:** The Education Department offers a variety of programs and field trips.

**AAZPA Member:** Yes

## COLLECTIONS & EXHIBITS

**Collection:** The Zoo's current collection includes the following number of species:
    Mammals: 57          Birds: 145          Reptiles: 27
    Amphibians: 4        Fish: 16            Invertebrates: 8

**Special Exhibits** at the Franklin Park Zoo include:
    African Tropical Forest - North America's largest open-space design tropical forest exhibit
    Birds World - includes a variety of indoor exhibits, a free-flight aviary and a waterfowl pond
    Hooves & Horns - features exotic hoofstock, including addax, mouflon, aoudad, wildebeest and Grevy's zebra
    Arthropod Exhibit
    Children's Zoo - features rare breeds of domestic animals

**Future Plans:**   A Birds of Prey (Eagles/Condors) Exhibit, a Warthog/Saddle-billed Stork Exhibit and Poisons-Toxins-Venoms of the African Tropical Forest will open in 1993. An African Predator-Prey Exhibit is slated for 1994.

## CAPTIVE BREEDING & RESEARCH

The Franklin Park Zoo has had special **breeding** success with the following species:

| | |
|---|---|
| Addax | Bali mynah |
| Grevy's zebra | Parrot species |
| Johnston's chameleon | Hadada ibis |

**Research projects** based at the Franklin Park Zoo include:
- Study of nest building in captive gorillas
- Research on female aggression in mandrills
- Study of feather picking behavior in parrots and macaws
- Nocturnal lighting and exhibit design in pottos

## SEASONAL FESTIVALS & PROGRAMS

Vacation in the Tropics - mid February
Easter Egg Hunt/Parade - March/April
Animal Olympics - late April
African Cultural Jamboree - July
Enchanted Forest - October
Festival of Lights - mid December to early January

## FOR MORE INFORMATION

Commonwealth Zoological Corporation, Franklin Park Zoo, Boston, Massachusetts 02121; 617-442-2002; Director: Sanders Lewallen

*The African Tropical Forest Pavilion at Franklin Park Zoo*
*(photo courtesy Franklin Park Zoo)*

# 3 WALTER D. STONE MEMORIAL ZOO
## Stoneham, Massachusetts

Informally known as "The Stone Zoo," this 25-acre suburban zoo boasts one of the largest aviaries in the country. Like the Franklin Park Zoo, it is managed by the Commonwealth Zoological Corporation.

The Zoo, established in 1905, stretches along the northeast shore of Spot Pond, 2 miles south of Stoneham.

## VISITOR INFORMATION

**Directions:** From downtown Boston, follow I-93 North. Drive approximately 7 miles and take Exit #34. Continue north and take a right at the first light; the Zoo will be on your right, on the northeast shore of Spot Pond.

**Open to the Public:** Daily, 10 AM-4 PM

**Closed:** Thanksgiving, Christmas and New Years Day

**Admission (1993):** Adult: $2.00   Child: $1.00   Senior: $1.00

**Parking Fee:** None

**Children's Zoo:** No

**Annual Membership** (includes membership to Franklin Park Zoo):
    Individual: $25   Family: $35

**Programs & Tours:** Educational programs and field trips are offered by the Zoo.

**AAZPA Member:** No

## COLLECTIONS & EXHIBITS

**Collection:** The Zoo's current collection includes the following number of species:
    Mammals: 5          Birds: 30

**Special Exhibits** at the Stone Zoo include:
    Aviary - one of the largest in the country; features 60 birds, representing 15 species; tropical plants offer shelter for macaws, Victoria-crowned pigeons, flamingos and other birds.
    Polar Bear Exhibit
    Black & White Colobus Monkey Exhibit
    Waterfowl Pond
    Mouflon and Aoudad

**Future Plans:** South America Grasslands and North American Tundra exhibits will open in 1993. A Penguin Exhibit is scheduled for completion in 1994.

## CAPTIVE BREEDING & RESEARCH

The Stone Zoo has had special **breeding** success with the following species:
    Capybara

**Research projects** at the Stone Zoo are in conjunction with those based at the Franklin Park Zoo.

## SEASONAL FESTIVALS & PROGRAMS

The Stone Zoo was recently brought under management of the Commonwealth Zoological Corporation. Renovations are underway and a schedule of seasonal programs is still in the planning stage. One event has been set:

Winter Carnival - late February

## FOR MORE INFORMATION

The Walter D. Stone Memorial Zoo, c/o Commonwealth Zoological Corporation, Franklin Park Zoo, Boston, Massachusetts 02121; 617-442-2002 or 617-438-5100; Director: Sanders Lewallen

# 4    ROGER WILLIAMS PARK ZOO
### Providence, Rhode Island

The Roger Williams Park Zoo is the third oldest zoo in the country and the first in New England to be accredited by the AAZPA. The 40-acre facility, established in 1872, participates in 13 species survival plans.

## VISITOR INFORMATION

**Directions:**   The Roger Williams Park Zoo is on the southern edge of Providence. Take Exit #16 from I-95N or Exit #17 from I-95S and follow the signs; the park is just east of the interstate.

**Open to the Public:**  9 AM-5 PM weekdays; 9 AM-6 PM weekends; Winter Hours 9 AM-4 PM

**Closed:** Thanksgiving, Christmas Day, New Years Day

**Admission (1993):** Adult: $3.50   Child: $1.50 (under 3 free)   Senior: $1.50

**Parking Fee:** None

**Children's Zoo:** Yes    **Separate Admission:** No

**Annual Membership:** Individual: $25   Family: $35   Senior: $25

**AAZPA Member:** Yes

## COLLECTIONS & EXHIBITS

**Collection:** The Zoo's current collection includes the following number of species:

Mammals: 46          Birds: 52          Reptiles: 32
Amphibians: 18       Fish: 8            Insects: 1
Other Invertebrates: 2

**Special Exhibits** at the Roger Williams Park Zoo include:

Tropical America - includes walk-through free-flight aviary, monkeys and reptiles
Underwater Viewing of Polar Bears, Sea Lions & Otters
African Plains Exhibit - includes elephants, giraffe, cheetahs, bongos, zebra and oryx.
Minor Breeds Farm
Australasian Building
Natural 5 Acre Wetland
North American Exhibits
Penguin Exhibit
Newly Renovated Menagerie (gift shop, bookstore, ice cream parlor) - this is the second oldest zoo building in the country

**Future Plans:** A Breeding & Research Center (off exhibit) will be completed in 1993. A new Education Center and a Snow Leopard Exhibit are scheduled to open in 1994. An Invertebrate House is slated for 1995.

## CAPTIVE BREEDING & RESEARCH

The Roger Williams Park Zoo has had special **breeding** success with the following species:

White-faced saki monkeys      Tree kangaroo
Parma wallabies               Dwarf mongoose
Naked mole-rats               Primates

As noted in the Introduction, the Roger Williams Park Zoo participates in 13 species survival plans. Other **research** based at the zoo includes:

- Study of the reproductive cycle of white-faced saki monkeys
- Research on cognitive learning in elephants and sea lions
- Field research on cotton-topped tamarins

## SEASONAL FESTIVALS & PROGRAMS

Farm Festival - mid April
Conservation Day - early June
Teddy Bear Rally - mid September
Halloween Festival - late October
Holiday Weekend - mid December

## FOR MORE INFORMATION

The Roger Williams Park Zoo, 1000 Elmwood Avenue, Providence, Rhode Island 02907-3600; 401-785-3510; Director: Tony Vecchio

# 5 MYSTIC MARINELIFE AQUARIUM
## Mystic, Connecticut

Located halfway between Boston and New York City, the Mystic Marinelife Aquarium is the most visited attraction in Connecticut. Originally founded as a privately owned, profit-making corporation in 1973, the Aquarium became a division of Sea Research Foundation, Inc., in 1977. This non-profit organization is dedicated to public education, research and marinelife conservation.

## VISITOR INFORMATION

**Directions:** The Aquarium is located in Stonington, Connecticut. Take Exit 90 from I-95; proceed to the south side of the Interstate and turn left (east) on Coogan Blvd. to the Aquarium.

**Open to the Public:** 9 AM-5:30 PM, July 1 through Labor Day;
9 AM-4:30 PM remainder of the year.
Visitors may remain in building until 6 PM all year.

**Closed:** Thanksgiving, Christmas Day, and the last full week of January

**Admission (1993):** Adult: $8.50   Child: $5.00 (under 4 free)   Senior: $7.50

**Parking Fee:** None

**Annual Membership:** Individual: $30   Family: $40   Senior: $20/$25 Family

**Programs & Tours:** The Education Department offers a wide variety of programs for the public and for regional school systems. These include field trips, workshops, behind-the-scenes tours, demonstrations, lectures and on-site labwork.

**AAZPA Member:** Yes

## COLLECTIONS & EXHIBITS

**Collection:** The Mystic Marinelife Aquarium features over 6000 specimens displayed in 50 exhibits.

**Special Exhibits** at the facility include:
Seal Island - this 2.5 acre outdoor exhibit features four species of seals/sea lions in three coastal habitats (New England Coast, Pribilof Islands, California Coast)
Penguin Pavilion - home to a breeding colony of African black-footed penguins
Apex Predator Exhibit - a mixed-species exhibit featuring a variety of sharks; the 30,000 gallon tank holds artificial sea water
The Deep Frontier - this large-screen film introduces visitors to marine life that thrive 2700 feet below the surface

Open Sea Exhibit - this 350,000 gallon, 16-window display features sand, tiger and nurse sharks

Adaptation Alcove - demonstrates how marine creatures adapt to their environment

Aquatic Communities Alcove - introduces the visitor to the symbiotic relationship of marine species in a variety of aquatic habitats

*The Penguin Pavilion at Mystic Marinelife Aquarium features a colony of African black-footed penguins.*

*(Photo by Paul Horton Photography, courtesy Mystic Marinelife Aquarium)*

## CAPTIVE BREEDING & RESEARCH

The Mystic Marinelife Aquarium has had special **breeding** success with the following species:

> Northern fur seals - the first facility in the U.S. to breed this species in captivity and the first to hand-rear a northern fur seal pup (after its mother failed to nurse). The Aquarium is the leading breeder of northern fur seals in the country.
>
> Harbor seals
> California sea lions
> African black-footed penguins
> Chain dogfish sharks

**Research** based at Mystic Marinelife Aquarium includes:

> - Pinniped eye research
> - Breeding inhibitor research in pinnipeds
> - Research on stranded animals; the Aquarium participates in the Northeast Regional Stranding Network
> - Studies on nutritional requirements of marine mammals
> - Research on monitoring toxic substances in sea water
> - Studies to characterize the chemistry of aquarium seawater

## SEASONAL FESTIVALS & PROGRAMS

The Mystic Marinelife Aquarium offers a summer internship program and hosts a variety of special events throughout the year.

## FOR MORE INFORMATION

Mystic Marinelife Aquarium, 55 Coogan Blvd., Mystic, Connecticut 06355-1997; 203-536-9631; President: Hugh P. Connell

# 6     BEARDSLEY ZOOLOGICAL GARDENS
## Bridgeport, Connecticut

The Beardsley Zoological Gardens, founded in 1922, covers 36 acres of parkland. The facility is primarily devoted to the display and conservation of North and South American species.

## VISITOR INFORMATION

**Directions:** From Routes 8 & 25 (between I-95 and Route 15) take Exit 5 and head southeast on Boston Avenue. Proceed to Noble Avenue and turn left. Follow this road to the Park and Zoo.

**Open to the Public:** Daily, 9 AM-4 PM

**Closed:** Thanksgiving, Christmas and New Years Day

**Admission (1993):** Adult: $3.75    Child: $2.00    Senior: $2.00

**Parking Fee:** $3.00

*New World Tropics Building*
*(photo by Ron Wolf, courtesy Beardsley Zoological Gardens)*

**Children's Zoo:** Yes      **Separate Admission:** No

**Annual Membership** (to Connecticut Zoological Society):
  Individual: $20      Family: $30

**Programs & Tours:** The Zoo offers a variety of public education including its Zoomobile outreach program and live animal demonstrations at the Children's Farmyard.

**AAZPA Member:** Yes

## COLLECTIONS & EXHIBITS

**Collection:** The Zoo's current collection includes the following number of species:

|            |             |                  |
|------------|-------------|------------------|
| Mammals: 32 | Birds: 51   | Reptiles: 32     |
| Amphibians: 8 | Insects: 8 | Invertebrates: 2 |

**Special Exhibits** at the Beardsley Zoological Gardens include:
  South American Rainforest - this naturalistic exhibit was designed to emphasize the Zoo's commitment to conservation.
  New England Farm Yard - this children's area permits close contact with a variety of domestic animals.

## CAPTIVE BREEDING & RESEARCH

The Beardsley Zoological Gardens participates in Species Survival Plans for the Siberian tiger, the red wolf and the golden lion tamarin.

## SEASONAL FESTIVALS & PROGRAMS

BunnyFest - late March
Earth Day - late April
Conservation Day - early June

Tricks for Treats - Halloween week
WinterFest - mid December

## FOR MORE INFORMATION

Beardsley Zoological Gardens, 1875 Noble Avenue, Bridgeport, Connecticut 06610; 203-576-8082; Director: Gregg Dancho

# 7    AQUARIUM OF NIAGARA FALLS
## Niagara Falls, New York

Established in 1965, this Aquarium is home to the largest collection of freshwater fish in the State of New York. The facility has also had unique success with the breeding of Peruvian penguins, the most endangered species of penguin in the world.

## VISITOR INFORMATION

**Directions:**   The Aquarium is on the north side of the city. From the NYS Thruway or from I-290, take I-190 north. Cross Grand Island; exit after north bridge onto the Robert Moses Parkway. Follow the parkway and the leaping dolphin signs to the Aquarium.

From Ontario, take the Rainbow Bridge across the Niagara River. Turn left on Rainbow Blvd. North and follow the dolphin signs.

**Open to the Public:** Daily, 9 AM-5 PM; open until 7 PM in Summer

**Closed:** New Years Day, Thanksgiving and Christmas

**Admission (1993):** Adult: $5.95   Child: $3.95   Senior: $3.95

**Parking Fee:** None

**Annual Membership:** Individual: $18   Family: $30   Senior: $10

**Programs & Tours:**   The Aquarium's Education Department works with local schools, libraries, youth centers and other social organizations to educate the public about regional and global aquatic ecosystems. The Department also coordinates educational workshops with Canisius College.

**AAZPA Member:** No

## COLLECTIONS & EXHIBITS

**Collection:**   The Aquarium's current collection includes the following number of species:

| | | |
|---|---|---|
| Mammals: 12 | Birds: 16 | Reptiles: 12 |
| Amphibians: 6 | Fish: Hundreds | Mollusks: Hundreds |
| Invertebrates: Hundreds | | |

**Special Exhibits** at the Aquarium of Niagara Falls include:
 Atlantic bottlenose dolphin exhibit
 Electric eel demonstrations
 Peruvian penguin exhibit
 Great Lakes: the Inland Seas - focuses on the fishlife, habitats and environmental health of the Great Lakes; deals with issues of acid rain, lamprey eel invasion, pollution and other threats to these Inland Seas.

**Future Plans:**   "Wonder Bay," a hands-on interactive exhibit for children, opens in 1993.

## CAPTIVE BREEDING & RESEARCH

The Aquarium of Niagara Falls participates in the Species Survival Plan for Peruvian penguins and has had special **breeding** success with this species.

**Research** at the Aquarium includes:
- the Marine Mammal Care Department conducts studies on Atlantic bottlenose dolphins and other marine mammals with emphasis on the conditioning of husbandry behaviors and on public education about these species
- research on and rehabilitation of stranded Kemp's Ridley turtles, an endangered species

## SEASONAL FESTIVALS & PROGRAMS

Sea'sonings of Niagara - March; regional foods festival
Annual Penguin Days - early March
Annual SEA'ster Egg Hunt - Easter week
Scouts Day - Spring
Aquarium Great Lakes Festival - June
Santa's Super Saturday - December

## FOR MORE INFORMATION

Aquarium of Niagara Falls, 701 Whirlpool Street, Niagara Falls, New York 14301; 716-285-3575; Director: Albert Clifton Jr.

# 8    BUFFALO ZOOLOGICAL GARDENS
### Buffalo, New York

The Buffalo Zoological Gardens, founded in 1875, has special breeding programs for rattlesnakes, pythons, boas and amphibians. Covering 23.5 acres, it is also the only U.S. zoo to have a science magnet school on the zoo grounds.

## VISITOR INFORMATION

**Directions:**    Take the Parkside Exit from Highway 33 and follow the signs to the Zoo.

**Open to the Public:**   Daily; 10 AM-5:30 PM, Memorial Day to Labor Day;
10 AM-4:30 PM, remainder of the year.

**Closed:** Thanksgiving and Christmas Day

**Admission (1993):** Adult: $5.00   Child: $3.00   Senior: $2.00

**Parking Fee:** $3.00 (car), $5.00 (bus)

**Children's Zoo:** Yes    **Separate Admission:** No

**Annual Membership:** Individual: $20   Family: $30   Grandparent: $25

**AAZPA Member:** Yes

## COLLECTIONS & EXHIBITS

**Collection:** The Zoo's current collection includes the following number of species:

| | | |
|---|---|---|
| Mammals: 67 | Birds: 52 | Reptiles: 60 |
| Amphibians: 13 | Fish: 6 | Invertebrates: 8 |

**Special Exhibits** at the Buffalo Zoological Gardens include:
White Tiger Exhibit
Tropical Rainforest/Lowland Gorilla Habitat
Lion/Tiger Habitat
Diversity of Life Exhibit - features insects, crustaceans and spiders
Austral-Asian Waterfowl Exhibit (new 1993)

**Future Plans:** The World of Wildlife education facility and a new Asian Elephant Exhibit will open in 1993. An Asian Forest Exhibit, featuring the Asian rhino, gaur and axis deer, is also planned.

## CAPTIVE BREEDING & RESEARCH

The Buffalo Zoological Gardens has had special **breeding** success with the following species:

| | |
|---|---|
| Wallaroo | Clouded leopard |
| Tamarins | Reindeer |
| Mandrills | Roan |
| Lowland gorillas | Bighorn sheep |
| Prehensile porcupine | Markor |
| Polar bears | |

*White Bengal Tiger*
*(photo by Margaret Smith, courtesy Buffalo Zoological Gardens)*

**Research projects** based at the Buffalo Zoological Gardens include:
- Husbandry of cotton-top tamarins
- Planning for mixed exhibits of South American mammals

## SEASONAL FESTIVALS & PROGRAMS

Leprechaun Village - early March
Easter Eggstravaganza - Easter season
Father's Day Car Show - June
Zoo-B-Que - late July
Children's Peace Festival - early August
Labor Day in the Zoo
Zooper Pumpkin Patch - October
Zoonderland - December

## FOR MORE INFORMATION

Buffalo Zoological Gardens, 300 Parkside Avenue, Buffalo, New York 14214-1999; 716-837-3900; Director: Minot H. Ortolani

# 9 SENECA PARK ZOO
### Rochester, New York

Situated on the east bank of the Genesee River, the Seneca Park Zoo was founded in 1894. The Zoo now encompasses 14 acres.

## VISITOR INFORMATION

**Directions:** The Zoo is on the northern edge of Rochester. Exit onto St. Paul St. from Route 104 (the Keeler Expressway) and proceed north to the Park and Zoo.

**Open to the Public:** 10 AM-5 PM Weekdays and throughout the Winter;
10 AM-7 PM Summer weekends and holidays

**Admission (1993):** Adult: $2.00   Ages 10-15: $1.50   Child: $1.00

**Parking Fee:** None
**Children's Zoo:** No
**AAZPA Member:** Yes

## COLLECTIONS & EXHIBITS

**Collection:** The Zoo's current collection includes the following number of species:

| | | |
|---|---|---|
| Mammals: 31 | Birds: 44 | Reptiles: 31 |
| Amphibians: 11 | Fish: 14 | Other Invertebrates: 2 |

**Future Plans:** The Discovery Building and three new outdoor North American Exhibits (Bald Eagle, Otter, Porcupine/Beaver) will open in 1993.

## CAPTIVE BREEDING & RESEARCH

The Seneca Park Zoo has had special **breeding** success with the following species:

| | |
|---|---|
| Snow leopard | White-handed gibbon |
| Siberian tiger | Corn snake |
| Polar bear | Black ratsnake |
| American bison | King vulture |
| Black-handed spider monkey | Reeve's pheasant |

## FOR MORE INFORMATION

The Seneca Park Zoo, 2222 St. Paul St., Rochester, New York 14621-1097; 716-266-6846; Director: Daniel R. Michalowski

# 10     BURNET PARK ZOO
### Syracuse, New York

The Burnet Park Zoo, founded in 1912, is owned by Onondaga County and managed by the County's Department of Parks. The Zoo covers 60 acres and is known for its work on the captive propagation of elephants.

## VISITOR INFORMATION

**Directions:** Directional signs are placed throughout the city and county.

**Open to the Public:** Daily, 10 AM-4:30 PM

**Closed:** Christmas and New Years Day

**Admission (1993):** Adult: $5.00  Child: $.200  Senior: $3.00

**Parking Fee:** None

**Children's Zoo:** Yes    **Separate Admission:** No

**Annual Membership:** Contact the Zoo

**AAZPA Member:** Yes

## COLLECTIONS & EXHIBITS

**Collection:** The Zoo's current collection includes the following number of species:

| | | |
|---|---|---|
| Mammals: 55 | Birds: 80 | Reptiles: 29 |
| Amphibians: 13 | Fish: 29 | Mollusks: 11 |
| Other Invertebrates: 20 | | |

**Special Exhibits** at the Burnet Park Zoo include:
Wild North - a collection of species from northern latitudes
Animals of Antiquity - a sequence of 18 exhibits depict the evolution of life on earth, from invertebrates to mammals

## CAPTIVE BREEDING & RESEARCH

The Burnet Park Zoo has had special **breeding** success with the following species:

| | |
|---|---|
| Elephants | Primate species |
| Sloths | Dart frogs |
| Pronghorn antelope | |

The Zoo conducts a variety of reproductive and contraceptive **research** on elephants, big cats, massasaugas, bog turtles and gibbons.

## SEASONAL FESTIVALS & PROGRAMS

Howling Good Time - March
Rainforest Celebration - April
Elephant Celebration Day - August

## FOR MORE INFORMATION

Burnet Park Zoo, 500 Burnet Park Drive, Syracuse, New York 13204; 315-435-8511; Director: David A. Raboy

# 11 UTICA ZOO
## Utica, New York

The Utica Zoo, established in 1914, now covers 80 acres.

## VISITOR INFORMATION

**Directions:** The Zoo is on the southern edge of Utica. From the downtown area, proceed south for one mile on Genesee St. Turn east on Memorial Parkway and continue .5 mile to the Zoo.

**Open to the Public:** 365 days per year, 10 AM-5 PM

**Admission (1993):** Adult: $3.00   Child: $1.50   Senior: $2.50

**Parking Fee:** None

**Children's Zoo:** Yes   **Separate Admission:** No

**Annual Membership:** Individual: $25   Family: $35

**AAZPA Member:** Yes

## COLLECTIONS & EXHIBITS

**Collection:** The Zoo's current collection includes the following number of species:

| | | |
|---|---|---|
| Mammals: 33 | Birds: 26 | Reptiles: 16 |
| Amphibians: 4 | Insects: 1 | |

**Special Exhibits** at the Utica Zoo include:
Sea Lion Exhibit - two shows daily
Siberian Tiger Exhibit - naturalistic; 1.5 acre enclosure

**Future Plans:** A Nature Trail will open in the spring of 1994.

## CAPTIVE BREEDING & RESEARCH

The Utica Zoo has had special **breeding** success with the following species:
Golden lion tamarin

## SEASONAL FESTIVALS & PROGRAMS

Animal Fair - Mother's Day Weekend in May
Earth Day
Easter Eggstravaganza
Halloween Spooktacular

## FOR MORE INFORMATION

The Utica Zoo, Steele Hill Road, Utica, New York 13501; 315-738-0472; Director:
Mark Rich

# 12       ROSS PARK ZOO
## Binghamton, New York

Home to "Valdessa," the first bald eagle rescued from the Exxon Valdez oil spill, the Ross Park Zoo was founded in 1875. The 25-acre zoo also harbors a 73-year-old carousel and offers free rides on its colorful, wooden steeds.

## VISITOR INFORMATION

**Directions:** From Interstate 81, take Exit 4 south and follow to Route 363 South; proceed to Route 434 West; take a left at the first light; continue straight ahead at the second light and then turn left at the stop sign. The Zoo will be .5 mile up the hill, on your right (entrance at 60 Morgan Road).

**Open to the Public:** Daily March 15 - November 30, 10 AM-5 PM;
Open weekends January to March 15

**Closed:** Thanksgiving Day, the month of December and New Years Day

**Admission (1993):** Adult: $3.00   Child: $2.25   Senior: $2.25

**Parking Fee:** None

**Children's Zoo:** Yes    **Separate Admission:** No

**Annual Membership:** Individual: $25   Family: $35   Senior: $20

**AAZPA Member:** Yes

## COLLECTIONS & EXHIBITS

**Collection:** The Zoo's current collection includes the following number of species:
Mammals: 25          Birds: 17          Reptiles: 16
Invertebrates: 1

As noted above, the Ross Park Zoo is home to "Valdessa," the first bald eagle rescued from the Exxon Valdez oil spill in Alaska.

**Future Plans:** A new Herpetarium is scheduled to open in 1996.

## CAPTIVE BREEDING & RESEARCH

The Ross Park Zoo has had special **breeding** success with the following species:
Red wolves
Siberian lynx

The Zoo is also participating in the species survival plan for the following endangered species:
Red wolf                    Golden lion tamarin
Snow leopard               Spectacled bear
Siberian tiger

## SEASONAL FESTIVALS & PROGRAMS

Old Fashioned Frolic Carnival - early June
Ice Cream Safari - mid July and mid August
Boo at the Zoo - Halloween weekend

## FOR MORE INFORMATION

The Ross Park Zoo, 185 Park Avenue, Binghamton, New York 13903; 607-724-5461; Director: Steven D. Contento


# 13 BRONX ZOO/INTERNATIONAL WILDLIFE CONSERVATION PARK
## Bronx, New York

The New York Zoological Society, founded in 1895, is an international organization dedicated to protecting wildlife and ecosystems across the globe. The society operates the Bronx Zoo, the Central Park Zoo, New York's Aquarium for Wildlife Conservation and the Queens Wildlife Conservation Center. In addition, the society manages 150 field projects in 41 countries.

Covering 265 acres, the Bronx Zoo, established in 1895, is the largest metropolitan wildlife park in the United States and is often praised as the best zoo in the country. The zoo is renowned for its Jungleworld Exhibit, an Asian rain forest habitat.

## VISITOR INFORMATION

**Directions:**   The Zoo is centrally located off the Bronx River Parkway; take Exit #6.

**Open to the Public:**   365 days per year; 10 AM-5 PM weekdays, 10 AM-5:30 PM weekends & holidays, March to October; 10 AM-4:30 PM November to February

**Admission (1993):**   Adult: $5.75 (Mar.-Oct.) / $2.50 (Nov.-Feb.)
Child/Senior: $2.00 (Mar.-Oct.) / $1.00 (Nov.-Feb.)
Under 2: Free all year

**Parking Fee:** $5.00

**Children's Zoo:** Yes     **Separate Admission:** Adult: $1.50   Child: $1.50

**Annual Membership:** (To New York Zoological Society)
   Individual: $38     Family: $54     Senior: $30

**AAZPA Member:** Yes

## COLLECTIONS & EXHIBITS

**Collection:** The Zoo's current collection includes the following number of species:
   Mammals: 175          Birds: 327          Reptiles: 155
   Amphibians: 25

**Special Exhibits** at the Bronx Zoo include:
   Jungleworld - this award-winning exhibit features a tropical Asian rain forest and the endangered species that inhabit that ecosystem
   Baboon Reserve - a re-creation of an Ethiopian mountain range; the exhibit is home to Gelada baboons & Nubian Ibex; also includes an African market
   Wild Asia - a 40-acre area which can be viewed from the Bengali Express Monorail
   World of Birds Exhibit
   World of Reptiles Exhibit
   World of Darkness Exhibit

*Snow leopard in Himalayan Highlands Exhibit*
*(courtesy New York Zoological Society)*

**Future Plans:**   New exhibits scheduled for completion over the next three years include White-lipped Deer (1993), Naked Mole Rat (1993-1994), Pere David Deer (1993), Babirusa (1995-1996) and Project Gorilla (1995-1996).

## CAPTIVE BREEDING & RESEARCH

The Bronx Zoo has had special **breeding** success with the following species:

| | |
|---|---|
| Snow leopards | Malay tapir |
| Proboscis monkeys | Cloud rat |
| Small-clawed otters | Red brockets |
| Silvered langurs | Slender-horned gazelles |
| Lowland gorillas | White-cheeked gibbons |
| Babirusa | Rodriguez fruit bats |
| Pudu | |

**Research projects** based at the Bronx Zoo include:
- Animal contraception research
- Elephant satellite tracking studies
- Social & reproductive behavior of Gelada baboons
- Gaur social & reproductive behavior
- Black howler translocation project
- Study of Babirusa infant development
- Artificial insemination of leopard cats

## SEASONAL FESTIVALS & PROGRAMS

Wildlife Conservation Month - March
Great Egg Even - March or April (Easter)
Zoobabies Weekend - June
Boo at the Zoo - October

## FOR MORE INFORMATION

Bronx Zoo/International Wildlife Conservation Park, mailing: 185th St. & Southern Blvd., Bronx, New York 10460; 718-220-5197; Info Line: 718-367-1010; General Director: William Conway

# 14 CENTRAL PARK WILDLIFE CONSERVATION CENTER
### New York, New York

Located in the green, urban oasis of Central Park, this 5.5 acre zoo first opened in 1864. Totally renovated and reopened as the Central Park Wildlife Conservation Center in 1988, the facility is managed by the New York Zoological Society.

The Center offers changing educational exhibits throughout the year and an on-site gallery, free of charge, features wildlife art displays. Nestled beneath the towers of Manhattan, this Zoo harbors one of the largest polar bear exhibits in the country.

## VISITOR INFORMATION

**Directions:**   The Central Park Wildlife Conservation Center is in the southeastern quadrant of Central Park; there is no on-site parking. Take the M1, M2, M3 or M4 bus to 64th St. Alternatively, catch the N or R train to the Fifth Avenue stop.

**Open to the Public:**   365 days per year; 10 AM-5 PM weekdays, 10:30 AM-5:30 PM weekends & holidays, April to October; 10 AM-4:30 PM, November through March

**Admission (1993):** Adult: $2.50   Child: $.50 (under 3 free)   Senior: $1.25

**Parking Fee:** No on-site parking

**Children's Zoo:** No (under renovation)

**Annual Membership:** (To New York Zoological Society)
   Individual: $38      Family: $54      Senior: $30

**AAZPA Member:** Yes

## COLLECTIONS & EXHIBITS

**Collection:** The Zoo's current collection includes the following number of species:
   Mammals: 13          Birds: 42          Reptiles: 30
   Amphibians: 10       Insects: 1         Fish: 1

**Special Exhibits** at the Central Park Wildlife Conservation Center include:
   Polar Circle - one of the largest polar bear exhibits in the country; three levels of observation, including underwater views
   Edge of the Icepack - indoor exhibit simulates the environment on an Antarctic ice floe; Gentoo and Chinstrap penguins can be observed swimming, feeding and nesting
   The Tropic Zone - indoor rainforest exhibit with all life zones represented, from floor to canopy; residents include piranha, leaf-cutter ants, broad-snouted caiman, golden-headed lion tamarins, tropical birds and other species

**Future Plans:** An aviary for endangered pheasants will open by 1996.

## CAPTIVE BREEDING & RESEARCH

The Central Park Wildlife Conservation Center has had special **breeding** success with the following species:

Tufted puffins                     Tropical forest bird species
Gentoo penguins                    Fruit doves
Chinstrap penguins                 Green & black poison arrow frogs
Burmese mountain tortoise

**Research** at the Zoo includes behavioral studies of African pygmy geese, Japanese macaques and black & white colobus monkeys. Crocodilian (Caiman) expert Peter Brazaitis is the Zoo's curator of animals.

## SEASONAL FESTIVALS & PROGRAMS
May Day Merriment - May 1
Jazz in June
Chill Out with the Polar Bears & Penguins - July
Birthday Party - August 8
Go Batty! For Halloween - late October
Winter Wildlife Weekends - December

## FOR MORE INFORMATION
The Central Park Wildlife Conservation Center, 830 Fifth Avenue at 64th St., New York, New York 10021; 212-861-6030; Director: Richard L. Lattis

*Sea lion Pool, Central Park Zoo*
*(courtesy New York Zoological Society)*

# 15  QUEENS WILDLIFE CONSERVATION CENTER
## Queens, New York

The Queens Zoo, located in Flushing Meadow Park, was founded in 1968. The 11-acre facility was closed for renovations and reopened in 1992 as the Queens Wildlife Conservation Center, devoted to the display of North American wildlife.

## VISITOR INFORMATION
**Directions:** The Center is located on the eastern side of Flushing Meadow Park, just west of the Grand Central Parkway/Long Island Expressway Interchange. Call 718-271-7761 for specific directions.

**Open to the Public:**  365 days per year; 10 AM-5 PM weekdays, 10 AM-5:30 PM weekends & holidays, April to October; 10 AM-4:30 PM, November to March.

**Admission (1993):** Adult: $2.50   Child: $.50 (under 3 free)   Senior: $1.25

**Children's Zoo:** Yes     **Separate Admission:** No

**Annual Membership:** (To New York Zoological Society)
   Individual: $38     Family: $54     Senior: $30

**AAZPA Member:** No

## COLLECTIONS & EXHIBITS

**Collection:** The Zoo's current collection includes the following number of species:

   Mammals: 25          Birds: 24
   Amphibians 1         Fish: 3

As noted above, the Queens Wildlife Conservation Center is devoted to North American wildlife. **Special Exhibits** at the center include:

   Buckminster Fuller Geodesic Dome - originally built for the 1964 World's Fair, the structure now serves as an aviary
   New naturalistic habitats for American black bear, bobcat and mountain lion
   Children's Zoo - close contact with domestic species and education about the domestication of plants & animals

**Future Plans:**   New otter and birds of prey exhibits will be completed by 1996

## SEASONAL FESTIVALS & PROGRAMS

Bison Bonanza - June
Fall Fling/Harvest Festival - September
Go Batty! For Halloween - late October

## FOR MORE INFORMATION

The Queens Wildlife Conservation Center, 53-51 111th St., Flushing Meadow Park, Queens, New York 11368; 718-271-7761 (recorded information); Director: Richard L. Lattis

# 16   NEW YORK'S AQUARIUM
## FOR WILDLIFE CONSERVATION
### Brooklyn, New York

Renowned for its success with the captive breeding of beluga whales, New York's Aquarium for Wildlife Conservation is owned by the city and managed by the New York Zoological Society. The 14 acre facility was established in 1896.

## VISITOR INFORMATION

**Directions:**   The Aquarium is located at Boardwalk and West 8th Street in Brooklyn. Take the 7S Exit from the Belt Parkway and follow the blue Beluga whale signs. Alternatively, take the D or F train to West 8th Street and walk across the road to the Aquarium.

**Open to the Public:**   365 days per year; 10 AM-7 PM, Memorial Day to Labor Day; 10 AM-5 PM remainder of year

**Admission (1993):**   Adult: $5.75   Child: $2.00   Senior: $2.00

**Parking Fee:**   $5.00

**Annual Membership:**  (To New York Zoological Society)
   Individual: $38     Family: $54

**AAZPA Member:**   Yes

## COLLECTIONS & EXHIBITS

**Collection:**   The Aquarium's current collection includes the following number of species:

| | | |
|---|---|---|
| Mammals: 8 | Birds: 1 | Reptiles: 4 |
| Amphibians: 3 | Fish: 338 | Invertebrates: 10 |

**Special Exhibits** at New York's Aquarium for Wildlife Conservation include:
   Discovery Cove - includes a touch-it-tank, a wave wall and many interactive exhibits (recognized by AAZPA with a significant achievement award)
   Coral Reef Conservation & Protection Exhibit

**Future Plans:**   Sea Cliffs Exhibit, depicting a rocky, Pacific coastal habitat, will open in 1993); a series of unique events are planned (from April to November) to highlight this new addition to the Aquarium.

## CAPTIVE BREEDING & RESEARCH

New York's Aquarium for Wildlife Conservation has had special **breeding** success with the following species:
   Beluga whales - recipient of the AAZPA Beane Award
   Endangered fresh water fish (poeciliios)
   Black-footed penguins
   Tropical salt water fish species

The Aquarium is currently participating in a host of **research** and conservation programs including:
- Study of breeding behavior in whales
- Study of fish parasitology
- Research on coral culture
- Propagation culture of fresh & salt water fish
- Studies on the physiology of deep sea fish and invertebrates
- Monitoring of local environmental conditions

## SEASONAL FESTIVALS & PROGRAMS
Penguin Weekend (includes annual Polar Bear Club ocean swim) - New Years Day
Wildlife Conservation Month - March
Mother's Day Weekend - May
Sea Scare - October
Ocean Holiday Weekends - late November through New Years Day

## FOR MORE INFORMATION
New York's Aquarium for Wildlife Conservation, West 8th St. and Surf Avenue, Brooklyn, New York 11224; 718-265-FISH; Director: Louis E. Garibaldi

*Beluga whales at New York's Aquarium for Wildlife Conservation*
*(photo courtesy New York Zoological Society)*

# 17 STATEN ISLAND ZOO
## Staten Island, New York

When this small Zoo opened in 1936, its bylaws proclaimed it to be "the first educational zoo in America." Today, the 8.5-acre facility is internationally recognized for its superb reptile display, including one of the largest collections of North American rattlesnakes.

## VISITOR INFORMATION

**Directions:** From the Staten Island Ferry, turn right onto Richmond Terrace; proceed 3.4 miles and turn left on Broadway; the Zoo will be 1.2 miles ahead.

Or take the S-48 Bus from the Ferry to the intersection of Forest Avenue and Broadway; turn left on Broadway and walk 2½ blocks to the Zoo.

From the Verrazano Narrows Bridge, follow I-278 West to Slosson Avenue Exit. Turn right onto Slosson and proceed to Martling Avenue. Turn right and drive to Clove Road; free parking will be on your right.

**Open to the Public:** Daily, 10 AM-4:45 PM

**Closed:** Thanksgiving, Christmas and New Years Day

**Admission (1993):** Adult: $3.00   Child: $2.00
Free Admission every Wednesday after 2 PM

**Parking Fee:** None

**Children's Zoo:** Yes   **Separate Admission:** No

**Annual Membership:** Individual: $25   Family: $45

**Programs & Tours:** The Zoo offers a variety of educational programs including tours, lectures, special classes, workshops, and outreach programs.

**AAZPA Member:** Yes

## COLLECTIONS & EXHIBITS

**Collection:** The Zoo's current collection includes the following number of species:
Mammals: 20        Birds: 25        Reptiles: 20
Amphibians: 5      Fish: 70         Insects: 2
Mollusks: 1        Other Invertebrates: 8

**Special Exhibits** at the Staten Island Zoo include:
Serpentarium - houses an internationally acclaimed display of reptiles, including one of the largest collections of North American rattlesnakes.
Ralph J. Lamberti Tropical Forest - a boardwalk leads visitors through this recreation of a South American Rainforest
John J. Marchi Aquarium - displays marine life from around the world
Children's Center - this New England farm permits close contact with an international collection of domestic animals

**Future Plans:**  African Savannah at Twilight, a naturalized, mixed-species habitat, will be completed in 1994.

## CAPTIVE BREEDING & RESEARCH

The Staten Island Zoo has had special **breeding** success with the following species:

| | |
|---|---|
| Ocelots | Waterfowl species |
| Cotton-top tamarins | Rattlesnake species |
| Black-handed spider monkeys | Anacondas |
| Leaf-nosed bats | Pine snakes |

## SEASONAL FESTIVALS & PROGRAMS

ZooOlympics - mid July
Seasonal floral displays

## FOR MORE INFORMATION

Staten Island Zoo, 614 Broadway, Staten Island, New York 10310; 718-442-3101; Director: Vincent N. Gattullo

*The Staten Island Zoo has had special breeding success*
*with the cotton-top tamarin.*
*(photo by V. Amesse; courtesy Staten Island Zoo)*

- 33 -

# 18

## THE ERIE ZOO
### Erie, Pennsylvania

Operated by the Erie Zoological Society, the Erie Zoo was founded in 1962. A highlight of the 15 acre Zoo is a train ride which takes visitors into Safariland, a refuge for deer and bison.

## VISITOR INFORMATION

**Directions:** From Interstate 90, take Exit 7 and drive north on Route 97. Proceed 3 miles to the first traffic light and turn left; this road takes you to the main entrance.

**Open to the Public:** Daily, 10 AM-5 PM; hours extended to 6 PM on Sundays in summer

**Closed:** Christmas and New Years Day

**Admission (1993):** Adult: $3.75   Child: $2.25   Senior: $3.50

**Parking Fee:** None

**Children's Zoo:** Yes   **Separate Admission:** No

**Annual Membership:** Individual: $35   Family: $35

**AAZPA Member:** Yes

## COLLECTIONS & EXHIBITS

**Collection:** The Zoo's current collection includes the following number of species:
| | | |
|---|---|---|
| Mammals: 49 | Birds: 27 | Reptiles: 6 |
| Amphibians: 2 | Fish: 5 | Invertebrates: 1 |

**Special Exhibits** at the Erie Zoo include:
The Main Zoo Building - combines traditional 1920s zoo architecture outside with state-of-the-art exhibits inside; renovation of the building will be complete in spring, 1993, featuring all African animals, to include gorillas, leopards, meerkats, and monkeys
Safariland - a natural setting with free ranging deer and bison

**Future Plans:** Completion of the main building renovation, as noted above.

## CAPTIVE BREEDING & RESEARCH

The Erie Zoo has had special **breeding** success with the following species:
| | |
|---|---|
| Giraffes | Polar Bears |
| Camels | Llamas |

## SEASONAL FESTIVALS & PROGRAMS
Dinamation's Dinosaurs Alive - scheduled from May 1 through mid August, 1993
ZooBoo - mid to late October
Zoolumination - over 100,000 lights adorn the Zoo throughout December
  (evenings except December 24 & 25)


## FOR MORE INFORMATION
The Erie Zoo, P.O. Box 3268, Erie, Pennsylvania 16508; 814-864-4091; Director:
James Rhea


# 19      PITTSBURGH ZOO
### Pittsburgh, Pennsylvania


The Pittsburgh Zoo, founded in 1898, has recently completed a massive renovation
project, dedicated to creating naturalized exhibits which foster natural behavior in the
zoo residents. This effort has included the extensive use of plantings which simulate
the native environment of the captive species. The 75 acre Zoo has thus re-committed
itself to the protection, display and propagation of earth's vanishing wildlife.

## VISITOR INFORMATION
**Directions:** From Downtown Pittsburgh, take 579 to Route 28 North; exit at the
Highland Park Bridge (Exit 6). Go across the bridge, staying in the
right lane; take the first right onto Butler Street. Go to the second light,
turn left and enter the Zoo lot.

**Open to the Public:** 10 AM-6 PM Memorial Day through Labor Day;
9 AM-5 PM the remainder of the year

**Closed:** Christmas Day

**Admission (1993):** Adult: $5.75   Child: $2.75   Senior: $2.75

**Parking Fee:** $2.00

**Children's Zoo:** Yes   **Separate Admission:** No

**Annual Membership:** Individual:: $25   Family: $40

**AAZPA Member:** Yes

*Lowland Gorilla*
*(photo by Rich Kilson; courtesy Pittsburgh Zoo)*

## COLLECTIONS & EXHIBITS

**Collection:** The Zoo's current collection includes the following number of species:

| | | |
|---|---|---|
| Mammals: 60 | Birds: 35 | Reptiles: 60 |
| Amphibians: 2 | Fish: 158 | Invertebrates: 83 |

**Special Exhibits** at the Pittsburgh Zoo include:

Tropical Forest Complex - home to 16 species of primate and adorned with more than 2000 plants

Asian Forest - landscaped with over 1500 types of trees, shrubs, perennials and grasses, this exhibit features Siberian tigers, barheaded geese and Demoiselle cranes

African Savannah - characterized by an arid terrain with over 4500 plants, the Savannah is home to African lions, elephants, white rhinos, reticulated giraffes, zebras, ostriches and flamingos
Aqua Zoo
Niches - a reptile and small mammal building
Bear Exhibits - feature black, sun, Kodiak and polar bears
North American Area - exhibits species native to our continent, including the endangered red wolf

**Future Plans:** An Insect Gallery, a Snow Leopard Exhibit, a new Entrance Plaza and an Education/Administration Building are all scheduled for completion in 1993.

## CAPTIVE BREEDING & RESEARCH

The Pittsburgh Zoo has had special **breeding** success with the following species:

| | |
|---|---|
| Western Lowland Gorilla | Giraffe |
| Mandrill | Gazelle |
| Howler Monkey | Zebra |
| Bornean Orangutan | |

The Zoo participates in Species Survival Plans of the AAZPA. **Research** based at the Pittsburgh Zoo include:
- an Orangutan study of two unrelated males living together
  (an adult and sub-adult)
- White Rhinoceros reproductive study
- Study of the effects of UV light on the living coral reef
- Visitor study
- Field research on Siberian Hamsters in cooperation with The Carnegie, Arizona State University and the Academy of Sciences of Russia

## SEASONAL FESTIVALS & PROGRAMS

Winter Festival - mid January
Easter Party - Saturday of the weekend before Easter
Food Festival - weekend before Memorial Day weekend
Conservation Day - June
Twilight Tours - June through August
Critter Craft Fair - July
Purina Big Cat Survival Fund - August
Senior Day - late September
Free Kids Month - October
ZooBoo - weekend (Thursday-Sunday) before Halloween
ZooLights - mid December through early January

## FOR MORE INFORMATION

Pittsburgh Zoo, P.O. Box 5250, Pittsburgh, Pennsylvania 15206; 412-665-3639; Director: Dr. Barbara Baker

# 20

## THE AVIARY
### Pittsburgh, Pennsylvania

First opened in 1952, the Aviary houses one of the world's finest collections of birds; more than 225 species, many of which are endangered, are represented here. Formerly known as the "Pittsburgh Conservatory-Aviary," the facility has been operated by Save-The-Aviary Inc., a private, nonprofit organization, since July, 1992.

The Aviary was accredited by the AAZPA in 1984 and has committed itself to public education, captive propagation and research. Among the many species bred at the facility are endangered birds such as Rothschild's mynah, the Guam rail and the Palawan peacock pheasant.

## VISITOR INFORMATION

**Directions:**   Located on Pittsburgh's historic North Side, the Aviary is a short distance north of Three Rivers Stadium. Proceed to the Stadium, turn north of Allegheny Avenue and then east on Western Avenue to West Park. Directional signs guide you from the Stadium exits to the Aviary.

**Open to the Public:** Daily, 9 AM-4:30 PM

**Closed:** Thanksgiving, Christmas and New Years Day

**Admission (1993):** Adult: $4.00    Child: $2.50    Senior: $3.00

**Parking Fee:** None

**Annual Membership:** Individual: $25    Family: $35

**Programs & Tours:**  The Volunteer Interpretive Program offers a variety of educational programs, including guided tours, outreach programs to schools and community groups and on-site demonstrations.

**AAZPA Member:** Yes

## COLLECTIONS & EXHIBITS

**Collection:**  The Aviary is home to over 400 birds representing more than 225 species.

**Special Exhibits** at the Aviary include:

The March Room - this walk-through greenhouse simulates a tropical wetland; part of the Scaife addition of 1969, this exhibit features waterfowl, egrets, herons, ibises and spoonbills.

**Future Plans:**   An outdoor Hummingbird Garden, to attract wild hummingbirds, is planned.

## CAPTIVE BREEDING & RESEARCH

The Aviary has had special **breeding** success with the following species:

| | |
|---|---|
| Blue-crowned mot mot | Scarlet ibis |
| African grey hornbills | Lilac-breasted roller |
| Bearded barbets | Inca terns |
| Blue-crowned pigeons | Snowy owls |

**Research** at the Aviary includes:
- Studies of avian parasitology
- Research on the causes of avian mortality
- Development of breeding and rearing strategies for birds that have been difficult to breed in captivity

## SEASONAL FESTIVALS & PROGRAMS

Children's Festival - mid May
Conservation Festival - early June
Hummingbirds & Natural Wonders - late July
Wings & Wildlife Nature Art Show - early November

## FOR MORE INFORMATION

The Aviary, Allegheny Commons West, Pittsburgh, Pennsylvania 15212; 412-323-7235; Director: Dayton Baker

# 21    CLYDE PEELING'S REPTILAND LTD.
### Allenwood, Pennsylvania

Landscaped with flowering trees, bamboo and ornamental grasses, this 2.5 acre facility was established in 1964. Reptiland uses natural outdoor habitats, indoor exhibits, live animal shows and hands-on demonstrations to introduce visitors to reptiles from across the globe. A second facility, open during the summer months, is located in the Catskill Mountains on Route 32, south of Cairo, New York.

## VISITOR INFORMATION

**Directions:** The original Reptiland is 13 miles southeast of Williamsport. From I-80, take Exit 30B and head north on Route 15. The facility is on Route 15, 6 miles north of the Interstate.

**Open to the Public:** Daily, 9 AM-7 PM, May to September;
10 AM-5 PM, October to April

**Closed:** Thanksgiving, Christmas and New Years Day

**Admission (1993):** Adult: $6.00   Child: $4.00

**Parking Fee:** None

**Children's Zoo:** No

**Annual Membership:** Not available

**Programs & Tours:** Four live animal shows are presented daily. The facility also offers reptile husbandry workshops and organizes photographic safaris to Kenya, the Amazon and the Galapagos Islands.

**AAZPA Member:** Yes

## COLLECTIONS & EXHIBITS

**Collection:** Reptiland's current collection includes the following number of species:

Birds: 5                     Reptiles: 50
Amphibians: 5             Fish: 1

**Special Exhibits** at Clyde Peeling's Reptiland include:

Outdoor Habitats - during the summer months, crocodiles, tortoises and lizards are displayed in naturalized exhibits

Enclosed Exhibits feature cobras, giant pythons, boas and vipers

**Future Plans:**   "The Beautiful & the Deadly," a multi-image show, is planned.

## CAPTIVE BREEDING & RESEARCH

Clyde Peeling's Reptiland has had special **breeding** success with the following species:

Siamese crocodile          Leopard tortoise

Reptiland conducts **research** on venomoid surgery and is actively involved in local environmental issues; the facility is currently aiding the fight against a proposed hazardous waste incinerator in Gregg Township.

## FOR MORE INFORMATION

Clyde Peeling's Reptiland, Ltd., RD #1, Box 388, Route 15, Allenwood, Pennsylvania 17810; 717-538-1869; Director: Clyde Peeling

# 22    ZOOAMERICA® NORTH AMERICAN WILDLIFE PARK
### Hershey, Pennsylvania

This unique Zoo, established in 1978, exhibits plants and animals that are native to North America. The 11-acre facility groups these species into 5 display areas, each representing a geographic region of the continent.

## VISITOR INFORMATION

**Directions:**   The Zoo is located one block north of U.S. 422 on State Route 743, in Hershey.

**Open to the Public:**   Daily, 10 AM-8 PM mid June through Labor Day;
10 AM-5 PM the remainder of the year

**Closed:** Thanksgiving, Christmas and New Years Day

**Admission (1993):** Adult: $4.00   Child: $2.75   Senior: $3.50

**Parking Fee:** None

**Children's Zoo:** No

**Annual Membership:** Individual: $15     Family: $35

**AAZPA Member:** Yes

## COLLECTIONS & EXHIBITS

**Collection:** The Zoo's current collection includes the following number of species:

| | | |
|---|---|---|
| Mammals: 21 | Birds: 17 | Reptiles: 17 |
| Amphibians: 1 | Mollusks: 1 | Insects: 5 |
| Other Invertebrates: 5 | | Fish: 5 |

**Special Exhibits** at ZOOAMERICA® include:

North American Habitats - the Zoo's exhibits are arranged in five groups, each representing a geographic region of North America; botanical collections are likewise distributed to reflect the native flora of each region.

**Future Plans:** A Collared Peccary Exhibit is scheduled for completion in 1993.

## CAPTIVE BREEDING & RESEARCH

ZOOAMERICA® has had special **breeding** success with the following species:
Golden eagle

## SEASONAL FESTIVALS & PROGRAMS

Creatures of the Night - last two Fridays & Saturdays in October, 6-10 PM

## FOR MORE INFORMATION

ZOOAMERICA® North American Wildlife Park, 100 W. Hershey Park Drive, Hershey, Pennsylvania 17033; 717-534-3860; Director: Troy E. Stump

*Kit Fox*
*(photo by Troy Stump; courtesy ZOOAMERICA® North American Wildlife Park)*

# 23 PHILADELPHIA ZOOLOGICAL GARDEN
## Philadelphia, Pennsylvania

The Philadelphia Zoo is owned and managed by the Zoological Society of Philadelphia which was founded in 1859. The Zoo itself opened in 1874 and now covers 42 acres.

Dave Wood, Assistant Curator of the Philadelphia Zoo, was one of the first zoologists in the world to breed naked mole rats in captivity. These rodents, housed in the Zoo's rare animal building, are the only mammals to display an insect-like social structure. Natives of Somalia and northern Kenya, naked mole rats form colonies in which only a single pair breeds.

## VISITOR INFORMATION

**Directions:** From Interstate 76, take the Girard Avenue Exit and follow the signs to the Zoo.

**Open to the Public:** Summer hours are 9:30 AM-5:30 PM weekdays, 9:30 AM-6:00 PM weekends; 9:30 AM-5:00 PM the remainder of the year

**Closed:** Thanksgiving, Christmas Eve, Christmas Day and New Years Day

**Admission (1993):** Adult: $7.00   Child: $5.75

**Parking Fee:** $3.00

**Children's Zoo:** Yes   **Separate Admission:** No

**Annual Membership** (to Zoological Society of Philadelphia):
  Individual: $30   Family: $40

**Programs & Tours:** The Zoo offers a variety of educational programs including guided tours, workshops, special classes, outreach programs and summer camp.

**AAZPA Member:** Yes

## COLLECTIONS & EXHIBITS

**Collection:** The Zoo's current collection includes the following number of species:
  Mammals: 111      Birds: 190
  Reptiles: 165     Amphibians: 28

**Special Exhibits** at the Philadelphia Zoological Garden include:
  Carnivore Kingdom - unique naturalistic habitats featuring jaguars, snow leopards and other carnivore species
  Rare Animal House - includes naked mole rats

**Future Plans:** Lion's Lookout is scheduled for completion in 1995. The Penrose Animal Health and Conservation Center is slated to open in 1996.

## CAPTIVE BREEDING & RESEARCH

The Philadelphia Zoological Garden has had special **breeding** success with the following species:

| | |
|---|---|
| Lowland gorillas | Geoffrey's marmosets |
| Indian rhinos | Crocodile lizards |
| Malayan tapirs | Prehensile-tailed skinks |
| Naked mole rats | Sun bitterns |

**Research** based at the Philadelphia Zoological Park includes:
- Participation in the Guam Bird Rescue Project
- Participation in Hawaiian Bird Project

## SEASONAL FESTIVALS & PROGRAMS

Zoobilee - June
Run Wild (10K Run) - November
Festival of Lights & Santa's Reindeer - November & December

## FOR MORE INFORMATION

Philadelphia Zoological Garden, 3400 West Girard Avenue, Philadelphia, Pennsylvania 19104-1196; 215-243-1100; Director: Pete Haskins

# 24     BERGEN COUNTY ZOOLOGICAL PARK
### Paramus, New Jersey

Established in 1960, the Bergen County Zoological Park encompasses 18 acres.

## VISITOR INFORMATION

**Directions:** Follow Route 4 to the Forest Avenue Exit. Bear right at the end of the ramp and proceed one mile to the Park (on your right).

**Open to the Public:** 365 days of the year; 10 AM-4:30 PM

**Admission (1993):** Adult: $2.00    Teens & Seniors: $1.00

**Parking Fee:** None

**Children's Zoo:** No (but have Farmyard Exhibit)

**Annual Membership:** Individual: $15    Family: $25

**AAZPA Member:** Yes

## COLLECTIONS & EXHIBITS

**Collection:** The Zoo's current collection includes the following number of species:

| | | |
|---|---|---|
| Mammals: 18 | Birds: 28 | Reptiles: 5 |
| Amphibians: 3 | Invertebrates: 2 | |

**Special Exhibits** at the Bergen County Zoological Park include:
   The Spider Monkey Pavilion
   North American Plains Exhibit
   Walk-Through Wetlands Aviary

**Future Plans:**   A new Farmyard will open in June, 1993.

## CAPTIVE BREEDING & RESEARCH

The Bergen County Zoological Park has had special **breeding** success with the following species:
   Black-handed spider monkeys
   Red brocket deer
   Ocelot

## SEASONAL FESTIVALS & PROGRAMS

Conservation Day - early June
Zoo Boo - late October

## FOR MORE INFORMATION

The Bergen County Zoological Park, 216 Forest Avenue, Paramus, New Jersey 07652; 201-262-3771; Director: Timothy R. Gunther

# 25   THOMAS H. KEAN NEW JERSEY STATE AQUARIUM AT CAMDEN
### Camden, New Jersey

Operated by the New Jersey Academy for Aquatic Sciences, this new aquarium, which opened to the public on February 29, 1992, is located on 4.5 acres along the east bank of the Delaware River. Construction of the Aquarium was funded by the New Jersey State Legislature and was prompted by a revitalization of the Camden waterfront, a project spearheaded by the Campbell Soup Company (based in Camden since 1869).

The facility's mission is to promote the understanding and protection of aquatic life and habitats, especially those found in and around the state of New Jersey. In that spirit, at least 70% of the specimens displayed at the Aquarium were collected from fresh and salt water habitats in the New Jersey region.

*Waterfront view of the Thomas H. Kean New Jersey State Aquarium*
*at Camden as seen from the "Delawhale" ferry*
*(photo courtesy of the Aquarium)*

## VISITOR INFORMATION

**Directions:** The Aquarium is easily accessible from Interstate 676; take the Nickle Blvd. Exit and follow the signs. The "Delawhale" ferry also transports visitors to Camden's waterfront from Penn's Landing in Philadelphia.

**Open to the Public:** Daily, 9:30 AM-5:30 PM

**Closed:** New Years Day, Easter, Thanksgiving, Christmas Day

**Admission (1993):** Adult: $8.50   Child: $5.50   Senior: $7.00

**Parking Fee:** $4.00-$7.00

**Annual Membership:** Individual: $45   Family: $55-$85

**Programs & Tours:** The Aquarium's Education Department offers daily and seasonal programs to increase public awareness of issues that affect regional and global aquatic habitats. School groups can schedule visits by calling 609-365-3300, Ext. 350.

**AAZPA Member:** No

## COLLECTIONS & EXHIBITS

**Collection:** The Aquarium's current collection includes the following number of species:

Mammals: 2          Birds: 15          Reptiles: 6
Amphibians: 6          Mollusks: 8          Fish: 220
Other Invertebrates: 46

**Special Exhibits** at the Thomas H. Kean New Jersey State Aquarium at Camden include:

Barrier Beach - an open, skylit area
Delaware River Exhibit - traces the course of this important waterway
Water Babies - an aquatic nursery
Open Ocean Tank - a 760,000 gallon tank featuring 400 fish and sharks of 40 different species
Seal Pool Exhibit - 170,000 gallons; this outdoor exhibit is one of the largest of its kind in the country
Rotunda Dome - color-coded lighting forecasts tomorrow's weather
Seaprobe - replica of an underwater research station
Edge of the Abyss - a view over the edge of the Continental Shelf through a 2-story window
Rocky Tide Pool - a "hands-on" exhibit
Sea Senses - interactive displays
Wet Lab - educational exhibits for children and adults
Under the Boardwalk - an underwater view of aquatic life that inhabits boardwalk pilings
Trout Stream - this outdoor exhibit includes a waterfall and a rushing mountain stream

**Future Plans:**  A 2-story Coral Reef Exhibit is scheduled for completion in 1994; additional educational displays are also planned.

## CAPTIVE BREEDING & RESEARCH

Since the facility just opened in 1992, a captive **breeding** record has not yet been established.

**Research** based at the Aquarium includes:
- reproductive biology and culture of Sea Ravens
- culture and captive rearing of Tile Fish
- study of the effects of bromate and other water pollutants on marine mammals

## FOR MORE INFORMATION

Thomas H. Kean New Jersey State Aquarium at Camden, 1 Riverside Drive, Camden, New Jersey 08103-1060; 609-365-3300, ext. 307; C.E.O.: Dr. Judith Wellington

# 26     CAPE MAY COUNTY PARK ZOO
## Cape May Court House, New Jersey

Located in a natural, wooded setting, the Cape May County Park Zoo is adorned with a large variety of botanical gardens. The 20-acre Zoo was founded in 1963.

## VISITOR INFORMATION

**Directions:** Take Exit #11 from the Garden State Parkway and follow the directional signs.

**Open to the Public:** Daily, 9 AM-5 PM

**Closed:** Christmas

**Admission:** Free

**Parking Fee:** None

**Children's Zoo:** No

**Annual Membership:** Contact the Cape May County Zoological Society at 609-465-9210

**AAZPA Member:** Yes

## COLLECTIONS & EXHIBITS

**Collection:** The Zoo's current collection includes the following number of species:

| | | |
|---|---|---|
| Mammals: 34 | Birds: 45 | Reptiles: 40 |
| Amphibians: 8 | Fish: 4 | Invertebrates: 4 |

**Future Plans:** An African Savanna Exhibit is scheduled for completion in 1994.

## CAPTIVE BREEDING & RESEARCH

The Cape May County Park Zoo has had special **breeding** success with the following species:

Leopard species
Ring-tailed lemurs
Cougars

The Diamond-back Terrapin Conservation Project is based at the Cape May County Park Zoo.

## SEASONAL FESTIVALS & PROGRAMS

Children's Zoo Camp - July and August

## FOR MORE INFORMATION

Cape May County Park Zoo, Route #9 and Pine Lane, Cape May Court House, New Jersey 08210; 609-465-5271; Director: Philip F. Judyski

# 27    OGLEBAY'S GOOD CHILDREN'S ZOO
## Wheeling, West Virginia

Part of a 1500 acre resort, this 65 acre Zoo features North American species in naturalized habitats. Founded in 1977, the Zoo also includes the Benedum Science Theater and offers a 1.5 mile train ride.

The Oglebay resort is the former site of Waddington Farm, the summer estate of Cleveland industrialist Col. Earl W. Oglebay. During the late 1800s and early 1900s, the Farm was a renowned agricultural center, pioneering experimental farming and animal husbandry techniques.

## VISITOR INFORMATION

**Directions:** From Interstate 70, take the Oglebay Park Exit (Exit 2A) and follow the signs on Route 88 north to the Park.

**Open to the Public:** 365 days per year; 10 AM-6 PM Summer;
10 AM-5 PM remainder of the year

**Closed:** Open every day of the year but hours restricted on Christmas Eve and Christmas Day

**Admission (1993):** Adult: $4.25   Child: $3.25 (under 2 free)
Senior discount available

**Parking Fee:** None

**Annual Membership:** Individual: $20   Family: $25
Family/Guest: $40 (6 guests at a time)

## COLLECTIONS & EXHIBITS

**Collection:** The Zoo's current collection includes the following number of species:

| | | |
|---|---|---|
| Mammals: 16 | Birds: 23 | Reptiles: 11 |
| Amphibians: 2 | Insects: 2 | Fish: 8 |

**Special Exhibits** at Oglebay's Good Children's Zoo include:
Red Wolf Exhibit
Otter Exhibit

## CAPTIVE BREEDING & RESEARCH

The Oglebay's Good Children's Zoo has had special **breeding** success with the following species:
Red Wolf
American Bison

## SEASONAL FESTIVALS & PROGRAMS
Good Easter Treasure Hunt - Easter weekend
Conservation Day - early June
Farm Days - late June
Oglebayfest - early October
Boo at the Zoo - late October
Festival of Lights - November to January

## FOR MORE INFORMATION
Oglebay's Good Children's Zoo, Oglebay Park, Wheeling, West Virginia 26003; 304-243-4030; Director: John A. Hargleroad

# 28    THE BALTIMORE ZOO
## Baltimore, Maryland

The Baltimore Zoo, established in 1876, is the third oldest zoo in the United States. Located on 160 acres in historic Druid Hill Park, the Zoo has undergone extensive redevelopment over the past decade.

Of special note is the new Children's Zoo, an 8-acre facility characterized by interactive exhibits and featuring fifty animal species native to Maryland. Its animal habitats, designed to place emphasis on education and conservation, reflect the diverse ecosystems of the State.

## VISITOR INFORMATION
**Directions:**   From southbound I-95, take Baltimore Beltway/West (I-695) to I-83/South. Take Exit 7 West to Druid Park Lake Drive and follow signs to the Zoo.

From northbound I-95, take Exit 49-B to Baltimore Beltway/West (I-695). Take Exit 18A to Liberty Road which becomes Liberty Heights Avenue. Proceed to Druid Hill Park and follow signs to the Zoo.

**Open to the Public:**   Daily, 10 AM-4 PM; open until 5 PM on weekends in summer (Memorial Day to Labor Day)

**Closed:** Christmas Day and on second Friday in June (for black-tie fundraiser)

**Admission (1993):** Adult: $6.50   Child: $3.50   Senior:  $3.50

**Parking Fee:** None

**Children's Zoo:** Yes     **Separate Admission:** No

**Annual Membership:** Individual: $25     Family: $40

**Programs & Tours:** The Zoo offers a wide variety of educational programs including lectures, behind-the-scenes tours, workshops, ecotravel, outreach programs and field trips.

**AAZPA Member:** Yes

## COLLECTIONS & EXHIBITS

**Collection:**   The Baltimore Zoo harbors over 1500 specimens, representing more than 230 species.

**Special Exhibits** at the Baltimore Zoo include:

Children's Zoo - this new, highly-acclaimed, 8-acre facility includes a farmyard and six natural Maryland habitats. Its 48 exhibits, many of which are interactive, house 50 species native to the State and place emphasis on education and conservation.

African Watering Hole Exhibit - this six acre habitat features zebra, ostrich, pink-backed pelicans, white rhinos, gazelle and other African species.

Kodiak Bear Exhibit - recently renovated

African Safari Trail - crosses 20 acres of plains, woodlands and rocky coastline.

**Future Plans:**   A Chimpanzee Forest is scheduled to open in 1994 and International Valley is slated for 1995.

## CAPTIVE BREEDING & RESEARCH

The Baltimore Zoo has had special **breeding** success with the following species:

Black-footed penguins - largest and most prolific colony in North America

African mud turtle - the Zoo's fortysomething female is the oldest member of her species in captivity

Eastern woodrat - only captive breeding program in U.S. devoted to rescuing this endangered species

Dumeril's ground boa

Bali mynah

Wattled crane

Siberian tiger

Lion-tailed macaque

**Research projects** based at the Baltimore Zoo include:

- Reproductive techniques in lion-tailed macaques
- Eastern woodrat conservation breeding program
- Research on avian malaria
- Studies on aardwolf nutrition

## SEASONAL FESTIVALS & PROGRAMS

Easter with the Beasts

Conservation Day - early June

Zoomerang! - second Friday in June (black-tie fundraiser)

Feast with the Beasts - mid September

Howl-o-ween Spooktacular - late October

## FOR MORE INFORMATION

The Baltimore Zoo, Druid Hill Park, Baltimore, Maryland 21217; 410-396-7102; Director: Brian A. Rutledge

# 29 THE NATIONAL AQUARIUM IN BALTIMORE
## Baltimore, Maryland

The National Aquarium's theme is to "make known the unity of life through water" by combining recreational and educational programs. Ground was broken for the Aquarium on August 1, 1978, and the facility first opened to the public on August 1, 1981. The seven-level structure, located at Pier #3, holds more than 2 million gallons of fresh and salt water. The Marine Mammal Pavilion, a 94,000 square foot addition to the original Aquarium, is located at Pier 4 and is attached to the Aquarium building by an enclosed footbridge.

## VISITOR INFORMATION

**Directions:** From I-95, take the I-395N Exit, heading downtown. Take the left fork and stay in the right lane; turn right onto Conway St., get in the center lane. At the end of Conway St., turn left onto Light St. Pass Harborplace (on your right), stay in the right lane and proceed to Piers 5 & 6 or to President Street for parking. Alternatively, turn left off of Light Street onto Gay Street to park at the Inner Harbor Garage.

**Open to the Public:** 10 AM-5 PM Daily (10 AM-8 PM Fridays), September 16 to May 14; from May 15 to September 15, 9 AM-5 PM Monday thru Thursday, 9 AM-8 PM Friday thru Sunday

**Closed:** Thanksgiving and Christmas Day

**Admission (1993):** Adult: $11.50   Child: $7.50   Senior: $9.50

**Parking Fee:** Variable; all parking is offsite

**Annual Membership:** Individual: $32   Family: $63/$95   Senior: $29

**Programs & Tours:** See Seasonal Festivals & Programs, page 53.

**AAZPA Member:** Yes

## COLLECTIONS & EXHIBITS

**Collection:** The National Aquarium in Baltimore harbors over 5000 specimens of more than 500 species of fish, birds, amphibians, invertebrates, plants and marine animals.

**Major Exhibits** in the **Aquarium Building** include:

Wings Under Water - the country's largest ray exhibit; feeding demonstrations daily at 10:45 AM & 2 PM

Atlantic Coral Reef - a 335,000 gallon exhibit of tropical fish, hawksbill turtles and simulated coral; feeding demonstrations at 11 AM, 1:30 PM and 3 PM

Open Ocean Exhibit - a 220,000 gallon tank housing sharks, rays and large gamefish

South American Rain Forest - enclosed by a 64-foot tall glass pyramid, more than 700 tropical plants and freshwater tanks provide refuge for tropical birds, two-toed sloths, tetras, piranhas and other fish

*National Aquarium in Baltimore and its Marine Mammal Pavilion*
*(photo by George Grall; courtesy National Aquarium in Baltimore)*

Seal Pool - outdoor, 70,000 gallon rock pool; the grey and harbor seals are fed at 10 AM and 4 PM; free to the public

Surviving Through Adaptations Gallery - 22 exhibits depict survival adaptations of marine species

North Atlantic to Pacific Gallery - a tour through the aquatic communities of earth's oceans; the Children's Cove offers hands-on contact with intertidal marine animals

Maryland: Mountains to Sea - four exhibits depict the aquatic habitats of Maryland: Allegheny Mountain Pond, Tidal Marsh, Coastal Beach and Atlantic Shelf.

**Major Exhibits** at the **Marine Mammal Pavilion** include:

The Dolphin Habitat - 1.2 million gallon pool and the Lyn P. Meyerhoff Amphitheater showcase Atlantic bottlenose dolphins

Scylla - life-size replica of a humpback whale

Educational Arcade - hands-on exhibits depict the nature and behavior of marine mammals

Discovery Room - collection of marine artifacts; part of the Jacob & Hilda Blaustein Aquatic Education Resource Center

## CAPTIVE BREEDING & RESEARCH

The National Aquarium in Baltimore has had special **breeding** success with:
Tropical Frogs - more than 1000 have been supplied to other institutions
Aquatic Birds - more than 150 sent to other U.S. zoos and aquariums
Neon Gobies - over 1800 sent to other institutions; for this achievement the National
    Aquarium was awarded the Propagator's Certificate by the AAZPA
Wood Ducks - placement of over 800 nesting boxes across Maryland has aided the
    comeback of this species

The National Aquarium has been working with the Nature Conservancy and other organizations to protect tropical rainforest in Central and South America. It has also been involved with many regional education, recycling and coastal restoration projects. Participation in the marine mammal stranding network offers support for the rehabilitation and release of sick or injured marine animals.

## SEASONAL FESTIVALS & PROGRAMS

The National Aquarium sponsors numerous educational and recreational programs throughout the year. These events are offered at a reduced fee for members. For information regarding membership and to obtain a schedule of these programs, contact the Members Office, National Aquarium in Baltimore, 501 East Pratt St., Baltimore, Maryland 21202, or call them at 410-727-FISH.

Special events and programs at the National Aquarium include:
Behind the Scenes Tours
Recycling Seminars
Breakfast with the Dolphins
Overnight Camps for Children & Adults
Field Trips sponsored by the Aquarium
Halloween Programs:
    Halloween Cabaret
    Creature Feature
    Bats in the Belfry
    Goblin Sharks & Ghost Crabs
    Murder on the Harbor - a murder mystery program
Gifts from the Sea - annual artisans events with holiday shopping (December)
Conservation Days (special program on Earth Day)

## FOR MORE INFORMATION

The National Aquarium in Baltimore, Pier 3, 501 East Pratt St., Baltimore, Maryland 21202-3194; 410-576-3822; Members Program Office 410-727-FISH; Director: Nicholas Brown

# 30 SALISBURY ZOOLOGICAL PARK
## Salisbury, Maryland

The Salisbury Zoological Park, established in 1954, stretches along a branch of the Wicomico River. This 12-acre Zoo is dedicated to the exhibition of Western Hemisphere species and boasts an outstanding collection of waterfowl.

## VISITOR INFORMATION

**Directions:** From U.S. 50, turn south on Highway 13 and proceed to Main St. Turn east on Main St. and drive one block to City Park.

**Open to the Public:** Daily; opens at 8 AM; closing time varies with seasons

**Closed:** Thanksgiving and Christmas

**Admission (1993):** Free; donations accepted

**Parking Fee:** None

**Children's Zoo:** No

**Annual Membership:** contact Friends of the Salisbury Zoo at 410-860-6880

**AAZPA Member:** Yes

## COLLECTIONS & EXHIBITS

**Collection:** The Zoo's current collection includes the following number of species:

Mammals: 18          Birds: 57
Reptiles: 13         Invertebrates: 2

**Special Exhibits** at the Salisbury Zoological Park include:
Waterfowl Collection

**Future Plans:** A North American Otter Exhibit is scheduled to open in 1996.

## CAPTIVE BREEDING & RESEARCH

The Salisbury Zoological Park has had special **breeding** success with the following species:

Spectacled bears - among the first zoos to breed this species
Llamas
Guanacos                Barnacled geese
Ocelots                 Tundra swans
Sun conures             Black-necked swans

The Zoo participates in Species Survival Plans for the Golden-headed Tamarin and Spectacled Bear.

## SEASONAL FESTIVALS & PROGRAMS

Earth Day Celebration - April
Zoobilee - May
Zoo Appreciation Day - August

## FOR MORE INFORMATION

Salisbury Zoological Park, Box 3163, Salisbury, Maryland 21802; 410-548-3188;
Director: Donald D. Bridgwater

# 31          BRANDYWINE ZOO
### Wilmington, Delaware

The Brandywine Zoo, founded in 1905, covers 12 acres. The facility boasts a fine
collection of tamarins and marmosets.

## VISITOR INFORMATION

**Directions:**   From I-95, take the Delaware Avenue Exit; proceed to the Zoo via
VanBuren Street and North Park Drive.

**Open to the Public:** 365 days per year, 10 AM-4 PM

**Admission (1993):**   Adult: $3.00   Child: $1.50   Senior: $1.50
Admission Free November through March

**Parking Fee:** None

**Children's Zoo:** No

**Annual Membership:** Individual: $20     Family: $30

**AAZPA Member:** Yes

## COLLECTIONS & EXHIBITS

**Collection:**     The Zoo's current collection includes the following number of species:
Mammals: 26          Birds: 18
Reptiles: 11         Invertebrates: 1

**Special Exhibits** at the Brandywine Zoo include:
Marmoset & Tamarin Exhibits
Bobcat Exhibit - a large, naturalized exhibit
North American River Otter Exhibit

**Future Plans:**  A Coatimundi Exhibit will open in 1993 and an Andean Condor
Exhibit is scheduled for completion in 1994.

## CAPTIVE BREEDING & RESEARCH

The Brandywine Zoo has had special **breeding** success with the following species:

Golden lion tamarins          Common Marmoset
Golden-headed tamarins        Capybaras
Red-handed tamarins

## SEASONAL FESTIVALS & PROGRAMS

Spring Fling - early April
Zippity Zoo Days - September

## FOR MORE INFORMATION

Brandywine Zoo, 1001 N. Park Drive, Wilmington, Delaware 19802; 302-571-7747; Director: Nancy M. Falasco


# 32  NATIONAL ZOOLOGICAL PARK
## Washington, D.C.

In 1887, William T. Hornaday, Chief Taxidermist for the National Museum, proposed a national zoo to exhibit and protect native American species. Two years later, on March 2, 1889, President Cleveland signed a bill to create the National Zoological Park. The Zoo now spreads across 163 acres of Rock Creek Park, a hilly, naturalistic setting in northwest Washington, D.C., and is accessed by over 2 miles of walking trails.

## VISITOR INFORMATION

**Directions:** The Zoo is located in northwest Washington, D.C. The main entrance is in the 3000 block of Connecticut Avenue; other entrances are off Beach Drive and at the junction of Harvard St. and Adams Mills Road.

**Open to the Public:** 8 AM-8 PM, April 15 to October 15;
8 AM-6 PM, October 16 to April 14;
Exhibit buildings are open 9 AM-6 PM, May 1 to September 15, and 9 AM-4:30 PM September 16 through April 30

**Closed:** Christmas Day

**Admission:** Free

**Parking Fee:** $1.00 flat rate before 10 AM; 10 AM-4:30 PM, $3.00 first 3 hours, $2.00 each additional hour; $2.00 flat rate after 4:30 PM; free handicapped parking in Lots B & D.

**Children's Zoo:** No

**Annual Membership:** Contact the Friends of the National Zoo at 202-332-WILD or write to them at the Zoo.

**Programs & Tours:**  Three learning centers (Zoolab, Birdlab & Herplab) are free and open to the public. Free tours are conducted on weekends. Feeding and training demonstrations are presented at the Giant Panda, Cheetah, Elephant, Seal & Sea Lion Exhibits.

**AAZPA Member:**  Yes

## COLLECTIONS & EXHIBITS

**Collection:**  The National Zoo's current collection includes the following number of species:

| | | |
|---|---|---|
| Mammals: 120 | Birds: 155 | Reptiles: 67 |
| Amphibians: 18 | Fish: 23 | Invertebrates: 14 |

**Special Exhibits** at the National Zoo include:

Amazonia - 15,000 sq. ft., climate-controlled habitat with 358 species of plants; Amazonian fish; aquatic and terrestrial animals

Komodo Dragon Exhibit - Indonesia donated a pair of these giant reptiles in 1988

Giant Panda Exhibit - Ling-Ling and Hsing-Hsing were presented to the U.S. by the People's Republic of China in 1972; Ling-Ling recently died at the age of 23.

Reptile Discovery Center - cooperative effort with Zoo Atlanta and the Dallas Zoo; 12 educational modules

Butterfly Gardens (seasonal)

Invertebrate Exhibit (open Wednesday thru Sunday) - explores the biology of earth's most primitive species

**Future Plans:**  The National Zoo has set the goal to become a "Biopark" with holistic exhibits combining plants and animals, thereby placing emphasis on the interdependence of species.

*"Kraken," the first Komodo dragon hatched outside of Indonesia;*
*hatching date was 9/13/92.*
*(photo by Jessie Cohen; courtesy National Zoological Park, Smithsonian Institution)*

## CAPTIVE BREEDING & RESEARCH

The National Zoo has had special **breeding** success with the following species:
Pygmy hippopotamus (more than any other zoo in the world)
Red panda
Greater one-horned rhinoceros
Golden lion tamarin
Komodo dragon
Cuban crocodile
Sumatran tiger
Tropical amphibians
Guam rail

The National Zoo coordinates **research** and captive breeding programs throughout the U.S. and across the globe. The Zoo participates in many of the Species Survival Plans governed by the AAZPA. Most of the National Zoo's research is based at its Conservation & Research Center in Front Royal, Virginia. Among the many projects are:
- Golden Lion Tamarin Species Survival Plan
- Guam Rail Reintroduction Project
- In Vitro Fertilization Research

## SEASONAL FESTIVALS & PROGRAMS

Zoonight, Zoofari & Seal Day - all sponsored and coordinated by Friends of the National Zoo; for info call 202-332-WILD
Sunset Serenades - outdoor summer concert series

## FOR MORE INFORMATION

The National Zoo, Smithsonian Institution, Washington, D.C. 20008; 202-332-WILD (Membership, Friends of the National Zoo); 202-673-4821 (Programs); 202-673-4840 (Public Affairs); Director: Michael H. Robinson

*Inside the National Zoo's new Amazonia exhibit which opened in November, 1992.*
*(photo by Jessie Cohen; courtesy National Zoological Park)*

# II. SOUTHEAST REGION

33. **Louisville Zoological Garden** (Louisville, Kentucky)
34. **Mill Mountain Zoo** (Roanoke, Virginia)
35. **Virginia Zoological Park** (Roanoke, Virginia)
36. **The Memphis Zoo & Aquarium** (Memphis, Tennessee)
37. **Grassmere Wildlife Park** (Nashville, Tennessee)
38. **Tennessee Aquarium** (Chattanooga, Tennessee)
39. **Knoxville Zoological Gardens** (Knoxville, Tennessee)
40. **North Carolina Zoological Park** (Asheboro, North Carolina)
41. **North Carolina Aquarium on Roanoke Island**
    (Manteo, North Carolina)
42. **North Carolina Aquarium at Pine Knoll Shores**
    (Atlantic Beach, North Carolina)
43. **North Carolina Aquarium at Fort Fisher**
    (Kure Beach, North Carolina)
44. **The Jackson Zoological Park** (Jackson, Mississippi)
45. **Birmingham Zoo** (Birmingham, Alabama)
46. **Montgomery Zoo** (Montgomery, Alabama)
47. **Zoo Atlanta** (Atlanta, Georgia)
48. **Greenville Zoo** (Greenville, South Carolina)
49. **Riverbanks Zoo & Botanical Garden**
    (Columbia, South Carolina)
50. **Brookgreen Gardens** (Murrells Inlet, South Carolina)
51. **The Zoo** (Gulf Breeze, Florida)
52. **Jacksonville Zoological Park** (Jacksonville, Florida)
53. **St. Augustine Alligator Farm, Inc.** (St. Augustine, Florida)
54. **Santa Fe Community College Teaching Zoo**
    (Gainesville, Florida)
55. **Central Florida Zoological Park** (Lake Monroe, Florida)
56. **Sea World of Florida** (Orlando, Florida)
57. **Discovery Island Zoological Park** (Lake Buena Vista, Florida)
58. **Busch Gardens Tampa** (Tampa, Florida)
59. **Lowry Park Zoo** (Tampa, Florida)
60. **Dreher Park Zoo** (West Palm Beach, Florida)
61. **Parrot Jungle & Gardens** (Miami, Florida)
62. **Miami MetroZoo** (Miami, Florida)

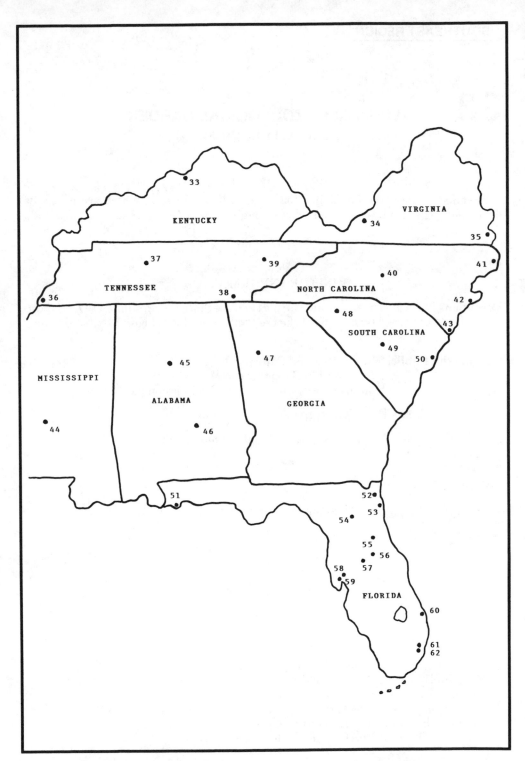

# SOUTHEAST REGION ZOOS & AQUARIUMS

# 33 LOUISVILLE ZOOLOGICAL GARDEN
## Louisville, Kentucky

Founded in 1968, the Louisville Zoo covers 133 acres, 74 of which are partially developed. The Zoo boasts an Arachnid Exhibit, the only one of its kind in North America.

## VISITOR INFORMATION

**Directions:** Located near the main airport and the State Fairgrounds, the Zoo is best reached from I-264. Take the Poplar Level Road North exit and follow the signs.

**Open to the Public:** Daily, 10 AM-5 PM April to August;
10 AM-4 PM September to March;
the Zoo closes 1 hour after the admission gate closes

**Closed:** New Years Day, Thanksgiving and Christmas

**Admission (1993):** Adult $5.00   Child: $2.50   Senior: $3.00

**Parking Fee:** None

**Children's Zoo:** No

**Annual Membership:** Individual: $20   Family: $40   One+One: $30

**AAZPA Member:** Yes

## COLLECTIONS & EXHIBITS

**Collection:** The Zoo's current collection includes the following number of species:
Mammals: 54        Birds: 53        Reptiles: 95
Amphibians: 26        Fish: 61        Other Invertebrates: 3

**Special Exhibits** at the Louisville Zoo include:
MetaZoo Education Center - combines classrooms, hands-on exhibits and living collections
HerpAquarium - houses reptiles, fish, amphibians and invertebrates
Arachnid Exhibit - the only one of its kind in North America
Polar Bear Exhibit - surface and underwater viewing

**Future Plans:**  The Louisville Zoo is currently preparing to implement Phases I & II of its Master Development Plan. New additions and exhibits will inlcude: Atrium and botanical collection, a Penguin Exhibit, Asian Elephant Logging Camp, Great Ape Exhibit and an Islands Exhibit. Completion dates are pending.

## CAPTIVE BREEDING & RESEARCH

The Louisville Zoo has had special **breeding** success with the following species:

| | |
|---|---|
| Woolly Monkeys | Black and White Ruffed Lemurs |
| Black-footed Ferrets | Guam Rail |
| Gila Monsters | Maned Wolves |
| Kirtland's Water Snake | Siberian Tigers |
| Hyacinth Macaws | Crested Screamers |
| Addax | Bongo |

**Research** based at the Louisville Zoo includes:
- Embryo Transfer of exotic to domestic equine
- Study of Hypertension in Woolly Monkeys
- Study of Subspeciation and relatedness in Woolly Monkeys

## SEASONAL FESTIVALS & PROGRAMS

Children's Environmental Festival - mid May
Summer Kickoff Celebration - late May
"Roarchestra" Orchestra Concert Series - mid June through July
Safari Day Camps - Summer
The World's Largest Halloween Party - last two weekends in October
Winter Light Safari - early December through early January
We Don't Hibernate Classes - January and February
Zooper Kids and 2X2 Programs - selected times throughout the year

## FOR MORE INFORMATION

Louisville Zoological Garden, 1100 Trevilian Way, P.O. Box 37250, Louisville, Kentucky 40233; 502-459-2181 (General), 502-459-2287 (Membership), 502-458-1940 (Campaign Office); Director: William R. Foster, D.V.M.

# 34

## MILL MOUNTAIN ZOO
### Roanoke, Virginia

Located atop Mill Mountain, this 10 acre Zoo yields broad views of the Roanoke Valley. The Zoo opened in 1952 and is operated by the Blue Ridge Zoological Society of Virginia.

## VISITOR INFORMATION

**Directions:** From I-81, exit onto I-581 and head south to downtown Roanoke. Take Exit #6 and turn right at the stoplight. Go through the first light and turn left at the second light (Jefferson St.). Proceed to 4th light and turn left onto Walnut Avenue which takes you up to the Mill Mountain Zoo.

**Open to the Public:** Daily; 10 AM-6 PM, mid April to October 1; 10 AM-4:30 PM, October 2 to mid April

**Closed:** Christmas Day

**Admission (1993):** Adult: $3.50   Child: $2.00

**Parking Fee:** None

**Children's Zoo:** No (however, Zoo has contact area for children)

**Annual Membership:** Individual: $10   Family: $25

**Programs & Tours:** The Zoo offers guided tours and educational programs; call in advance for schedules and reservations.

**AAZPA Member:** No

## COLLECTIONS & EXHIBITS

**Collection:** The Zoo's current collection includes the following number of species:
  Mammals: 20         Birds: 9         Reptiles: 9

**Future Plans:** A Manchurian Crane Exhibit is scheduled to open in 1993. A Japanese Macaque Exhibit and a Domestic Minor Breeds area will be completed in 1994. A Siberian Tiger Exhibit is slated for 1996. "Animals of the Orient" and a Northern Asia Exhibit are also planned.

## CAPTIVE BREEDING & RESEARCH

The Mill Mountain Zoo has had special **breeding** success with the following species:
  Red panda

The Zoo participates in Species Survival Plans for the golden lion tamarin, the red panda and Matschie's tree kangaroo. The American Center for Rare & Endangered Species, located at the Zoo, is devoted to breeding endangered North American animals.

## SEASONAL FESTIVALS & PROGRAMS

Zoobilation! - mid April
Sister City Day - mid May
Conservation Festival - mid June
Picnic Night - mid June
Fourth of July Picnic Night
Breakfast with the Animals - early July
ZooDo! - mid July
Membership Night - mid August
Breakfast with the Animals - early October
Zoo Boo! - Halloween

## FOR MORE INFORMATION

Mill Mountain Zoo, Blue Ridge Zoological Society of Virginia, P.O. Box 13484, Roanoke, Virginia 24034; 703-343-3241; Director: Mrs. Beth Poff

# 35   VIRGINIA ZOOLOGICAL PARK
### Norfolk, Virginia

Established in 1937, the Virginia Zoological Park is owned and operated by the City of Norfolk. The 55-acre Zoo participates in six Species Survival Plans.

## VISITOR INFORMATION

**Directions:**   The Zoo is north of the downtown area. From I-64, on the north side of Norfolk, exit onto Granby St. Head south on Granby Street for approximately 4 miles; the Zoo is at 3500 Granby.

**Open to the Public:** Daily, 10 AM-5 PM

**Closed:** Christmas and New Years Day

**Admission (1993):** Adult: $2.00   Child: $1.00   Senior: $1.00

**Parking Fee:** None

**Children's Zoo:** Yes     **Separate Admission:** No

**Annual Membership:** Contact the Virginia Zoological Society at 804-624-9937

**AAZPA Member:** Yes

## COLLECTIONS & EXHIBITS

**Collection:** The Zoo's current collection includes the following number of species:

| | | |
|---|---|---|
| Mammals: 37 | Birds: 26 | Reptiles: 36 |
| Amphibians: 5 | Insects: 1 | Other Invertebrates: 1 |

**Future Plans:** A Tiger Exhibit will open in 1993.

## CAPTIVE BREEDING & RESEARCH

The Virginia Zoological Park participates in Species Survival Plans for Clouded leopards, Red ruffed lemurs, Rhinos, Elephants, Baird's tapirs and Virgin Island tree boas.

The Zoo conducts **research** on: Infrasonic communication in Rhinos.

## SEASONAL FESTIVALS & PROGRAMS

Breakfast with the Animals - Spring
Early Bloomers - Spring
Summer Safari - all Summer
Zoo Tots
Zoo Snooze
Zoo to Do - early September

## FOR MORE INFORMATION

Virginia Zoological Park, 3500 Granby Street, Norfolk, Virginia 23504; 804-441-5240, 804-441-2374; Superintendent: Gary Ochsenbein

# 36 THE MEMPHIS ZOO & AQUARIUM
## Memphis, Tennessee

Having originated as an animal menagerie in Overton Park, establishment of the Memphis Zoo was spearheaded by Colonel Robert Galloway. Today, the 70-acre facility, founded in 1906, is undergoing major renovations. An Egyptian style entryway and orientation court lead into the wooded setting which was once known as the "Hippo Capital of the World" due to its prolific hippo residents.

## VISITOR INFORMATION

**Directions:** From the downtown area, travel east on Poplar Avenue. Proceed approximately 5 miles and turn left into Overton Park at Kenilworth (look for Zoo sign); follow the banners to the front gate.

**Open to the Public:** Daily; 9 AM-5 PM April through September;
9 AM-4:30 PM October through March

**Closed:** Thanksgiving, Christmas Eve, Christmas Day

**Admission (1993):** Adult: $5.00   Child: $3.00   Senior: $3.00

**Parking Fee:** None

**Children's Zoo:** Yes   **Separate Admission:** No

**Annual Membership:** Individual: $25   Family: $40   Senior: $40 (grandparent)

**AAZPA Member:** Yes

## COLLECTIONS & EXHIBITS

**Collection:** The Zoo & Aquarium's current collection includes the following number of species:

| | | |
|---|---|---|
| Mammals: 291 | Birds: 105 | Reptiles: 88 |
| Amphibians: 16 | Fish: 163 | Insects: 1 |
| Mollusks: 1 | Other Invertebrates: 10 | |

**Special Exhibits** at the Memphis Zoo & Aquarium include the following:

Hoofed Mammal Collection - includes 35 species

Nocturnal Exhibit - features the New Zealand Boobook owl, pigeon and dove collection - includes 15 species, among them the world's rarest pigeon (the Mauriturus pink pigeon)

Cat Country Exhibit - covers four acres

New Zealand Kiwi Breeding Facility

**Future Plans:** The Cat Country Exhibit, an education complex, the Children's Village and the Orientation Plaza will all be completed in 1993. Expansion of the forest exhibit, the opening of Primate Canyon, completion of the World of Darkness and dedication of a Zoo Tram are all scheduled for 1994.

## CAPTIVE BREEDING & RESEARCH

The Memphis Zoo & Aquarium has had special **breeding** success with the following species:

| | |
|---|---|
| Fruit Dove Species | King Cobra |
| Hooded pitta | Cuban ground iguana |
| Fairy bluebird | Lowland gorilla |
| West African dwarf crocodile | Hippopotamus |
| Radiated tortoise | Pere David deer |
| Gila monster | Snow leopard |
| Indian python | |

Among the **research projects** currently underway at the Memphis Zoo & Aquarium are:

- Reproductive ecology of South African cobras
- Behavioral research on aard wolves and Fennec foxes (a cooperative effort with Memphis State University)
- Behavioral and reproductive studies of the Lowland anoa
- Captive husbandry program for lesser Antilles iguana

## SEASONAL FESTIVALS & PROGRAMS

Zoo Grass - early June
Zoo Rendezvous - early September
Zoo Boo - late October
Winter Lights - December

## FOR MORE INFORMATION

The Memphis Zoo & Aquarium, 2000 Galloway, Memphis, Tennessee 38112; 901-276-WILD: Director: Charles Wilson

# 37     GRASSMERE WILDLIFE PARK
## Nashville, Tennessee

The 200-acre Grassmere Wildlife Park, established in 1990, takes advantage of the local, natural landscape to display animals indigenous to Tennessee. The Park also features the Croft House; built in the early 1800s, this antebellum home is listed on the National Register of Historic Places.

## VISITOR INFORMATION

**Directions:** The Park is southeast of the downtown area, between I-65 and I-24.
From I-65, take the Harding Place Exit (Exit 78-A), proceed east to Nolensville Road and then north to the Wildlife Park.
From I-24, take the Harding Place Exit (Exit #56), proceed west to Nolensville Road and then north to the Park.

**Open to the Public:** 10 AM-5 PM, Memorial Day to Labor Day; 10 AM-4 PM remainder of the year; the Park remains open 1 hour after the entrance gate closes

**Closed:** Thanksgiving, Christmas and New Years Day

**Admission (1993):** Adult: $5.00   Child: $3.00 (under 3 free)   Senior: $3.00

**Parking Fee:** None

**Children's Zoo:** No

**Annual Membership:** Individual: $25   Family: $35   Grandparent: $35

**AAZPA Member:** Yes

## COLLECTIONS & EXHIBITS

**Collection:** The Wildlife Park's current collection includes the following number of species:

Mammals: 38 specimens    Birds: 35 specimens
Reptiles: 32 specimens    Amphibians: 7 specimens
Fish: 95 specimens

**Special exhibits** at the Grassmere Wildlife Park include:
North American River Otter Exhibit - surface and underwater viewing
Citicorp Aviary - a collection of native birds
Cumberland River Exhibit - features a variety of fish, reptiles and other aquatic life
Croft Family Home - daily tours of this antebellum house; listed on National Register of Historic Places. The farm was deeded to Cumberland Museums by Elise and Margaret Croft with the stipulation that it be used as a nature and wildlife center.

**Future Plans:** A Golden Eagle Exhibit will be completed in 1993. A Red Wolf Exhibit and Survival Facility and a Wetlands Habitat are also planned.

## CAPTIVE BREEDING & RESEARCH

The Grassmere Wildlife Park has had special **breeding** success with the following species:

Bison                          North American river otter
American elk               Fulvous whistling duck
Black bear                  House finch

**Research projects** based at the Park include:
- Captive breeding of western pygmy rattlesnakes
- Study of pair bonding in captive North American otters
- DNA fingerprinting of captive North American otters

## SEASONAL FESTIVALS & PROGRAMS

Nashville Earth Day Festival - April
Grassmere Wildlife Park Birthday Party - early June
Halloween Howl - Halloween Week
Teddy Bear Rally - early November

## FOR MORE INFORMATION

Grassmere Wildlife Park, 3777 Nolensville Road, Nashville, Tennessee 37204; 615-833-1534; Director: Bill Cook

# 38     TENNESSEE AQUARIUM
### Chattanooga, Tennessee

Tennessee is home to more freshwater fish species than any other State in the Union. It is thus fitting that the world's first freshwater life center, the Tennessee Aquarium, opened here in 1992.

This 12-story, 130,000 square-foot complex is the "crown jewel" of Chattanooga's 20-year Redevelopment Plan. Located in Ross's Landing Park & Plaza, on the banks of the Tennessee River, the Aquarium is a private, nonprofit, educational facility, dedicated to the understanding, conservation and enjoyment of rivers. Its exhibits trace the course of earth's major rivers, depicting the flora and fauna of aquatic habitats along the way.

*Amazon River Exhibit*
*(photo by Richard T. Bryant; courtesy Tennessee Aquarium)*

## VISITOR INFORMATION

**Directions:** From I-24, take Exit 178, drive north on Market Street and turn left (west) on 2nd Street to the Aquarium.

From U.S. 27, take Exit 1C. Proceed east on 4th Street and then north on Broad Street to the Aquarium.

**Open to the Public:** Daily, 10 AM-6 PM; open until 8 PM Fri.-Sat.-Sun., May 1 through Labor Day

**Closed:** Thanksgiving and Christmas Day

**Admission (1993):** Adult: $8.75  Child: $4.75

**Parking Fee:** $3.00-$5.00

**Annual Membership:** Individual: $29  Family: $49  Senior: Discount available

**Programs & Tours:** The Aquarium harbors extensive educational facilities including a 200-seat auditorium, classrooms, a computer lab and a wet lab.

**AAZPA Member:** No (new facility)

## COLLECTIONS & EXHIBITS

**Collection:** The Tennessee Aquarium is home to over 4000 specimens, representing more than 350 species of fish, birds, mammals, reptiles and amphibians.

**Special Exhibits** at the Tennessee Aquarium include:

Appalachian Cove Forest - housed beneath the pyramidal glass roof of the Aquarium, this exhibit changes with the seasons; its three component habitats are the mountain sink, the mountain stream and the otter pool.

Tennessee River Gallery - this exhibit compares the Tennessee River before and after construction of the TVA Dams. The 138,000 gallon Nickajack Lake habitat is the largest freshwater aquarium tank in the world. The exhibit also examines the natural history of Reelfoot Lake, created by an earthquake in 1812.

Discovery Falls - a series of interactive exhibits focus on small life forms along the Tennessee River and offer tips to anglers.

Mississippi Delta - this cypress swamp habitat is home to alligators, redbellied and map turtles, alligator snapping turtles and a variety of snakes; shallow pools harbor gar, bass and sunfish. This exhibit also includes the only saltwater tank at the Aquarium, featuring residents of the Gulf of Mexico (fish, stingrays, sharks and tarpon)

Rivers of the World - examines six river systems from around the world, placing emphasis on their ecology and on the importance of protecting these ribbons of life.

## SEASONAL FESTIVALS & PROGRAMS

Anniversary Celebration - May 1
Other seasonal events still in the planning stage.

## FOR MORE INFORMATION

Tennessee Aquarium, One Broad Street, Chattanooga, Tennessee 37402; 615-265-0695; Director: William S. Flynn

*The Tennessee Aquarium*
*(photo by Richard T. Bryant; courtesy Tennessee Aquarium)*

# 39 KNOXVILLE ZOOLOGICAL GARDENS
## Knoxville, Tennessee

Nestled among the forested hills of eastern Tennessee, the Knoxville Zoological Gardens was established in 1946. Its 75 acres are adorned with 125 varieties of trees and shrubs.

## VISITOR INFORMATION

**Directions:** The Zoo is northeast of the downtown area. From Interstate 40, take Exit #392 and follow the signs.

**Open to the Public:** 9:30 AM-6 PM Summer; 9:30 AM-4:30 PM Winter

**Closed:** Christmas Day

**Admission (1993):** Adult: $6.00   Child: $3.50   Senior: $3.50

**Parking Fee:** $1.00

**Children's Zoo:** Yes   **Separate Admission:** $.50

**Annual Membership:** Individual: $30 ($35, + Guest)   Family: $45   Senior: $25

**AAZPA Member:** Yes

## COLLECTIONS & EXHIBITS

**Collection:** The Zoo's current collection includes the following number of species:
Mammals: 63        Birds: 60        Reptiles: 105
Amphibians: 4        Insects: 6

**Special Exhibits** at the Knoxville Zoological Gardens include:
Red Panda Exhibit
Cheetah Savannah
Red Wolf Exhibit
Asiatic Lion Exhibit
Andean Condor Exhibit
Drill Baboon Exhibit
Children's Zoo - new Log Barn completed in 1992

**Future Plans:** New Gorilla and Chimpanzee Exhibits are planned for 1993.

## CAPTIVE BREEDING & RESEARCH

The Knoxville Zoological Gardens has had special **breeding** success with the following species:

White Rhino            Red Wolf
Red Panda              California Sea Lion
Reticulated Giraffe    Polar Bear
African Elephant       Bog Turtle
Snow Leopard           Bali Mynah
Chimpanzee

**Research projects** based at the Knoxville Zoological Gardens include:
- Study of social behavior and influence of environmental factors on development of drill baboons
- Red Panda reproduction and early development
- Infant social development of chimpanzee: hand-reared vs. maternal-reared chimps
- Study of red wolf behavior
- Physiology and behavioral development of African Elephants

## SEASONAL FESTIVALS & PROGRAMS

"Zoolympics" (Fundraiser for underprivileged children) - early Spring
Zoofari (Zoo Fundraiser Dinner & Dance) - early June
Zooper Kids - Summer Day Camps
Teddy Bear Picnic - late July
Boo! at the Zoo - late October
Zoo Lights before Christmas - mid December to December 23; a Festival of over 100,000 sparkling lights

## FOR MORE INFORMATION

Knoxville Zoological Gardens, P.O. Box 6040, Knoxville, Tennessee 37914; 615-637-5331; Acting Director: Michael Fouraker

# 40   NORTH CAROLINA ZOOLOGICAL PARK
## Asheboro, North Carolina

Founded in 1974, the North Carolina Zoological Park was the world's first zoo to be planned entirely around the natural habitat philosophy. Encompassing 1448 acres, it is one of the largest zoo's, by area, in the country.

## VISITOR INFORMATION

**Directions:**   From U.S. 220 and U.S. 64, follow directional signs to the Zoo Parkway (N.C. 159) and drive 6 miles southeast of Asheboro to the Zoo.

**Open to the Public:**   9 AM-5 PM weekdays, 10 AM-6 PM weekends and holidays, April through October; 9 AM-4 PM daily, November through March

**Closed:**   Visitor services are closed December 24-25 but the animal exhibits are open (weather permitting)

**Admission (1993):** Adult: $5.00   Child: $3.00   Senior: $3.00

**Parking Fee:** None

**Children's Zoo:** No

**Annual Membership:** Individual: $25   Family: $39

**AAZPA Member:** Yes

*Meerkats*
*(photo by Jim Page; courtesy North Carolina Zoological Park)*

## COLLECTIONS & EXHIBITS

**Collection:** The Zoo's current collection includes the following number of species:

Mammals: 40          Birds: 67          Reptiles: 10
Amphibians: 2        Fish: 2

**Special Exhibits** at the North Carolina Zoological Park include:

R.J. Reynolds Forest Aviary - recreating a tropical forest, this exhibit features over 150 exotic birds; selected by *USA Today* as one of the 10 best natural habitat exhibits in the country

African Wart Hogs - the only East Coast zoo to exhibit this species

African Pavilion - houses 200 animals and over 3000 plants representing a variety of Africa's major ecosystems. Among the residents are Colobus monkeys, dwarf crocodiles, meerkats, leopards and mandrills.

African Plains - a 37 acre rolling grassland; features 12 species of antelope

Forest Glade Habitat - home to a family of lowland gorillas

Forest Edge Habitat - a 3.5 acre open woodland simulates the savanna country of Kenya; home to reticulated giraffes, Grant's zebras, marabou storks and ostriches

**Future Plans:**    A four-million dollar Desert Pavilion will open in 1993; this indoor habitat recreates a Sonoran Desert environment and is the first exhibit to open in the Zoo's new 200-acre North American Region. Sixty-four additional North American habitats, featuring 100 new animals and 200 new plant species, will open in October, 1994.

## CAPTIVE BREEDING & RESEARCH

The North Carolina Zoological Park has had special **breeding** success with the following species:
African Pied Barbet - first U.S. captive breeding of this bird
Red-face Liocichla - first U.S. captive breeding of this Asian songbird
African spoonbills - the only breeding colony of this bird in the U.S.

## SEASONAL FESTIVALS & PROGRAMS

Zoo Fling - educational programs and live entertainment each weekend in April
8 KM Road Race - late April
Zoo & Aquarium Month - June; special programs on weekends
Grandparents Day - mid September
ZooFest - educational programs and live entertainment each weekend in October
Zoo Walk - October
Boo at the Zoo - October 30 & 31
Christmas at the Zoo - December 24-26; free admission for all visitors

## FOR MORE INFORMATION

North Carolina Zoological Park, Route 4, Box 83, Asheboro, North Carolina 27203; 919-879-7000; Director: Robert L. Fry

# 41 NORTH CAROLINA AQUARIUM ON ROANOKE ISLAND
## Manteo, North Carolina

This 14.5 acre complex is one of three Aquariums spaced along the coast of North Carolina. Originally established as marine resource centers in 1976, these facilities were renamed the North Carolina Aquariums in 1986. The private, nonprofit North Carolina Aquarium Society was established to manage the trio and to solicit funds for development of the Aquarium exhibits.

The North Carolina Aquariums are devoted to exhibiting marine life native to the mid Atlantic Coast, educating the public on marine conservation issues and conducting reseearch on the diverse inhabitants of this fragile life zone.

*North Carolina Aquarium on Roanoke Island*
*(photo courtesy North Carolina Aquarium)*

*Residents of The North Carolina Aquarium on Roanoke Island*
*(photo courtesy North Carolina Aquarium)*

## VISITOR INFORMATION

**Directions:**  The North Carolina Aquarium on Roanoke Island is three miles north of Manteo on Airport Road.

**Open to the Public:** 9 AM-5 PM Monday-Saturday; 1 PM-5 PM Sunday

**Closed:** Thanksgiving, Christmas and New Years Day

**Admission:** Free; admission charge under consideration

**Parking Fee:** None

**Annual Membership** (to North Carolina Aquarium Society):
Individual: $20      Family: $35
Contact the Society at 417 N. Blount St., Raleigh, North Carolina 27601;
1-800-832-FISH

**Programs & Tours:**  The Aquarium offers a wide variety of educational programs including field trips, a lecture series, on-water programs and special workshops.

**AAZPA Member:** Yes

## COLLECTIONS & EXHIBITS

**Collection:** The Zoo's current collection includes the following number of species:
Fishs 40                Reptiles: 10        Invertebrates: 9

**Special Exhibits** at the North Carolina Aquarium on Roanoke Island include:
Grady-White Shark Gallery - features sharks of northeastern North Carolina
Coastal Carolina Wetlands Exhibit - home to alligators, turtles and fresh water fish
Marine Aquarium Gallery - marine life of northeastern coastal North Carolina

**Future Plans:**  A Skate & Ray Touch Tank and an Estuarine Interpretive Trail are both scheduled to open in 1993.

## CAPTIVE BREEDING & RESEARCH

The Aquarium participates in the North Carolina Division of Marine Fisheries red drum tagging program and juvenile fish study.

## SEASONAL FESTIVALS & PROGRAMS

Annual Earth Day Celebration
Conservation Day - first weekend in June
Hurricane Awareness Week
Wildfoods Weekend - first weekend in October

## FOR MORE INFORMATION

North Carolina Aquarium on Roanoke Island, P.O. Box 967, Manteo, North Carolina 27954; 919-473-3493; Director: Rhett B. White

# 42

## NORTH CAROLINA AQUARIUM
## AT PINE KNOLL SHORES
### Atlantic Beach, North Carolina

The three North Carolina Aquariums are strategically located at the three most densely populated, and most heavily visited, areas along the North Carolina coast. All three facilities are dedicated to educating the public about the diversity and fragility of the State's coastal ecosystems.

## VISITOR INFORMATION

**Directions:** From New Bern, follow U.S. 70 southeast to Morehead City and then take the causeway south to Atlantic Beach. The Aquarium is 5 miles west of Atlantic Beach on N.C. 58.

**Open to the Public:** 9 AM-5 PM, Monday to Saturday; 1 PM-5 PM Sunday

**Closed:** Thanksgiving, Christmas and New Years Day

**Admission:** Has been free; decision regarding an admission fee is pending

**Parking Fee:** None

**Annual Membership** (to North Carolina Aquarium Society):
  Individual: $20      Family:$35

  Contact the Society at 417 N. Blount St., Raleigh, North Carolina 27601; 1-800-832-FISH

**Programs & Tours:** The Aquarium offers a wide variety of educational programs, including field trips, films, live animal demonstrations, behind-the-scenes tours, canoeing, snorkeling, boat trips, nautical craft workshops and seafood demonstrations.

**AAZPA Member:** Yes

## COLLECTIONS & EXHIBITS

**Collection:** The Aquarium's current collection includes the following number of species:

Reptiles: 5                 Fish: 50              Mollusks: 5
Other Invertebrates: 12

**Special Exhibits** at the North Carolina Aquarium at Pine Knoll Shores include:
   Touch Tank
   Loggerhead Sea Turtle Exhibit
   North Carolina Marine Life Gallery
   Living Shipwreck Display
   Precious Waters Exhibit - features alligators and salt marsh
   Nature Trail through maritime forest

## SEASONAL FESTIVALS & PROGRAMS

The Aquarium offers numerous programs and festivals through the year. Among these are:
   North Carolina Dive Weekend - Fall
   North Carolina Aquarium Surf Fishing Workshop - Fall

## FOR MORE INFORMATION

North Carolina Aquarium at Pine Knoll Shores, Atlantic Beach, North Carolina 28512-0580; 919-247-4003; Director: Jay Barnes

*Diver at North Carolina Aquarium, Pine Knoll Shores*
*(photo courtesy of the Aquarium)*

# 43 NORTH CAROLINA AQUARIUM AT FORT FISHER
## Kure Beach, North Carolina

Located 20 miles south of Wilmington, North Carolina, this 12-acre facility displays marine and coastal life characteristic of the Cape Fear region. Surrounded by undeveloped beach, coastal dunes, marshlands and the Cape Fear estuary, the Aquarium offers a wide variety of educational programs throughout the year.

## VISITOR INFORMATION

**Directions:** From Wilmington, drive south on U.S. 421 (Carolina Beach Road). Proceed approximately 20 miles to Kure Beach; the Aquarium is located just beyond this coastal town.

**Open to the Public:** 9 AM-5 PM, Monday to Saturday; 1 PM-5 PM Sunday

**Closed:** Thanksgiving, Christmas and New Years Day

**Admission:** Has been free but admission charge currently under consideration

**Parking Fee:** None

**Annual Membership** (to North Carolina Aquarium Society):
Individual: $20      Family: $35
Contact the Society at 417 N. Blount St., Raleigh, North Carolina 27601;
1-800-832-FISH

**Programs & Tours:** Educational programs based at the Aquarium include field trips, workshops, lectures, films, summer camps and seasonal events.

**AAZPA Member:** Yes

## COLLECTIONS & EXHIBITS

**Collection:** The Aquarium's current collection includes the following number of species:

| | | |
|---|---|---|
| Reptiles: 15 | Amphibians: 6 | Mollusks: 4 |
| Insects: 2 | Fish: 60 | Other Invertebrates: 33 |

**Special Exhibits** at the North Carolina Aquarium at Fort Fisher include:
Marine Life of the Cape Fear Coast
Shark Tank - 20,000 gallon exhibit
Stingray & Skate Exhibit
Touch Tank
Replica of Humpback Whale (49 ft. long)

**Future Plans:**  A Sea Turtle Exhibit is scheduled to open in 1993. An Open Ocean Tank (225,000 gallons) and a Green Swamp Exhibit are planned for 1996.

*Moray Eel*
*(photo by Jim Lanier; courtesy North Aquarium at Fort Fisher)*

## SEASONAL FESTIVALS & PROGRAMS

Earth Day
Conservation Day
Zoo & Aquarium Month - June

## FOR MORE INFORMATION

North Carolina Aquarium at Fort Fisher, 2201 Fort Fisher Blvd. South, P.O. Box 130, Kure Beach, North Carolina 28449-0130; 919-458-8257; Director: Dr. James A. Lanier III

# 44 THE JACKSON ZOOLOGICAL PARK
### Jackson, Mississippi

Established in 1919, this 110 acre Zoo has received wide acclaim for its Children's Discovery Zoo which features a variety of "hands-on" educational displays. The Zoo also works closely with city schools, offering a curriculum package called "The Jackson Zoo - A Living Classroom."

## VISITOR INFORMATION

**Directions:** The Jackson Zoological Park is northwest of the downtown area. From I-220, take the Capitol Street Exit. Drive east on Capitol Street; the Zoo will be approximately 2 miles, on your left.

**Open to the Public:** Daily, 9 AM-6 PM June-August; 9 AM-5 PM September-May

**Closed:** Christmas and New Years Day

**Admission (1993):** Adult: $3.50    Child: $1.75    Senior: $1.75

**Parking Fee:** None

**Children's Zoo:** Yes    **Separate Admission:** No

**Annual Membership:** Individual: $15    Family: $30

**AAZPA Member:** Yes

## COLLECTIONS & EXHIBITS

**Collection:** The Zoo's current collection includes the following number of species:
    Mammals: 61          Birds: 50          Reptiles: 28
    Amphibians: 1

**Special Exhibits** at the Jackson Zoological Park include:
    African Boardwalk Rain Forest - this exhibit features a ½ acre chimpanzee island
    African Plains Exhibit - home to cheetahs
    Children's Discovery Zoo - includes four "hands-on" barns full of interactive displays for children

**Future Plans:** The Zoo Gift Shop and The Elephant House Cafe were both scheduled to open in February, 1993. The Zoo's masterplan for future development places emphasis on naturalized exhibits, grouped by region; continuous work is scheduled for the next three years.

## CAPTIVE BREEDING & RESEARCH

The Jackson Zoological Park has had special **breeding** success with the following species:

| | |
|---|---|
| Cheetahs | Colobus monkeys |
| Serval cats | Sitatunga |
| Clouded leopards | King vultures |
| Chimpanzees | |

## SEASONAL FESTIVALS & PROGRAMS

ZOO Blues - first weekend in April
ZOOparty - third weekend in April
Conservation Day - first weekend in June
Fright Night at the Zoo - third week in October
Zoo Unto Others - Thanksgiving Days
Christmas at the Zoo - first two weekends in December

## FOR MORE INFORMATION

The Jackson Zoological Park, 2918 West Capitol Street, Jackson, Mississippi 39209; 601-352-2585; Director: Barbara A. Barrett

# 45        BIRMINGHAM ZOO
### Birmingham, Alabama

Spreading across 100 acres of wooded parkland, the Birmingham Zoo was founded in 1955. The Zoo is owned and operated by the city of Birmingham and receives support from the Alabama Zoological Society.

## VISITOR INFORMATION

**Directions:** The Zoo is located on the southern edge of Birmingham. Follow U.S. 280/U.S. 31 to the Mountain Brook Exit.

**Open to the Public:** Daily, 9 AM-5 PM; extended hours to 7 PM during summer

**Closed:** Zoobilee Day (in September), Thanksgiving and Christmas Day

**Admission (1993):** Adult: $4.00   Child: $1.50 (under 2 free)   Senior: $1.50

**Parking Fee:** None

**Children's Zoo:** No

**Annual Membership:** Individual: $25   Family: $40   Senior: $15

**Programs & Tours:** "Zoo to You" program brings expertise of zoo professionals to regional classrooms

**AAZPA Member:** Re-accreditation in progress

*Hamadryas Baboons*
*(photo by Liz Hicks; courtesy Birmingham Zoo)*

## COLLECTIONS & EXHIBITS

Collection:  The Zoo's current collection includes the following number of species:

| | | |
|---|---|---|
| Mammals: 68 | Birds: 78 | Reptiles: 68 |
| Amphibians: 6 | Fish: 5 | Insects: 3 |
| Other Invertebrates: 6 | | |

**Special Exhibits** at the Birmingham Zoo include:

Predators Building
Social Animals Building - includes Hamadryas baboons, natives of rocky, desert areas of Ethiopia, Somalia and the Middle East
Panther Chameleons - recent addition to the Zoo

**Future Plans:**   A Cheetah Exhibit is scheduled to open in the spring of 1993.

## CAPTIVE BREEDING & RESEARCH

The Birmingham Zoo has had special **breeding** success with the following species:
Spider monkeys
Besia oryx
Siberian tiger

The Zoo participates in species survival plans for the White-handed Gibbon, Orangutan, Snow Leopard, Siberian Tiger, Asian Elephant, Southern White Rhinoceros, White-naped Crane, Bali Mynah and Lowland Gorilla.

## SEASONAL FESTIVALS & PROGRAMS

Zoobilee (Black-Tie Fund Raiser) - mid September
Boo in the Zoo - Halloween
Holiday with the Animals - December

## FOR MORE INFORMATION

The Birmingham Zoo, 2630 Cahaba Road, Birmingham, Alabama 35223; 205-879-0458; Director: Jerry Wallace

# 46 MONTGOMERY ZOO
### Montgomery, Alabama

The Montgomery Zoo, established in 1972, covers 40 acres. The facility is home to nine endangered species and will be adding a South American Realm in 1993. The latter will feature brocked and pampas deer, tapirs, capybaras, peccaries, rheas, guanocos and coscoroba swans.

## VISITOR INFORMATION

**Directions:** The Zoo is on the northern edge of Montgomery. From I-65, exit onto North Blvd. (Route 152), heading northeast. Turn right (south) on Lower Wetumpka Road and then left (east) on Vandiver Blvd. to the Zoo.

**Open to the Public:** Daily, 10 AM-7 PM summer;
10 AM-5 PM the remainder of the year

**Closed:** Christmas and New Years Day

**Admission (1993):** Adult: $3.50   Child: $1.50 (under 4 free)   Senior: $2.00

**Parking Fee:** None

**Children's Zoo:** No

**Annual Membership:** Individual: $25   Family: $35   Grandparent: $35

**AAZPA Member:** Yes

*Chimpanzee Habitat*
*(photo by William Fiore; courtesy Montgomery Zoo)*

## COLLECTIONS & EXHIBITS

**Collection:** The Zoo's current collection includes the following number of species:
    Mammals: 45        Birds: 98        Reptiles: 31

**Future Plans:** Work is underway on a Bengal Tiger Exhibit. In addition, a collection of South American habitats, "The South American Realm," is scheduled for 1993.

## CAPTIVE BREEDING & RESEARCH

The Montgomery Zoo has had special **breeding** success with the following species:

| | |
|---|---|
| Chimpanzees | Slender-horned gazelles |
| Red kangaroos | Eld's deer |
| Banteng | Ne Ne geese |

## SEASONAL FESTIVALS & PROGRAMS

Zoo Weekend - second weekend in March
Ballet and the Beasts - mid April
Summer Concert Series - May through August
Zoo Boo - October
Christmas Light Festival - November to December

## FOR MORE INFORMATION

Montgomery Zoo, 329 Vandiver Blvd., Montgomery, Alabama 36110; 205-240-4900; Director: Mr. William J. Fiore

# 47

## ZOO ATLANTA
### Atlanta, Georgia

Home to the famous Willie B., a silverback gorilla who spent almost three decades in solitude, Zoo Atlanta was founded in 1889. When the 37-acre Zoo opened its naturalized gorilla exhibit in 1988, Willie B. was reunited with other members of his species and has since sired offspring. His earlier plight and his newfound "freedom" characterize a shift in zoo management: from confinement and entertainment to conservation, humane care, education and research.

## VISITOR INFORMATION

**Directions:** From downtown Atlanta, take Interstate 75 South to Interstate 20; go east on Interstate 20 and exit onto Boulevard (Exit #26); follow the signs to Zoo Atlanta which is located in Grant Park.

**Open to the Public:** Daily; 10 AM-5 PM weekdays (10 AM-6 PM summer); 10 AM-6 PM weekends

**Closed:** New Years Day, Martin Luther King Jr.'s Birthday, Thanksgiving Day, Christmas Day

**Admission (1993):** Adult: $7.00    Child: $3.50    Senior: $6.00

**Parking Fee:** None

**Children's Zoo:** Yes    **Separate Admission:** No

**Annual Membership:** Individual: $30    Family: $49

**AAZPA Member:** Yes

## COLLECTIONS & EXHIBITS

**Collection:** The Zoo's current collection includes the following number of species:
Mammals: 33          Birds: 57          Reptiles: 126
Amphibians: 14       Fish: 1            Invertebrates: 14

**Special Exhibits** at Zoo Atlanta include:
Ford African Rain Forest - 18 western lowland gorillas in natural habitat and family groupings
Masai Mara - re-creation of East African plains featuring giraffes, zebra, black rhino, ostriches, antelope, gazelle, African lions and exotic birds

**Future Plans:** An Okefenokee Swamp Exhibit, Tropical Islands Exhibit and Conservation Center are scheduled to open in 1994. Completion of an Australian Outback Exhibit is slated for 1996.

*The famous Willie B.*
*(photo by J. Sebo;*
*courtesy Zoo Atlanta)*

## CAPTIVE BREEDING & RESEARCH

Zoo Atlanta has had special **breeding** success with the following species:
  Sumatran tigers
  Western lowland gorilla

Current **research projects** at the Zoo include:
  - Primate behavioral studies
  - Chilean flamingo breeding
  - Nocturnal behavior of African elephants
  - Golden lion tamarin re-introduction program

## SEASONAL FESTIVALS & PROGRAMS

Tortoise Race Weekend - June
Willie B.'s Birthday Party - July
Rainforest Weekend - October
Great Halloween Caper - October
Starlet the Elephant's Big Birthday Party - November

## FOR MORE INFORMATION

Zoo Atlanta, 800 Cherokee Avenue, S.E., Atlanta, Georgia 30315-1440; 404-624-5600;
Director: Dr. Terry L. Maple

# 48

## GREENVILLE ZOO
### Greenville, South Carolina

The Greenville Zoo, established in 1960, was completely renovated in 1986. The 15-acre Zoo is now characterized by spacious, naturally landscaped exhibits, grouped into geographic regions.

## VISITOR INFORMATION

**Directions:** From I-385, take Exit #42 and follow signs to the Zoo.

**Open to the Public:** Daily, 10 AM-4:30 PM

**Closed:** Thanksgiving, Christmas and New Years Day

**Admission (1993):** Adult: $3.00    Child: $1.25

**Parking Fee:** None

**Children's Zoo:** No

**Annual Membership:** Individual: $20    Family: $30    Senior: $15

**Programs & Tours:** The Zoo offers educational programs for children, families and community groups.

**AAZPA Member:** Yes

## COLLECTIONS & EXHIBITS

**Collection:** The Zoo's current collection includes the following number of species:
    Mammals: 25          Birds: 19          Reptiles: 34
    Amphibians: 7        Insects: 3         Fish: 5

**Special Exhibits** at the Greenville Zoo include:
    White Bengal Tiger Exhibit
    Red Panda Exhibit
    Waterfowl Lagoon

## SEASONAL FESTIVALS & PROGRAMS

Zoo Camp - Summer
Boo in the Zoo - late October
Christmas Light Program - December

## FOR MORE INFORMATION

Greenville Zoo, 150 Cleveland Park Drive, Greenville, South Carolina 29601; 803-467-4300; Director: Lee Sims

# 49 RIVERBANKS ZOO & BOTANICAL GARDEN
## Columbia, South Carolina

Often cited as one of the ten best zoos in America, the Riverbanks Zoo was founded in 1974. The 50-acre Zoo will be complemented by a 70-acre Botanical Garden, to open in 1994; the Garden will be located across the Saluda River from the Zoo.

Despite its location in a relatively small State, the Riverbanks Zoo is the 14th most visited zoo in the country. Furthermore, it has received accolades for its Aquarium Reptile Complex and is internationally renowned for its captive breeding of threatened bird and reptile species.

## VISITOR INFORMATION

**Directions:** The Riverbanks Zoo is located along the Saluda River, west of downtown Columbia. Take the Greystone Boulevard Exit from Interstate 126; the Zoo is just south of the Interstate.

**Open to the Public:** Daily, 9 AM-4 PM; 9 AM-5 PM on Summer weekends

**Closed:** Thanksgiving and Christmas Day

**Admission (1993):** Adult: $4.00    Child: $1.75    Senior: $2.50

**Parking Fee:** None

**Children's Zoo:** No

**Annual Membership:** Individual: $25    Family: $35    Grandparent: $39

**Programs & Tours:** The Zoo's Education Department offers a variety of programs which complement elementary school curricula throughout South Carolina.

**AAZPA Member:** Yes

## COLLECTIONS & EXHIBITS

**Collection:** The Zoo's current collection includes the following number of species:
    Mammals: 47          Birds: 121          Reptiles: 84
    Amphibians: 14       Fish: 185

**Special Exhibits** at the Riverbanks Zoo include:
    Aquarium Reptile Complex - more than 80 exhibits featuring habitats of South Carolina, the Desert Southwest, the Tropics and the Open Ocean; the Ocean Gallery includes a 60,000 gallon Indo-Pacific coral reef aquarium. The Complex, which opened in 1989, was named one of the top three new exhibits by the AAZPA.
    African Plains Exhibit - renovated in 1991, this mixed-species habitat features black rhinos, zebras, giraffes and ostriches

*African Plains Exhibit*
*(photo by E. Short; courtesy Riverbanks Zoo)*

*Siberian Tiger Exhibit*
*(photo courtesy Riverbanks Zoo)*

Riverbanks Farm - having opening in 1988, this exhibit is home to a variety of domestic animals and is the site of seasonal festivals

**Future Plans:** A New Animal Hospital is planned and the Riverbanks Botanical Garden will open in 1994 on a 70 acre site across the Saluda River from the Zoo. The Garden will feature walking trails through natural areas, formal flower gardens, a home demonstration garden and a Visitor Center.

## CAPTIVE BREEDING & RESEARCH

The Riverbanks Zoo has had special **breeding** success with the following species:

Black Howler Monkeys - the zoo has the largest captive colony of this species in the world and has been recognized by the AAZPA for its breeding success with this monkey

Toco Toucan - first Zoo in the world to breed this species

Crimson Seedcracker - first Zoo in the world to breed this species

Milky Eagle Owl - first Western Hemisphere Zoo to breed this species

Blue-billed Weaver - first Western Hemisphere Zoo to breed this species

Cinereous Vulture - first captive breeding in Western Hemisphere

| | |
|---|---|
| Bali Mynah | Renauld's Ground Cuckoos |
| Golden Lion Tamarin | Eclectus Parrots |
| Radiated Tortoise | Pied Hornbills |
| Aruba Island Rattlesnake | King Cobra |
| White-faced Saki Monkeys | Siberian Tiger |

The Riverbanks Zoo participates in many of the Species Survival Plans administered by the AAZPA. The Zoo established a Raptor Rehabilitation Program in 1979 and has been involved in projects to breed and re-introduce endangered Bali mynahs and Golden lion tamarins. **Research** at the Zoo also includes:

- Study of variation in bill size in black-bellied seedcracker species (a National Science Foundation study in conjunction with the University of California at Berkeley)
- Reproductive studies on Baird's tapir, African elephants and radiated tortoises
- Funding of graduate animal pathology research at the University of Georgia (a cooperative effort with Zoo Atlanta)

## SEASONAL FESTIVALS & PROGRAMS

Springtime at Riverbanks Farm - early spring
Annual Taste of Columbia at Riverbanks Zoo - early spring
Annual Southern Garden Show - early spring
Conservation Day - May
Summer Day Camps - June through August
Fridays After Five - performing arts series, June-August
Lights Before Christmas at Riverbanks Zoo - December
Free Fridays - January & February

## FOR MORE INFORMATION

The Riverbanks Zoo & Botanical Garden, 500 Wildlife Parkway, P.O. Box 1060, Columbia, South Carolina 29202; 803-779-8717; Director: Palmer E. Krantz

# 50     BROOKGREEN GARDENS
## Murrells Inlet, South Carolina

Brookgreen Gardens, founded in 1931, is the oldest public sculpture garden in America. The Park's botanical collection includes a 250 year-old live oak, a palmetto garden and a native plant garden with 70 woody plant species of the Southeastern U.S. The wildlife park is home to sixteen species native to the region.

## VISITOR INFORMATION

**Directions:** Brookgreen Gardens is on the west side of U.S. 17, mid-way between Myrtle Beach and Georgetown.

**Open to the Public:** Daily, 9:30 AM-4:45 PM

**Closed:** Christmas Day

**Admission (1993):** Adult: $5.00     Child (6-12): $2.00 (under 6 free)

**Parking Fee:** None

**Children's Zoo:** No

**Annual Membership:** Individual: $25     Family: $35

**AAZPA Member:** Yes

## COLLECTIONS & EXHIBITS

**Collection:** Brookgreen Gardens' current animal collection includes the following number of species:
Mammals: 5     Birds: 10       Reptiles: 1

**Special Exhibits** at Brookgreen Gardens include:
Cypress Bird Sanctuary - built in 1977; a 90-foot net covers a cypress swamp which is home to waterfowl, egrets, ibis and herons
Otter Pond & Alligator Swamp Exhibits - in tidal fresh water
Virginia White-Tailed Deer Exhibit - 23 acres with rotterdam moat
Raptor Aviary - completed 1988
Fox & Raccoon Glade
Native Plant Garden - includes 70 woody plant species native to the Southeastern U.S.

**Future Plans:** Enlargement of the nature center with expanded educational programs is scheduled for 1994.

## SEASONAL FESTIVALS & PROGRAMS
Brookgreenfest - October

## FOR MORE INFORMATION
Brookgreen Gardens, 1931 Brookgreen Drive, Murrels Inlet, South Carolina 29576; 803-237-4218; Director: Gurdon L. Tarbox, Jr.

# 51

## THE ZOO
### Gulf Breeze, Florida

Covering 50 acres along the northern Gulf Coast, the ZOO opened in 1984. Sixty percent of the facility is covered by The Preserve, a mixed-species exhibit where animals roam free in their natural habitat. The ZOO's Safari Line Limited boards visitors at the Nairobi Station and carries them through The Preserve, offering a taste of the African continent.

## VISITOR INFORMATION

**Directions:** The ZOO is located on the Gulf Breeze Parkway (U.S. 98), 8 miles east of Gulf Breeze and 19 miles west of Fort Walton Beach.

**Open to the Public:** 9 AM-5 PM Summer, 9 AM-4 PM Winter

**Closed:** Thanksgiving and Christmas Day

**Admission (1993):** Adult: $8.50 + tax    Child: $5.00 + tax    Senior: $7.50 + tax

**Parking Fee:** None

**Children's Zoo:** Yes    **Separate Admission:** No

**Annual Membership:** Individual: $50    Family: $95    Grandparents: $95

**Programs & Tours:** Animal shows are presented daily at the Outdoor Amphitheater (late May to Labor Day)

**AAZPA:** Yes

## COLLECTIONS & EXHIBITS

**Collection:** The ZOO's current collection includes the following number of species:
    Mammals: 63          Birds: 110
    Reptiles: 10         Fish: 6

**Special Exhibits** at The ZOO include:
    The Preserve - 30 acres of free-roaming animals in their natural habitat
    Japanese Gardens - features a reflecting pool, a variety of horticulture and
        authentic deer scare
    Alligator Exhibit - recent addition to The ZOO
    White Bengal Tiger Exhibit
    Pygmy Hippo Exhibit - three specimens of this rare species

**Future Plans:** The ZOO will open an Orangutan Exhibit in 1993. New Rhinoceros, Elephant and Chimpanzee Exhibits are scheduled for completion in 1996.

## CAPTIVE BREEDING & RESEARCH

The ZOO has had special **breeding** success with the following species:

| | |
|---|---|
| Colobus monkey | Sarus crane |
| Red-handed tamarin | Bali mynah |
| de Brazza's monkey | Sacred ibis |
| Siamang | Addax |
| Gibbon | Gemsbok |
| Lemur | Thomson's Gazelle |

**Research** at The ZOO has included behavioral studies of the greater apes in cooperation with students from the University of West Florida.

## SEASONAL FESTIVALS & PROGRAMS

ZOO HOP - Easter Celebration
ZOO BOO - Halloween Carnival
ZOOCamp - One week summer program for children (ages 5-12)

## FOR MORE INFORMATION

The ZOO, 5701 Gulf Breeze Parkway, Gulf Breeze, Florida 32561; 904-932-2229; Director: Pat Quinn

*Giraffe Feeding Station*
*(photo courtesy E. W. Bullock*
*Associates and The ZOO*
*at Gulf Breeze, Florida)*

# 52 JACKSONVILLE ZOOLOGICAL PARK
### Jacksonville, Florida

Established in 1914, the Jacksonville Zoological Park harbors a fine collection of rare and unusual birds and reptiles, many of which have been successfully bred at the facility. The 71-acre Zoo, located on the north bank of the Trout River, also boasts a 432-foot pier which provides convenient access for boaters.

## VISITOR INFORMATION

**Directions:** The Zoo is north of the downtown area on the north bank of the Trout River. From I-95, take Exit 124-A and proceed east on Heckscher Drive. Follow signs to the Park.

**Open to the Public:** Daily, 9 AM-5 PM

**Closed:** Thanksgiving, Christmas and New Years Day

**Admission (1993):** Adult: $4.00   Child: $2.50   Senior: $3.00

**Parking Fee:** None; also, free docking at Zoo's pier on Trout River

**Children's Zoo:** Yes    **Separate Admission:** No

**Annual Membership:** Individual: $25    Family: $35    Senior: $20

**Programs & Tours:** "Elephant Encounter" is presented daily. "Animals & Us" is presented on weekends and holidays.

**AAZPA Member:** Yes

## COLLECTIONS & EXHIBITS

**Collection:** The Zoo's current collection includes the following number of species:
| | | |
|---|---|---|
| Mammals: 59 | Birds: 84 | Reptiles: 48 |
| Amphibians: 5 | Fish: 1 | Invertebrates: 1 |

**Special Exhibits** at the Jacksonville Zoological Park include:

Mahali Pa Simba - Swahili for "Place of the Lion," this natural exhibit immerses the visitor in the lion's habitat, offering views from three perspectives.

Grizzled Grey Tree Kangaroo - one of only three zoos in the world to exhibit this species

South African Crested Porcupine - one of only three zoos in North America to exhibit this species

African Veldt - an 11 acre re-creation of the African savannah; home to ostriches, greater kudu, Thomson's gazelles and other plains species

Okavango Trail - a boardwalk leads visitors past and through exhibits that feature natives of the Okavango River region of South Africa: crocodiles, caracal lynx, blue duikers, Kirk's dik-dik, tropical birds and other species.

Florida Wetlands Exhibit - this naturally occuring habitat features plants and animals native to northeast Florida

Aviary - home to Marabou storks and rare Pondicherry vultures

**Future Plans:** The Jacksonville Zoological Park is in the midst of a major redevelopment project: ZOO-2000. The Mahali Pa Simba Exhibit was the first step in this ambitious program.

## CAPTIVE BREEDING & RESEARCH

The Jacksonville Zoological Park has had special **breeding** success with the following species:

Aldabra tortoise
Eastern indigo snake
Florida pine snake
Pondicherry vulture
Southern ground hornbill
Toco toucan
Marabou stork - one of only two successful captive breeding programs in the world

**Research projects** based at the Jacksonville Zoological Park include:

- Participation in Florida Panther captive breeding program
- Captive breeding and release programs for Eastern indigo snake and Florida pine snake (cooperative effort with Florida Game & Fresh Water Fish Commission)
- Participation in Species Survival Plans of the AAZPA

## SEASONAL FESTIVALS & PROGRAMS

Animal Magnetism - February
Teddy Bear Affair - April
Girl Scout Day - April
Earth Day/Conservation Day - June
Back to School - August
Boy Scout Day/Zoofair - October
Spooktacular - October
Christmas on Main Street - December

## FOR MORE INFORMATION

Jacksonville Zoological Park, 8605 Zoo Road, Jacksonville, Florida 32218; 904-757-4463; Executive Director: Dale Tuttle

# 53  ST. AUGUSTINE ALLIGATOR FARM, INC.
## St. Augustine, Florida

Home to almost 3000 reptiles representing over 75 species, the St. Augustine Alligator Farm has been educating and entertaining visitors since 1893. The 17 acre facility is opening a new exhibit, "Crocodilians of the World," on Memorial Day, 1993, which will feature specimens from all 22 crocodile species.

## VISITOR INFORMATION

**Directions:**  Take Highway A1A South; the Alligator Farm is 1.5 miles off the Bridge of Lions.

**Open to the Public:**  365 days per year; 9 AM-6 PM Summer; 9 AM-5 PM the remainder of the year

**Admission (1993):**  Adult: $7.95   Child: $5.25   Senior: $7.20

**Parking Fee:**  None

**Children's Zoo:**  Yes      **Separate Admission:**  No

**Annual Membership:**  Individual: $11.95

**AAZPA Member:**  Yes

## COLLECTIONS & EXHIBITS

**Collections:**  The St. Augustine Alligator Farm's current collection includes the following number of specimens:

Mammals: 45 specimens                    Birds: 57 specimens
Reptiles: 2875 specimens

**Special Exhibits** at the Alligator Farm include:
Wildlife Shows - presented every hour starting at 10 AM
Gomek - this giant crocodile from New Guinea is the largest specimen on exhibit (17.5 feet, 1700 pounds)
Crocodilians of the World - new in Summer, 1993; features all 22 species of crocodile

## CAPTIVE BREEDING & RESEARCH

The St. Augustine Alligator Farm has had special **breeding** success with the following species:
Siamese crocodiles
Chinese alligators
Cuban crocodiles

## FOR MORE INFORMATION

St. Augustine Alligator Farm, Inc., A1A South, St. Augustine, Florida 32084; 904-824-3337; Director: Mark A. Wise

# 54 SANTA FE COMMUNITY COLLEGE
## TEACHING ZOO
### Gainesville, Florida

In addition to serving as the Zoo for the Gainesville area, this 14-acre facility, established in 1972, is a teaching laboratory for the Zoo Animal Technology Program of Santa Fe Community College. This program is a 5-semester course of study that trains students for a career in zookeeping; one of only two such programs in the U.S., the course is also part of a joint program in animal technology that combines study at both Santa Fe Community College and the State University of New York at Oswego.

## VISITOR INFORMATION

**Directions:** Exit onto State Road 222 from Interstate 75. Go one mile to NW 83rd St. (the Frontage Road for the college). Turn down the drive marked "Gymnasium, Zoo;" the Zoo driveway and parking area are just past the gym, on the left.

**Open to the Public:** Weekdays, 9 AM-3 PM; weekends, 9 AM-2 PM

**Closed:** During school semester breaks (typically late April, mid August and the December-January holiday period)

**Admission:** Free

**Parking Fee:** None

**Children's Zoo:** No

**Annual Membership:** No membership program

**AAZPA Member:** Yes

## COLLECTIONS & EXHIBITS

**Collection:** The Zoo's current collection includes the following number of species:
Mammals: 13          Birds: 30          Reptiles: 30
Amphibians: 3

**Special Exhibits** at the Teaching Zoo include:
Bald Eagle Exhibit
Red-Ruffed Lemur Exhibit - an S.S.P. species
Asian Small-Clawed Otter Exhibit - an S.S.P. species

**Future Plans:** A new habitat for the African grey parrots is scheduled to open in 1993.

## CAPTIVE BREEDING & RESEARCH

The Santa Fe Community College Teaching Zoo has had special **breeding** success with the following species:

Eclectus Parrots

Hawk-headed Parrots

Yellow-crowned Amazons

In addition to its role as a teaching facility, the Zoo also conducts **research**. One such program is the study of alligator development, a project coordinated with reproductive biologists at the University of Florida.

## FOR MORE INFORMATION

The Santa Fe Community College Teaching Zoo, 3000 NW 83rd St., Gainesville, Florida 32606; 904-395-5604; Director: Jack A. Brown

# 55  CENTRAL FLORIDA ZOOLOGICAL PARK
### Lake Monroe, Florida

Established in 1975, the Central Florida Zoological Park covers 109 acres. Feeding demonstrations and animal encounter programs are offered on weekends.

## VISITOR INFORMATION

**Directions:** From Orlando, take I-4 East to Exit 52 and follow the signs to the Central Florida Zoological Park.

From Daytona Beach, take I-4 West to Exit 52 and head south on Highway 17/92. The Zoo will be on your right.

**Open to the Public:** Daily, 9 AM-5 PM

**Closed:** Thanksgiving Day and Christmas

**Admission (1993):** Adult: $5.00   Child: $2.00   Senior: $3.00

**Parking Fee:** None

**Children's Zoo:** Yes   **Separate Admission:** No

**Annual Membership:** Individual: $20   Family: $40   Senior: $15

**Programs & Tours:** Nature Niche, an education program for children, is based at the Zoo. Weekend feeding demonstrations and Animal Encounters. Tours available by reservation.

**AAZPA Member:** Yes

## COLLECTIONS & EXHIBITS

**Collection:** The Zoo's current collection includes the following number of species:

Mammals: 33          Birds: 32          Reptiles: 48
Amphibians: 10       Invertebrates: 5

**Special Exhibits** at the Central Florida Zoological Park include:
Animal Adventure - a Children's Zoo
Herpetarium - includes monitor lizards and neotropical pit vipers
Neotropical Primates
Aviaries - planted with natural vegetation

Future Plans:    Bali Mynah, Saffron Toucanet, Tamarin, Clouded Leopard and
                 Caribbean Iguana Exhibits will open in 1993. Cheetah, Mixed
                 Antelope and Invertebrate Exhibits will be completed by 1994.

## CAPTIVE BREEDING & RESEARCH

The Central Florida Zoological Park has had special **breeding** success with the following species:

Black-handed Spider Monkey          Bali Mynah
Capuchin Monkey                     Macaws
Black Howler Monkey                 Amazons
Siamang                             Alligator
Caracal                            Arboreal Pit Viper
Serval                             Boas

**Research** at the Central Florida Zoological Park includes:
- Behavioral and Reproductive studies in felines

## FOR MORE INFORMATION

Central Florida Zoological Park, 3755 N. Highway 17/92, P.O. Box 309, Lake Monroe, Florida 32747; 407-323-4450; Director: Edward S. Posey

# 56

## SEA WORLD OF FLORIDA
### Orlando, Florida

Owned and operated by Anheuser-Busch Companies, Inc., Sea World of Florida opened in December, 1973, and has since become the world's most popular marine life park. With a commitment to entertainment, education, research and conservation, the Park offers an increasing variety of shows, exhibits and "hands-on" displays for its 4-million-plus annual visitors.

## VISITOR INFORMATION

**Directions:** Located at the intersection of Interstate 4 and the Bee Line Expressway, 10 minutes south of downtown Orlando.

**Open to the Public:** 365 days per year; 9 AM-7 PM; hours vary during summer and on holidays; Sea World recommends that you allow 8 hours to see all shows and exhibits.

**Admission (1993):** Adult: $31.95   Child: $27.95   Senior: $27.95

**Parking Fee:** $4.00 per car

**Annual Membership:** (subject to change)
Individual: $54.95   Child: $44.95   Senior: $39.95

**Programs & Tours:** Sea World offers Behind-the-Scenes tours and "Let's Talk Training" presentations; the latter introduces visitors to animal behavior and training techniques. Daily animal shows highlight the natural abilities of marine mammals.

**AAZPA Member:** Yes

## COLLECTIONS & EXHIBITS

**Collection:** The Park's current collection includes the following number of species:
Mammals: 10        Birds: 104                Reptiles: 7
Fish: 210          Invertebrates: 75

**Special Exhibits** at Sea World of Florida include:
Manatees: The Last Generation - this 3.5 acre exhibit, new in 1993, introduces visitors to the natural habitat of the endangered Florida manatee
Pacific Point - this 2.5 acre habitat duplicates the rocky, northern Pacific Coast; home to California sea lions, harbor seals and fur seals; the exhibit is new in 1993
Shamu Breeding & Research pool - newest addition to Shamu Stadium; permits underwater viewing of killer whales
Mission: Bermuda Triangle - flight-simulator technology used in this "voyage" into the Bermuda Triangle
Terrors of the Deep - largest collection of dangerous sea creatures ever assembled; includes sharks, eels, venomous fish and barracuda
Penguin Encounter - home to hundreds of penguins and alcids; a living laboratory for understanding behavior of polar species

Tropical Reef - this 160,000 gallon exhibit is home to over 1,000 tropical fish

Caribbean Tide Pool - permits close examination of sea urchins, starfish, anemones and other marine life

Community Pools - allows "hands-on" interaction with dolphins, sea lions and sting rays

## CAPTIVE BREEDING & RESEARCH

Sea World of Florida has had special **breeding** success with the following species:

| | |
|---|---|
| Killer whales | Penguin species |
| Dolphins | Flamingos |
| Sea lions | Common puffins |
| Otters | Tufted puffins |
| Nene geese | White-winged wood ducks |

Sea World funds the Beached Animal Rescue and Rehabilitation Program which was established in 1973. This program aids sick, injured, stranded and orphaned marine animals, including manatees, dolphins, whales, sea turtles, otters and coastal birds. **Research** conducted in concert with these rescue and rehabilitation activities, is vital to the future welfare of these species.

Sea World is the largest facility in Florida authorized to rescue, treat, rehabilitate and release manatees.

## FOR MORE INFORMATION

Sea World of Florida, 7007 Sea World Drive, Orlando, Florida 32821; 407-351-3600; Executive Vice President and General Manager: William A. Davis

*Shamu and Baby Shamu perform in Sea World of Florida's "Shamu: New Visions" show.*
*(® 1993, Sea World Inc. Reproduced by permission)*

# 57   DISCOVERY ISLAND ZOOLOGICAL PARK
### Lake Buena Vista, Florida

Discovery Island Zoological Park opened in 1974. This 11.5 acre Zoo, owned and managed by Walt Disney World Company, specializes in the display of tropical birds.

## VISITOR INFORMATION

**Directions:** Take I-4 west to the Magic Kingdom Exit. Follow signs to the Contemporary Resort. A boat carries visitors to Discovery Island from the Contemporary Resort Marina.

**Open to the Public:** Daily, mid March to mid February; 10 AM-7 PM Summer; 10 AM-5 PM the remainder of the season.

**Closed:** for 4 weeks from late February through mid March

**Admission (1993):**   (subject to change)
Adult: $8.50 + tax      Child: $4.75 + tax

**Parking Fee:** $4.00

**Children's Zoo:** No

**Annual Membership:** Not Available

**AAZPA Member:** Yes

## COLLECTIONS & EXHIBITS

**Collection:** The Zoo's current collection includes the following number of species:
Mammals: 11         Birds: 100         Reptiles: 11
Amphibians: 2       Invertebrates: 3

**Special Exhibits** at Discovery Island Zoological Park include:
South American Aviary - this walk-through exhibit covers 3 acres
Tropical Bird Exhibits - the Zoo's specialty
Animal Nursery

**Future Plans:** Lemur and Bald Eagle Exhibits will open in 1993.

## CAPTIVE BREEDING & RESEARCH

Discovery Island Zoological Park has had special **breeding** success with the following species:
Maguari stork                 King vulture
American flamingo             Scarlet ibis

## SEASONAL FESTIVALS & PROGRAMS

Earth Day - late April
Conservation Day - first Saturday in June

## FOR MORE INFORMATION

Discovery Island Zoological Park, P.O. Box 10,000, Lake Buena Vista, Florida 32830; 407-824-3784; Director: Mary Healy

# 58 BUSCH GARDENS TAMPA
## Tampa, Florida

Both a theme park and a renowned zoo, Busch Gardens Tampa opened in 1959. This 300 acre facility, owned by Anheuser-Busch Companies, Inc., features entertainment, shopping, dining, amusement rides and animal exhibits, grouped into nine cultural/geographic regions.

The Park's 80-acre Serengeti Plains, a naturalized setting for 800 free-roaming African animals, can be viewed from a monorail, a skyride, a steam-powered train or an adjacent walkway.

## VISITOR INFORMATION

**Directions:** Located at the corner of Busch Blvd. and 40th Street, eight miles northeast of downtown Tampa. Take Exit 54 from I-75 and head west for 2 miles; follow signs to the Park.

Alternatively, drive north on I-275 from the downtown area. Exit onto Busch Blvd. and head east; the Park will be 2 miles ahead.

**Open to the Public:** 365 days per year; call 813-987-5082 for hours (vary with season)

**Admission (1993):** (subject to change)
Adult: $29.75     Child (3-9): $24.45

**Parking Fee:** $4.00 per car

**Children's Zoo:** Yes     **Separate Admission:** No

**Annual Membership:** (subject to change)
Adult: $79.95     Child: $49.95     Senior: $59.95

**AAZPA Member:** Yes

## COLLECTIONS & EXHIBITS

**Collection:** The Park's animal collection includes the following number of species:
Mammals: 71     Birds: 201     Reptiles: 62
Amphibians: 3     Arachnids: 3

**Special Exhibits** at Busch Gardens Tampa include:

Myombe Reserve: The Great Ape Domain - this three-acre habitat is landscaped with thick, tropical foliage and is home to gorillas and chimpanzees.

Koala Display - located in the Bird Gardens area, this exhibit features koalas, Dama wallabies and rose-breasted cockatoos.

Nairobi Field Station - an animal nursery

Serengeti Plain - this 80-acre replica of the African Veldt features mixed herds of giraffe, zebra, antelope and other Plains species. The vast exhibit may be viewed from a monorail, from a steam-powered train, from a skyride or from a promenade that borders the habitat.

## CAPTIVE BREEDING & RESEARCH

Busch Gardens Tampa has had special **breeding** success with the following species:

| | |
|---|---|
| Black rhinoceros | Chimpanzee |
| Golden conure | Nile crocodile |
| Grevy's zebra | Asian elephant |

## FOR MORE INFORMATION

Busch Gardens Tampa, 3000 E. Busch Blvd., Tampa, Florida 33612; 813-987-5082; General Manager & Executive Vice President: Joe Fincher

# 59        LOWRY PARK ZOO
## Tampa, Florida

Recognized by the AAZPA as one of the top three zoos of its size, the Lowry Park Zoo opened in 1957. Owned by the City of Tampa, this 24-acre Zoo is beautifully landscaped with woodlands, rockwork, naturalized exhibits and waterfalls. Visitors view the animals from ground level and overhead walkways.

## VISITOR INFORMATION

**Directions:** From downtown Tampa, take Ashley Street North to I-275. Proceed north on I-275 to the Sligh Blvd. Exit (Exit #31). Turn left on Sligh Blvd. and proceed to North Blvd. Turn right on North Blvd., the Zoo entrance will be 200 feet, on your left.

**Open to the Public:** 9:30 AM-6 PM, Summer; 9:30 AM-5 PM, Winter

**Closed:** Christmas Day

**Admission (1993):** Adult: $5.50   Child: $3.50 (under 4 free)   Senior: $4.50

**Parking Fee:** None

**Children's Zoo:** Yes

**Annual Membership:** Individual: $20   Family: $40   Senior: $12

**Programs & Tours:** The Zoo participates in the curriculum of Hillsborough County elementary schools. The Education Department has also developed self-guided tours and educational packets for visitors. Other programs include Saturday Zooper Classes, Zoo Tots, "Breakfast With ..." programs, Behind the Scenes, Overnight Camp-ins and the Girl Scout Badge Program.

**AAZPA Member:** Yes

## COLLECTIONS & EXHIBITS

**Collection:** The Zoo's current collection includes the following number of species:
    Mammals: 49        Birds: 138        Reptiles: 69
    Amphibians: 15

**Special Exhibits** at the Lowry Park Zoo include:
Free-flight Aviary - over 65 species of tropical birds
Primate World - features orangutans, mandrills and chimpanzees
Asian Domain - home to Sumatran tigers, Sarus cranes, sloth bears and the rare Indian rhinoceros (one of only 30 in the U.S. and 2000 in the world)
Children's Village - includes a petting zoo
Florida Manatee Hospital & Aquatic Center and Florida Wildlife Center - this 7-acre addition to the Zoo features native flora and fauna. The Florida Manatee Hospital & Aquatic Center includes an exhibit building, three 25,000 gallon manatee treatment tanks, a manatee emergency treatment clinic, a hydroponics unit and an associated life support system.

The Florida Wildlife Center features American alligators, red wolves and the rare Florida panther.

## CAPTIVE BREEDING & RESEARCH

The Lowry Park Zoo has had special **breeding** success with the following species:

| | |
|---|---|
| Arabian oryx | Bali mynah |
| Chimpanzee | Guam rail |
| Orangutan | Golden lion tamarin |
| Siamang | Sumatran tiger |

There are over a dozen ongoing **research** projects at the Lowry Park Zoo, many of which are joint projects with regional universities and governmental agencies. Among these studies are:
- Manatee hearing research
- Baseline immunology in manatees
- Manatee food preference studies
- Conditioning of Golden lion tamarins for reintroduction in the wild

## SEASONAL FESTIVALS & PROGRAMS

Seniors Month - January
Lowry Park Zoo Birthday - March
Karamu (formal fundraiser) - April
Kids Week - July
Ralston Big Cat Survival - August
ZooBoo - October
Zoofari (informal fundraiser) - November
Teddy Bear Affair - November
Santa Parade - December

## FOR MORE INFORMATION

Lowry Park Zoo, 7530 North Boulevard, Tampa, Florida 33604; 813-935-8552; Interim Director: Al Trayner

# 60

## DREHER PARK ZOO
### West Palm Beach, Florida

Visitors to this 22-acre Zoo are treated to an impressive variety of wild, native species in addition to the captive animals. The Park's lush, tropical gardens, planted over 40 years ago, attract herons, egrets, anhingas, coot, kingfishers and other birds to the Zoo grounds.

## VISITOR INFORMATION

**Directions:** The Zoo is just east of I-95. From southbound I-95, take the Southern Blvd. Exit. Proceed east to Parker Avenue and then south on Parker. Turn right on Summit Blvd. to the Zoo.

From northbound I-95, take the Forest Hill Blvd. Exit. Go east to Parker Avenue then north on Parker to Summit Blvd. Turn left on Summit Blvd. to the Zoo.

**Open to the Public:** 365 days per year; 9 AM-5 PM

**Admission (1993):** Adult: $5.00    Child: $3.50    Senior: $4.50

**Parking Fee:** None

**Children's Zoo:** Yes    **Separate Admission:** No

**Annual Membership:** Individual: $30    Family: $40    Senior: $25

**AAZPA Member:** Yes

## COLLECTIONS & EXHIBITS

**Collection:** The Zoo's current collection includes the following number of specimens:
- Mammals: 101 specimens
- Reptiles: 117 specimens
- Invertebrates: 1 specimen
- Birds: 253 specimens
- Fish: 41 specimens

**Special Exhibits** at the Dreher Park Zoo include:
Florida Panther Exhibit
Nature Trail - 1650 foot boardwalk
Southern Bald Eagle Exhibit
Small primates - outdoor, naturalistic exhibits for rare, endangered primate species
Reptile Collection

**Future Plans:** The Zoo will add a boat ride on the Park's lake in 1993.

## CAPTIVE BREEDING & RESEARCH

Brazilian tapir
Gopher tortoise
Goeldi monkey
Rhinoceros iguana
Hoffman's sloth

Cotton-top tamarin
Yellow-footed tortoise
Cuban boa
Toco toucan
African hedgehog

## SEASONAL FESTIVAL & PROGRAMS

Taykee's Birthday Party - January
Teddy Bear Rally - February
Photo Safari - March
Egg-Citement - April
Folk Arts Festival - May
Conservation Day - June
Zoo After 5 - July to September
Boo at the Zoo - October
Feast for Beasts - November
Winter Wonderland - December

## FOR MORE INFORMATION

Dreher Park Zoo, 1301 Summit Blvd., West Palm Beach, Florida 33405-3098; 407-533-0887; Director: Robert M. Callahan

# 61 PARROT JUNGLE & GARDENS
## Miami, Florida

A popular Miami attraction since 1936, Parrot Jungle & Gardens is more than an aviary. This 32-acre facility features tropical bird exhibits, a petting zoo, trained bird shows, botanical gardens, cultural displays and more.

## VISITOR INFORMATION

**Directions:** From U.S. 1 in South Miami, turn south on S.W. 57th Avenue. Parrot Jungle & Gardens is at S.W. 57th Avenue and Killian Drive (S.W. 112th St.)

**Open to the Public:** 365 days per year; the Parrot Cafe opens at 8 AM; Park hours are 9:30 AM-6 PM

**Admission (1993):** Adult: $10.50    Child: $6.00    Senior: $9.50

**Parking Fee:** None

**Children's Zoo:** Yes    **Separate Admission:** No

**Annual Membership:** Individual: $25    Family: $55    Senior: $20

**Programs & Tours:** Educational programs at the Park include bird and animal shows, behind-the-scenes tours, guided tours for school and community groups, slide presentations, conservation activities for scout troops, and outreach programs ("Jungle Reach")

**AAZPA Member:** Yes

## COLLECTIONS & EXHIBITS

**Collection:**   The Park's current collection includes over 1200 specimens, representing more than 150 species of birds, mammals and reptiles.

**Special Exhibits** at Parrot Jungle & Gardens include:
Alligator Habitat
Miccosukee Indian Village
Flamingo Lake
Children's Petting Zoo
Exotic Bird Aviaries

**Future Plans:**  A Birds of Prey Exhibit will open in 1993.

## CAPTIVE BREEDING & RESEARCH

Parrot Jungle & Gardens has had special **breeding** success with the following species:
Parrot species
Macaws
Cockatoos

## SEASONAL FESTIVALS & PROGRAMS

Annual Easter Egg Hunt Festival
Holiday Happening - December

## FOR MORE INFORMATION

Parrot Jungle & Gardens, 11000 S.W. 57th Avenue, Miami, Florida 33156; 305-666-7834; Director: Dr. Bern Levine

# 62

## MIAMI METROZOO
### Miami, Florida

With over 60 exhibits on 740 acres, the Miami MetroZoo is one of the largest zoos in the world. The MetroZoo opened in 1981 and is now home to over 2000 animals, representing more than 300 species.

Renowned for its tropical beauty, this is a "cageless" zoo and its spacious, naturalized exhibits are grouped into four geographic regions. Visitors can wander along its beautifully-landscaped pathways or tour the Zoo on the Zoofari Monorail.

Heavily damaged by Hurricane Andrew in August, 1992, the MetroZoo was closed for several months but has now reopened.

## VISITOR INFORMATION

**Directions:**   The MetroZoo is southwest of Miami. From U.S. 1, take SW 152nd St. west; drive 3 miles to the Zoo.

**Open to the Public:**  Daily, 9:30 AM-5:30 PM

**Admission (1993):**   Subject to change; temporarily reduced.
Adult: $5.00     Child: $2.50

**Children's Zoo:**  Yes

**Annual Membership:**  Contact the Zoological Society of Florida at 305-255-5551

**Programs & Tours:**  The Zoo offers a variety of educational programs including tours, special classes, workshops and outreach programs.

**AAZPA Member:**  Yes

## COLLECTIONS & EXHIBITS

**Collection:**   The MetroZoo is home to over 2000 animals, representing more than 300 species.

**Special Exhibits** at the Miami MetroZoo include:
   Asian River Life - landscaped with tropical plants, a waterfall and artificially-created fog, this new habitat features Asian small-clawed otters.
   African Plains - a mixed-species habitat is home to zebra, giraffe, antelope and other African animals.
   White Bengal Tiger Exhibit
   Koala Exhibit
   Wings of Asia - this 1.5 acre, free-flight aviary displays more than 300 exotic Asian birds

## CAPTIVE BREEDING & RESEARCH

More than 2000 animals have been born at the Miami MetroZoo since it was established. Many of these species are endangered in the wild and some of the births were the first ever in captivity.
The birth of a koala at the MetroZoo was the first in the U.S. outside of California.

## FOR MORE INFORMATION

Miami MetroZoo, 12400 S.W. 152nd Street, Miami, Florida 33177; 305-251-0401; Director: Robert Yokel

# III. GREAT LAKES REGION

63. **International Crane Foundation** (Baraboo, Wisconsin)
64. **Henry Vilas Zoo** (Madison, Wisconsin)
65. **Milwaukee County Zoo** (Milwaukee, Wisconsin)
66. **Racine Zoological Gardens** (Racine, Wisconsin)
67. **Clinch Park Zoo** (Traverse City, Michigan)
68. **Saginaw Children's Zoo** (Saginaw, Michigan)
69. **John Ball Zoological Garden** (Grand Rapids, Michigan)
70. **Binder Park Zoo** (Battle Creek, Michigan)
71. **Potter Park Zoo** (Lansing, Michigan)
72. **Detroit Zoological Park** (Royal Oak, Michigan)
73. **Belle Isle Zoo** (Detroit, Michigan)
74. **Belle Isle Aquarium** (Detroit, Michigan)
75. **Lincoln Park Zoological Gardens** (Chicago, Illinois)
76. **John G. Shedd Aquarium** (Chicago, Illinois)
77. **The Brookfield Zoo** (Brookfield, Illinois)
78. **Cosley Animal Farm & Museum** (Wheaton, Illinois)
79. **Peoria's Glen Oak Zoo** (Peoria, Illinois)
80. **Miller Park Zoo** (Bloomington, Illinois)
81. **Henson Robinson Zoo** (Springfield, Illinois)
82. **Scovill Children's Zoo** (Decatur, Illinois)
83. **Fort Wayne Children's Zoo** (Fort Wayne, Indiana)
84. **The Indianapolis Zoo** (Indianapolis, Indiana)
85. **Mesker Park Zoo** (Evansville, Indiana)
86. **The Toledo Zoo** (Toledo, Ohio)
87. **Cleveland Metroparks Zoological Park** (Cleveland, Ohio)
88. **Sea World of Ohio** (Aurora, Ohio)
89. **Akron Zoological Park** (Akron, Ohio)
90. **Columbus Zoo** (Columbus, Ohio)
91. **Cincinnati Zoo & Botanical Garden** (Cincinnati, Ohio)

# GREAT LAKES REGION ZOOS & AQUARIUMS

# 63 INTERNATIONAL CRANE FOUNDATION
## Baraboo, Wisconsin

Dedicated to the protection of cranes and their native wetlands around the world, the International Crane Foundation was established in 1973. The 225-acre facility is home to the most complete collection of cranes on earth; of 15 species represented here, seven are threatened with extinction.

The Foundation is funded almost entirely by memberships, tour admissions and private donations.

## VISITOR INFORMATION

**Directions:** From I-90, take the Portage/Baraboo Exit onto Route 33. Head into Baraboo and turn right at the first traffic light onto County A. Proceed 4 miles and turn left on Shady Lane Road; the Foundation will be .75 mile, on your right.

**Open to the Public:** 9 AM-5 PM, Daily, May through October

**Closed:** November through April

**Admission (1993):** Adult: $5.00    Child: $2.50    Senior: $4.50

**Parking Fee:** None

**Children's Zoo:** No

**Annual Membership:** Individual: $20    Family: $20

**Programs & Tours:** Guided tours are offered at 10 AM, 1 PM and 3 PM daily, Memorial Day through Labor Day and on weekends in May, September and October.

Evening tours are offered at 6:30 PM on Thursdays in July and August.

Group tours are available April 15 to October 31; call in advance for reservations.

**AAZPA Member:** Yes

## COLLECTIONS & EXHIBITS

**Collection:** The International Crane Foundation houses 150 specimens, representing 15 species of cranes.

**Special Exhibits** at the Foundation include:
African Crane Exhibit
Chick Exercise Yard
Nature trails - through restored prairie, past wetlands and into oak and cherry woodlands.

**Future Plans:** The Foundation will open a Whooping Crane Exhibit in 1993-1994.

## CAPTIVE BREEDING & RESEARCH

The Foundation has had special **breeding** success with the following species:

| | |
|---|---|
| Whooping cranes | Sandhill cranes |
| Black-necked cranes | Brolgas |
| Siberian cranes | |

The International Crane Foundation coordinates field **research** across the globe. Specific studies include reintroduction programs for Whooping cranes, Siberian cranes and Sandhill cranes.

## FOR MORE INFORMATION

The International Crane Foundation, E-11376 Shady Lane Road, Baraboo, Wisconsin 53913; 608-356-9462; Director: Dr. George Archibald

# 64 HENRY VILAS ZOO
### Madison, Wisconsin

Located on the north shore of Lake Wingra, the Henry Vilas Zoo occupies land donated by Colonel and Mrs. William Vilas in memory of their son. Admission has been free since the Zoo first opened, a tribute to the Henry Vilas Zoological Society, founded in 1914 to support Zoo improvements. Daily operation is funded by Dane County and the City of Madison.

## VISITOR INFORMATION

**Directions:** From Interstate 90, take the Highway 12/18 West Exit. From Highway 12/18 exit north onto Park St. Proceed to Drake Street, turn left and continue 6 blocks to the Zoo entrance.

**Open to the Public:** Buildings open year-round from 9:30 AM-4:45 PM; Grounds open 9:30 AM-8 PM, June through Labor Day and 9:30 AM-5 PM, September through May.

**Closed:** The afternoons of Martin Luther King Day, Good Friday, Thanksgiving Day, the day after Thanksgiving, Christmas Eve, Christmas Day, New Years Eve, and New Years Day.

**Admission (1993):** Free

**Parking Fee:** None

**Children's Zoo:** Yes (open 10 AM-4:45 PM, Memorial Day Weekend through Labor Day); No admission charge.

**Annual Membership** (to Henry Vilas Zoological Society):
Individual: $10    Family: $25    Senior: $15

**Programs & Tours:** The Zoo offers a variety of educational programs including tours, classes and outreach programs.

**AAZPA Member:** Yes

## COLLECTIONS & EXHIBITS

**Collection:** The Zoo's current collection includes the following number of species:

| | | |
|---|---|---|
| Mammals: 56 | Birds: 62 | Reptiles: 28 |
| Amphibians: 4 | Insects: 14 | Fish:10 |

**Special Exhibits** at the Henry Vilas Zoo include:

Discovery Center/Herpetarium - this building opened in 1992; the Discovery Center features interactive, educational exhibits highlighting the diversity of animal life and the vital role that zoos play in wildlife conservation.

The Herpetarium is home to a wide variety of reptiles and amphibians, displayed in naturalized exhibits; the facility features underwater viewing of alligators, anacondas, turtles and native fish.

Children's Zoo - located on an island in Wingra Lagoon; includes a petting area.

**Future Plans:** A new Primate Complex will open in 1994 and a Large Cat Complex is scheduled for completion in 1997. A new Aviary is slated for the year 2000.

## CAPTIVE BREEDING & RESEARCH

The Henry Vilas Zoo has had special **breeding** success with the following species:

| | |
|---|---|
| Orangutans | Camels |
| Siberian tigers | Penguins |
| Spectacled bears | |

**Research** based at the Henry Vilas Zoo includes:

- Studies on Rhinoceros Reproduction

## SEASONAL FESTIVALS & PROGRAMS

Opening of Children's Zoo - Memorial Day Weekend
Zoo Benefit - last Saturday night in July
Halloween at the Zoo - Friday to Sunday during or just preceding Halloween

## FOR MORE INFORMATION

Henry Vilas Zoo, 702 S. Randall Avenue, Madison, Wisconsin 53715; 608-266-4732; Director: David C. Hall, DVM

# 65      MILWAUKEE COUNTY ZOO
## Milwaukee, Wisconsin

The Milwaukee County Zoo originated in 1892 as a small collection of mammals and birds in the City's Washington Park. Having come under the jurisdiction of the Milwaukee County Park Commission during the 1930s, the Zoo moved to its present 200-acre site in 1958.

Recognized as one of the best zoos in the country, the Milwaukee County Zoo is known for its predator/prey exhibits where natural enemies, though separated by moats, appear to occupy the same enclosures.

## VISITOR INFORMATION

**Directions:** Take I-94 west, toward Madison and exit on Highway 100 (Exit 304B). Drive north on this highway and turn right on Bluemound Rd.

**Open to the Public:** 365 days per year; 9 AM-5 PM, May 1 through Labor Day (open until 6 PM on Sundays and Holidays; 9 AM-4:30 PM, September through April

**Admission (1993):** April to October:    Adult: $6.00   Child: $4.00   Senior: $5.00
                    November to March:   Adult: $4.00   Child: $2.50   Senior: $3.00

**Parking Fee:** $4.00

**Children's Zoo:** Yes     **Separate Admission:** No

**Annual Membership:** Individual: $35     Family: $45

**Programs & Tours:** The Zoo offers a variety of educational programs, including animal shows, demonstrations, group tours, zoomobile and special events.

**AAZPA Member:** Yes

## COLLECTIONS & EXHIBITS

**Collection:** The Zoo's current collection includes the following number of species:
    Mammals: 95        Birds: 103        Reptiles: 60
    Amphibians: 2       Fish: 106        Invertebrates: 14

**Special Exhibits** at the Milwaukee County Zoo include:
    Koala Exhibit - this pair of Aussies was donated by the San Diego Zoo in celebration of Milwaukee County Zoo's 100th birthday
    Apes of Africa Exhibit - a replica of the West African rain forest; home to lowland gorillas and bonobos
    Stackner Heritage Farm - this working dairy farm celebrates Wisconsin's dairy heritage; includes a petting zoo of domestic animals during summer months
    Lake Wisconsin - a 65,000 gallon tank in the center of the Aquarium/Reptile Building; features hundreds of native fish in a naturalistic setting

**Future Plans**   Renovation of the Primate Building will be completed in 1993. The Aquarium/Reptile Building is scheduled for renovation by 1995.

## CAPTIVE BREEDING & RESEARCH

The Milwaukee County Zoo has had special **breeding** success with the following species:

Trumpeter swans
Humboldt penguins
Ruwenzori mountain fruit bats
Vampire bats
Straw-colored fruit bats
Reticulated giraffes

Greater kudu
American elk
Japanese macaques
Mandrills
Siberian tigers
Snow leopards

**Research** projects based at the Milwaukee County Zoo include:
- Thermal preference and thermoregulation behavior in broadsnout caiman
- Karotype of giant yellowfoot tortoises
- Surgical sterilization of white-tailed deer
- Vitamin and mineral status of Humboldt penguins
- Reproductive studies in rhinoceros
- Acclimation of golden lion tamarins

## SEASONAL FESTIVALS & PROGRAMS

First Wisconsin Day - January 1
Zoo's Snow Ball (Snow Sculpting) - January
Egg Days - Easter season
Conservation Weekend - Spring
Zoo's Birthday - July
Teddy Bear Days - July
July Concert Series
Milwaukee a la Carte - late August
Harvest Zoobilee Show - mid September
Dungeon of Darkness - late October
Halloween Spooktacular - October 31
Turkey Walk ( American Heart Assoc.) - November
Breakfast/Lunch with Santa - December weekends
Holiday Night Lights - mid December

## FOR MORE INFORMATION

Milwaukee County Zoo, 10001 W. Bluemound Road, Milwaukee, Wisconsin 53226; 414-256-5412; Director: Mr. Charles Wikenhauser

# 66 RACINE ZOOLOGICAL GARDENS
## Racine, Wisconsin

Founded in 1923, this 28-acre Zoo is managed by the Racine Zoological Society.

## VISITOR INFORMATION

**Directions:** The Zoo is located on the north side of Racine, near Lake Michigan. Proceed north on Main St. from the downtown area.

**Open to the Public:** 9 AM-8 PM Memorial Day to Labor Day; 9 AM-4:30 PM remainder of the year.

**Closed:** Christmas Day

**Admission:** Free

**Parking Fee:** None

**Children's Zoo:** Yes

**Annual Membership** (to Racine Zoological Society):
Individual: $25     Family: $35     Senior: $20

**AAZPA Member:** Yes

## COLLECTIONS & EXHIBITS

**Collection:** The Zoo's current collection includes the following number of species:
Mammals: 28          Birds: 27          Reptiles: 13
Fish: 10             Invertebrates: 1

**Special Exhibits** at the Racine Zoological Gardens include:
White Bengal Tiger Exhibit
Asian Elephant Exhibit
Orangutan Exhibit

**Future Plans:** Renovation of the Elephant Yard, the Big Cat House and the Primate House is scheduled.

## CAPTIVE BREEDING & RESEARCH

The Racine Zoological Gardens has had special **breeding** success with:
Llamas              Penguins
Camels              Capybaras

## SEASONAL FESTIVALS & PROGRAMS

Zoofari Education Day - June
Jazz Concert Series - June through August
Black-tie Dinner Dance - August
Halloween Festival - October
Christmas Light Festival - December

## FOR MORE INFORMATION

Racine Zoological Gardens, 2131 N. Main St., Racine, Wisconsin 53402; 414-636-9189; Director: Dr. Thomas Torhorst

*Capybaras*
*(photo courtesy Racine Zoological Gardens)*

# 67

## CLINCH PARK ZOO
### Traverse City, Michigan

Located on the shore of Grand Traverse Bay, the Clinch Park Zoo, founded in 1932, exhibits native Michigan wildlife. Most of Zoo's specimens were rehabilitated after sustaining injuries, many from gunshots, in the wild.

A ¼ scale steam engine, the "Spirit of Traverse City," has provided visitors with a ride around the 3.5 acre Zoo since 1982.

### VISITOR INFORMATION

**Directions:** The Zoo is located in downtown Traverse City at the corner of Cass St. and Grandview Parkway.

**Open to the Public:** Daily, April 15 to November 1; opens at 9:30 AM; closes 7:30 PM Memorial Day to Labor Day; closes 4:30 PM remainder of season

**Closed:** November 2 through April 14 (except holiday program)

**Admission (1993):** Adult: $1.50    Child: $1.00

**Parking Fee:** None

**Children's Zoo:** No

**Annual Membership:** Individual: $10    Family: $15

**Programs & Tours:** Educational programs include tours, resource materials for class work, special rates for school and scouting groups, and community/school outreach programs.

**AAZPA Member:** No

## COLLECTIONS & EXHIBITS

**Collection:** The Zoo's current collection includes the following number of species:

| | | |
|---|---|---|
| Mammals: 12 | Birds: 6 | Reptiles: 8 |
| Amphibians: 3 | Fish: 10 | |

**Special Exhibits** at the Clinch Park Zoo include:

Birds of Prey Aviary

Aquarium Building - its six large tanks display fish native to Michigan waters; also features an indoor/outdoor otter display

Education Center - dedicated in 1990; this $60,000 facility includes an ecology lab, video displays, touch tables and small animal exhibits.

Predator Exhibits - renovated enclosures for lynx, raccoon, red fox, bobcats and coyotes

**Future Plans:**   Renovation of the Hoofstock Area is scheduled for completion in 1993. The Aquarium will be updated by 1996.

## SEASONAL FESTIVALS & PROGRAMS

Family Fun Day - first Sunday in June

Christmas for Animals - second Sunday in December

## FOR MORE INFORMATION

Clinch Park Zoo, 161 Grandview Parkway, Traverse City, Michigan 49684; 616-922-4904; Director: Ken Gregory

*Bobcat*
*(photo courtesy*
*Clinch Park Zoo)*

# 68 SAGINAW CHILDREN'S ZOO
## Saginaw, Michigan

The Saginaw Children's Zoo, established in 1967, focuses on education and is designed to introduce children to wildlife. The 8.5-acre Zoo is located in Celebration Square near the banks of the Saginaw River.

In addition to the animal exhibits, the Children's Zoo features a miniature train ride, the "Ibershoff Special."

## VISITOR INFORMATION

**Directions:** From I-75, take Exit 149-B and head west on Michigan 46. Follow signs to Celebration Square.

**Open to the Public:** Mother's Day weekend to Labor Day; 10 AM-5 PM, Monday-Saturday; 11 AM-6 PM Sundays & Holidays

**Closed:** Day after Labor Day to mid May (except holiday programs)

**Admission (1993):** Adult: $1.50    Child: $.75    Senior: $.75

**Parking Fee:** None

**Annual Membership:** Individual: $20    Family: $30

**AAZPA Member:** No

## COLLECTIONS & EXHIBITS

**Collection:** The Zoo's current collection includes the following number of specimens, representing 28 species:

Mammals: 40 specimens          Birds: 50 specimens
Reptiles: 10 specimens         Amphibians: 2 specimens

**Special Exhibits** at the Saginaw Children's Zoo include:
Timber Country - completed 1992; features wildlife native to Michigan including timber wolves, porcupines and red-tailed hawks
Contact Area - opened in 1992; a "hands-on" exhibit

## CAPTIVE BREEDING & RESEARCH

The Saginaw Children's Zoo has had special **breeding** success with the following species:
Blue & Gold macaws
African pygmy goats

## SEASONAL FESTIVALS & PROGRAMS

Earth Day - spring
Mother's Day - free for moms
Father's Day - free for dads
Halloween at the Zoo - October (2 nights)
Holiday Lights - December (2 weekends)

## FOR MORE INFORMATION

Saginaw Children's Zoo, 1720 S. Washington, Saginaw, Michigan 48601; 517-759-1657; Director: Caryn A. Amacher

# 69 JOHN BALL ZOOLOGICAL GARDEN
### Grand Rapids, Michigan

This 14-acre Zoo, founded in 1891, boasts a large collection of amphibians and reptiles.

## VISITOR INFORMATION

**Directions:**  From U.S. 131, take the Pearl St. Exit and proceed west to Valley. Turn left on Valley. The Zoo is at Fulton & Valley.

**Open to the Public:**  365 days per year; 10 AM-6 PM summer; 10 AM-4 PM winter

**Admission (1993):** Adult: $2.50    Child: $1.00    Senior: $1.00

**Parking Fee:** None

**Children's Zoo:** Yes    **Separate Admission:** No

**Annual Membership:** Individual: $20    Family: $35

**AAZPA Member:** Yes

## COLLECTIONS & EXHIBITS

**Collection:** The Zoo's current collection includes the following number of species:
Mammals: 40          Birds: 49          Reptiles: 64
Amphibians: 16        Insects: 1

**Special Exhibits** at the John Ball Zoological Garden include:
The Nocturnal Building
Reptile & Amphibian Collection

**Future Plans:**  The Living Shores Aquarium will open in June, 1994; an African Veldt Exhibit is scheduled for completion in September, 1994.

## CAPTIVE BREEDING & RESEARCH

The John Ball Zoological Garden has had special **breeding** success with the following species:
Snow leopards
Bald eagles

A Wildlife Conservation Fund is administered by the Zoo.

## SEASONAL FESTIVALS & PROGRAMS

Rendezoo Gala - early June
Zoo Daze - mid August
Boo at the Zoo - late October
Christmas for the Animals - early December

## FOR MORE INFORMATION

The John Ball Zoological Garden, 1300 W. Fulton, Grand Rapids, Michigan 49504; 616-776-2591; Director: John Lewis

# 70
## BINDER PARK ZOO
### Battle Creek, Michigan

Located on the southern edge of Battle Creek, Michigan, the Binder Park Zoo recently increased its land lease to 405 acres, setting in motion an ambitious master plan to expand and revitalize the Zoo. Founded in 1977, the Zoo prides itself as a regional conservation center for threatened and endangered species.

Access to the Zoo's naturalized exhibits is via shaded boardwalks, brick paths and a scenic, .75 mile, wood-chip trail. The Z.O. & O. Railroad also loops through the center of the Park.

## VISITOR INFORMATION

**Directions:** From Interstate 94, take Exit 100 and drive south on Beadle Lake Road; proceed 3 miles to the Zoo.

**Open to the Public:** Daily, April 13 to October 13; 9 AM-5 PM M-F; 9 AM-6 PM Saturday; 11 AM-6 PM Sunday; Open until 8 PM on Wednesdays & Thursdays from June through August

**Closed:** October 14 through April 12 (except for Halloween and Christmas programs)

**Admission (1993):** Adult: $4.50     Child: $2.50     Senior: $3.50

**Parking Fee:** None

**Children's Zoo:** Yes     **Separate Admission:** No

**Annual Membership:** Individual: $25     Family: $37     Senior: $37 (Grandparent)

**AAZPA Member:** Yes

## COLLECTIONS & EXHIBITS

**Collection:** The Zoo's current collection includes the following number of species:
| | | |
|---|---|---|
| Mammals: 31 | Birds: 25 | Reptiles: 15 |
| Amphibians: 5 | Insects: 1 | Other Invertebrates: 3 |

**Special Exhibits** at the Binder Park Zoo include:
   Miller Children's Zoo - two acres; includes eleven domestic animal exhibits, one of the world's largest accurate dinosaur replicas and many "hands-on" interactive displays

## CAPTIVE BREEDING & RESEARCH

The Binder Park Zoo has had special **breeding** success with the following species:
| | |
|---|---|
| Ring-tailed lemurs | Bennett's wallabies |
| White-handed gibbons | Trumpeter swans |
| Formosan sika deer | Grant's zebras |

*White-handed Gibbon*
*(photo courtesy Binder Park Zoo)*

**Research** projects at the Zoo include:
- Red Panda nutrition research
- Cheetah reproduction, nutrition & behavior
- Trumpeter Swan Restoration Program
- Mexican Wolf Recovery Program
- Cooperative conservation programs with Sichuan Wildlife Conservation
    Association, China

## SEASONAL FESTIVALS & PROGRAMS

Zooper Day Camps
The Great Zoo Boo - late October
Christmas at the Zoo - late November through December

## FOR MORE INFORMATION

The Binder Park Zoo, 7400 Division Drive, Battle Creek, Michigan 49017; 616-979-1351; Director: Gregory B. Geise

# 71

## POTTER PARK ZOO
### Lansing, Michigan

Located on the north bank of the Cedar River, the Potter Park Zoo, founded in 1917, is also adjacent to a beautiful hardwood forest preserve.

## VISITOR INFORMATION

**Directions:** The Zoo is southeast of the downtown area. From Interstate 496, take the Pennsylvania Avenue exit and drive south for four blocks to the Zoo.

**Open to the Public:** 9 AM-7 PM Summer; 9 AM-5 PM Winter; open every day of the year

**Admission (1993):** Adult: $2.00   Child: $1.00

**Parking Fee:** $1.50

**Children's Zoo:** Yes     **Separate Admission:** No

**Annual Membership:** Individual: $25     Family: $40

**AAZPA Member:** Yes

## COLLECTIONS & EXHIBITS

**Collection:** The Zoo's current collection includes the following number of species:
    Mammals: 40              Birds: 59              Reptiles: 26
    Amphibians: 4            Other Invertebrates: 2

**Special Exhibits** at the Potter Park Zoo include:
    New Farmyard Exhibit
    Penguin Exhibit
    Primate Building
    Lion House

**Future Plans:** A new Monkey Island and completion of the central core revitalization project are scheduled for 1994-1995.

## CAPTIVE BREEDING & RESEARCH

The Potter Park Zoo has an ongoing **research** program on animal nutrition.

## SEASONAL FESTIVALS & PROGRAMS

"Zoo Fest" - Spring
Farm Days at the Zoo - Summer
Zoo Boo - late October
Twelve Days of Christmas - December

## FOR MORE INFORMATION

The Potter Park Zoo, 1301 S. Pennsylvania Avenue, Lansing, Michigan 48912; 517-483-4221; Associate Director: Gerald Brady

# 72     DETROIT ZOOLOGICAL PARK
### Royal Oak, Michigan

The Detroit Zoological Park, founded in 1928, was the first zoo in North America to feature barless exhibits extensively, pioneering the use of water and dry moats to confine animals. The 125-acre zoo is thus characterized by open, naturalized exhibits which give visitors unobstructed views of the animals and their habitats.

## VISITOR INFORMATION

**Directions:** The Zoo is 2 miles north of the Detroit city limits, at the intersection of I-696 and Woodward Avenue in Royal Oak. From downtown Detroit, take I-75 north to I-696; proceed west on I-696; the Zoo exit is clearly marked.

**Open to the Public:** 10 AM-5 PM, May through September; 10 AM-4 PM, October through April

**Closed:** Thanksgiving, Christmas Eve through New Years Day

**Admission (1993):** Adult: $6.00     Child: $3.00     Senior: $4.00

**Parking Fee:** $3.00 (cars & vans), $6.00 (buses)

**Children's Zoo:** No

**Annual Membership** (to Detroit Zoological Society):
    Individual: $25     Family: $40

**Programs & Tours:** Log Cabin Learning Center, open May through Labor Day

**AAZPA Member:** Yes

## COLLECTIONS & EXHIBITS

**Collection:** The Zoo's current collection includes the following number of species:
    Mammals: 50        Birds: 125        Reptiles: 75
    Amphibians: 25       Mollusks: 1

**Special Exhibits** at the Detroit Zoological Park include:
    Several large outdoor mixed-species exhibits
    Chimpanzee Exhibit - 4 acres, indoor/outdoor
    Penguinarium

**Future Plans:** The Toco Toucan Exhibit and a Mandrill Exhibit will open in 1993.

## CAPTIVE BREEDING & RESEARCH

The Detroit Zoological Park has had special **breeding** success with the following species:

| | |
|---|---|
| Matschie's tree kangaroo | Scarlet ibis |
| Polar bear | Boat-billed heron |
| Chimpanzee | King vulture |
| African greater flamingo | |

## SEASONAL FESTIVALS & PROGRAMS

Log Cabin Learning Center - open May through Labor Day
Free Days for Children - Mondays, July and August
Isabella Fiesselmann Day - late August; seniors receive free admission and free
    tractor-train tours
Zoo Boo - late October; pumpkin art, treats and entertainment for children

## FOR MORE INFORMATION

The Detroit Zoological Park, P.O. Box 39, Royal Oak, Michigan 48068-0039;
313-398-0903; Acting Director: Mrs. Khadejah Shelby


# 73

## BELLE ISLE ZOO
### Detroit, Michigan


Located on an island in the Detroit River, the 13-acre Belle Isle Zoo opened in 1980.
The Zoo is characterized by a .75 mile elevated walkway from which visitors view the
animals in large, naturalized exhibits.


## VISITOR INFORMATION

**Directions:** Belle Isle is an island in the Detroit River, 2.5 miles east of downtown
Detroit. Access is via the Douglas MacArthur Bridge located at East
Jefferson Avenue and East Grand Boulevard. Once on the island, signs
direct you to the Zoo.

**Open to the Public:** 10 AM-5 PM May through September; 10 AM-4 PM in October

**Closed:** November through April

**Admission (1993):** Adult: $2.00    Child: $.50    Senior: $1.00

**Parking Fee:** None

**Children's Zoo:** No

**Annual Membership** (to Detroit Zoological Society):
    Individual: $25    Family: $40

**AAZPA Member:** Yes

**Collection:** The Zoo's current collection includes the following number of species:
Mammals: 20          Birds: 15          Reptiles: 8
Amphibians: 8

As mentioned above, the main section of the Zoo is characterized by a .75 mile elevated walkway which provides access to the large, naturalized exhibits.

**Future Plans:** A Carnivore Complex, which will house Sumatran tigers, African lions and Mexican wolves, is scheduled to open in 1993.

### CAPTIVE BREEDING & RESEARCH

The Belle Isle Zoo has had special **breeding** success with the following species:
Spectacled bear
Red kangaroo

### SEASONAL FESTIVALS & PROGRAMS

Opening Day Zoobilee - May 1
Free Admission for Children - Tuesdays, July & August
Halloween Zoobilee - October 31

### FOR MORE INFORMATION

The Belle Isle Zoo, P.O. Box 39, Royal Oak, Michigan 48068-0039; 313-267-7160; Acting Director: Mrs. Khadejah Shelby

# 74          BELLE ISLE AQUARIUM
## Detroit, Michigan

The Belle Isle Aquarium, founded in 1904, is the oldest continuously-operating, municipally-owned aquarium in the United States. The original building is still in use. The Aquarium has been honored by the AAZPA for its outstanding success with the captive breeding of freshwater stingrays.

### VISITOR INFORMATION

**Directions:** Belle Isle is an island in the Detroit River, 2.5 miles east of downtown Detroit. Access is via the Douglas MacArthur Bridge, located at East Jefferson Avenue and East Grand Blvd. Once on the island, follow the signs to the Aquarium.

**Open to the Public:** Open 365 days per year, including weekends and holidays, 10 AM-5 PM

**Admission (1993):** Adult: $1.00     Child: $1.00 (under 2 free)

**Parking Fee:** None

**Annual Membership** (to Detroit Zoological Society): Individual: $25     Family: $40

**AAZPA Member:** Yes

## COLLECTIONS & EXHIBITS

**Collection:** The Aquarium's current collection includes the following number of species:

Reptiles: 3        Amphibians: 1        Fish: 140
Mollusks: 5        Insects: 1

## CAPTIVE BREEDING & RESEARCH

The Belle Isle Aquarium has had special **breeding** success with the following species:

Ocellated stingray               Butterfly goodeid
Dwarf stingray                   Golden skiffia
Checkerboard stingray            Green goodeid
Blue-tailed goodeid              Lake Victoria mouthbrooders

The Aquarium is most famous for its success with breeding and rearing the three freshwater stingray species listed above. The ocellated stingray has now been bred and reared through three captive generations. Honors for these accomplishments were awarded by the AAZPA in 1976, 1980 and 1985.

## FOR MORE INFORMATION

The Belle Island Aquarium, P.O. Box 39, Royal Oak, Michgan 48068-0039; 313-267-7159; Acting Director: Mrs. Khadejah Shelby

# 75 LINCOLN PARK ZOOLOGICAL GARDENS
## Chicago, Illinois

Located in the heart of Chicago, the Lincoln Park Zoological Gardens is one of the last free-admission, major-city zoos in the world. This 35-acre facility, established in 1868, boasts the finest lowland gorilla collection in the country, producing 38 offspring to date.

America's oldest and most visited Zoo, Lincoln Park Zoological Gardens has undergone a dramatic transformation over the past two decades. Though historic, neo-classical buildings still adorn the grounds, their old, iron cages have given way to naturalized habitats. At least one new or renovated exhibit has opened every year since the mid 1970s.

*Lowland Gorilla Exhibit*
*(photo by Susan Reich; courtesy Lincoln Park Zoological Society)*

## VISITOR INFORMATION

**Directions:**   Follow Lakeshore Drive to Fullerton (2400 N); turn west and proceed 1 block to Cannon Drive which leads to parking area.

From I-90/I-94, exit onto Fullerton Avenue and head east to the Park; turn on Cannon Drive to reach parking area.

Buses 151 and 156 take passengers to the West Entrance.

**Open to the Public:**  9 AM-5 PM each day; open 365 days per year.

**Admission (1993):**  Free

**Parking Fee:**  None

**Children's Zoo:**  Yes

**Annual Membership:**  Contact the Lincoln Park Zoological Society at 312-935-6700.

**Programs & Tours:**  The Zoo's award-winning education programs include lectures, field trips, workshops, curriculum formats, seminars, outreach programs and sponsorship of field research.

**AAZPA Member:**  Yes

## COLLECTIONS & EXHIBITS

**Collection:**   The Lincoln Park Zoological Gardens is home to over 1500 animals, representing more than 335 species.

| | |
|---|---|
| Mammals: 116 | Reptiles/Amphibians: 98 |
| Birds: 115 | Invertebrates: 6 |

**Special Exhibits** at the Lincoln Park Zoological Gardens include:
  Lowland Gorilla Exhibit - the finest collection in the U.S.
  The Farm-in-the-Zoo - a 5 acre replica of a Midwestern farm
  Helen Brach Primate House - newly renovated, naturalized habitats for monkeys,
    lemurs and gibbons
  McCormick Bird House - features a free-flight rainforest aviary
  Polar Bear Exhibit - largest polar bear pool in the world

**Future Plans:**   Renovation of the Kovler Lion House has just been completed.
                    Upcoming projects include a new reptile/small mammal facility, a
                    new conservation center, a modern visitor center and renovation of
                    the sea lion pool. Completion dates are pending.

## CAPTIVE BREEDING & RESEARCH

The Lincoln Park Zoological Gardens has had special **breeding** success with the
following species:
  Lowland gorilla - a world leader in the captive propagation of this species
  Snow leopard                    Maned wolf
  Cheetah                         Grant's gazelle
  Spectacled bear                 Arabian oryx
  Bali mynah                      Bactrian camel

The Lincoln Park Zoo participates in 25 Species Survival Plans established by the
AAZPA. **Research** projects based at the Zoo include:
  - Studies of gorilla reproductive behavior
  - Research on thermal regulation in spectacled bears
  - Tabulation of gorilla sex ratios at birth

## SEASONAL FESTIVALS & PROGRAMS

Zooperbowl - January
Earth Day Celebration
Run for the Zoo - first Sunday in June
Zoo Ball - July
World's Longest Birthday Card - to be created at the Children's Zoo in 1993 to celebrate
  the 125th Birthday of the Lincoln Park Zoo
SpookyZoo Spectacular - Halloween festival
Caroling to the Animals - first week in December

## FOR MORE INFORMATION

Lincoln Park Zoological Gardens, 2200 N. Cannon Drive, Chicago, Illinois 60614;
312-294-4660, 312-294-4662; Director: David F. Hales

# 76 JOHN G. SHEDD AQUARIUM
### Chicago, Illinois

Located on the shore of Lake Michigan, just southeast of downtown Chicago, the John G. Shedd Aquarium opened in 1930. Home to over 6000 aquatic animals, representing 600 species, the facility dedicated a new Oceanarium in April, 1991. The latter features a 3 million gallon, saltwater habitat, designed to simulate the coastal environment of the Pacific Northwest.

## VISITOR INFORMATION

**Directions:** The Aquarium is on Lake Shore Drive, a mile southeast of the downtown area. Parking is available near Soldier's Field, just south of the Aquarium.

**Open to the Public:** Daily, 9 AM-6 PM

**Closed:** Christmas Day and New Years Day

**Admission (1993):** Adult: $3.00 Aquarium / $7.00 Aquarium & Oceanarium
Child/Senior: $2.00 Aquarium / $5.00 Aquarium & Oceanarium

**Parking Fee:** Paid and metered lots near Soldier's Field, south of the Aquarium

**Annual Membership:**
Individual: $35     Family: $50 (up to 6 immediate family members)

**Programs & Tours:** Shedd Aquarium offers on-site classes for all age groups ranging from underwater photography to marine mammal anatomy. The facility also sponsors excursions to aquatic environments across the country and around the globe.

**AAZPA Member:** Yes

## COLLECTIONS & EXHIBITS

**Collection:** The Aquarium's current collection includes over 6000 specimens, representing 600 species of aquatic life.

**Special Exhibits** at the Shedd Aquarium include:
Coral Reef - this exhibit re-creates a Caribbean coral reef ecosystem and features 200 aquatic animals; divers feed the animals three times each day.
Oceanarium - this 3 million gallon, saltwater habitat was designed to simulate ocean waters off the coast of the Pacific Northwest. The exhibit features beluga whales, Pacific white-sided dolphins, harbor seals and Alaskan sea otters; a few of the otters were orphaned by the Exxon Valdez oil spill in 1989. The facility is designed to permit underwater viewing of the whales, dolphins and sea otter. It also includes a Penguinarium, featuring gentoo, rockhopper and magellanic penguins.

## CAPTIVE BREEDING & RESEARCH

The John G. Shedd Aquarium has had special **breeding** success with the following species:

Lake Victoria African cichlids
Tahitian land snail
South American bonytongue

## SEASONAL FESTIVALS & PROGRAMS

Haunted Shedd - late October

## FOR MORE INFORMATION

John G. Shedd Aquarium, 1200 S. Lake Shore Drive, Chicago, Illinois 60605; 312-986-2300; Director: William P. Braker

# 77     THE BROOKFIELD ZOO
## Brookfield, Illinois

Formally named the Chicago Zoological Park, this 215 acre zoo opened in 1934. The facility is internationally renowned for its innovative work with naturalistic, multi-species exhibits and has been a leader in captive breeding, research and wildlife conservation.

Owned by the Forest Preserve District of Cook County, the Brookfield Zoo is managed by the Chicago Zoological Society. Displaying 2500 animals, the Park is also a botanical gardens and is adorned with more than 35,000 annuals in spring and summer.

## VISITOR INFORMATION

**Directions:** The Zoo is located at First Avenue and 31st St in Brookfield, 14 miles west of downtown Chicago. It is accessible via the Stevenson (I-55) and Eisenhower (I-290) Expressways, via the Tri-State Tollway (I-294) via the Burlington Northern commuter line or by the PACE bus service.

**Open to the Public:** 365 days per year; 9:30 AM-5:30 PM Memorial Day to Labor Day; 10 AM-4:30 PM remainder of year

**Admission (1993):** Adult: $3.50    Child: $1.50    Senior: $1.50

**Parking Fee:** $4.00

**Children's Zoo:** Yes    **Separate Admission:** Adult: $1.00   Child: $.50

**Annual Membership:** Individual: $30    Family: $47    Senior: $27

**AAZPA Member:** Yes

## COLLECTIONS & EXHIBITS

**Collection:** The Zoo's current collection includes the following number of species:

Mammals: 164          Birds: 126          Fish: 2

Reptiles & Amphibians: 119                  Invertebrates: 4

**Special Exhibits** at the Brookfield Zoo include:

Tropic World - one of the world's largest indoor zoo exhibits; representing rainforest regions of Africa, Asia and South America, the display features 100 primates, 30 tropical birds and a variety of mammals.

Seven Seas Panorama - a 2000 seat dolphinarium, pools holding over 1 million gallons of saltwater and a rocky shores exhibit (seals, sea lions, walruses)

The Fragile Kingdom - an African desert, an Asian rain forest and Big Cat exhibits stress the interdependence of species and their adaptation to the environment.

Discovery Center Theater - a multi-image guide to the Brookfield Zoo

Children's Zoo - permits close encounters with North American wildlife

Aquatic Bird House - includes a "Be a Bird" exhibit which allows visitors to exercise their flight muscles; also features a nocturnal kiwi exhibit

Walkabout in Australia House - includes free-flying fruit bats among other "down-under" species

**Future Plans:** Habitat Africa! will open in 1993; this 7-acre habitat will feature giraffes, zebras, wild dogs and other residents of the African savannah.

## CAPTIVE BREEDING & RESEARCH

The Brookfield Zoo has had special **breeding** success with the following species:

Snow leopards                  Lowland gorillas

Siberian tigers                  Humboldt penguins

Golden lion tamarins

## SEASONAL FESTIVALS & PROGRAMS

National Pig Day - March 1

Animals in Action - shows held at Children's Zoo Seabury Arena, Memorial Day to Labor Day

Teddy Bear Picnic - first weekend in August

Boo! at the Zoo - Halloween weekend

Holiday Magic Festival - first three weekend evenings in December

## FOR MORE INFORMATION

The Brookfield Zoo, 3300 Golf Rd., Brookfield, Illinois 60513; 708-485-0263; Director: Dr. George Rabb

# 78  COSLEY ANIMAL FARM & MUSEUM
### Wheaton, Illinois

In November, 1973, Miss Paula Jones donated 2.5 acres of land to the Wheaton Park District in memory of her cousin's husband, Harvey H. Cosley. Miss Jones stipulated that this land should be maintained as a farm.

Cosley Animal Farm, a recreational and educational facility, opened to the public in 1974. Now covering 11 acres, the Farm features domestic animal exhibits, an historical, 1887 train station, the oldest barn in Wheaton, antique farm implements, gardens and the Vern Kiebler Learning Center. The latter building, named for an original board member of the Cosley Foundation, opened in 1987.

## VISITOR INFORMATION

**Directions:** The Farm is 30 miles west of Chicago, in Wheaton, Illinois. From Route 38 (Roosevelt Road), turn north on Main St., left (west) on Harrison and then right (north) on Gary Avenue to the Farm.

**Open to the Public:** April to October, 9 AM-4 PM weekdays, 10 AM-6 PM Fri.-Sun.; November to March, 9 AM-4 PM daily; open until 9 PM December 1-24

**Closed:** Thanksgiving, Christmas and New Years Day

**Admission (1993):** Free ($.50 per child for out-of-district groups)

**Parking Fee:** None

**Annual Membership:** Not available

**Programs & Tours:** The Cosley Farm has an active volunteer program (call 708-665-5534). A variety of educational classes and workshops are offered to community and school groups.

**AAZPA Member:** No

## COLLECTIONS & EXHIBITS

**Collection:** The Farm's current animal collection includes the following number of species:

| | | |
|---|---|---|
| Mammals: 15 | Birds: 32 | Reptiles: 1 |
| Amphibians: 1 | Fish: 2 | |

**Special Exhibits** at the Cosley Animal Farm & Museum include:

Duck Pond - home to resident waterfowl; utilizes a re-circulation system to conserve water

Domestic Farm Animals - typical, Midwest farm species

Wildlife Area - displays native wildlife species that are often seen in farm environments; all specimens here were either injured or were raised by humans and are thus not releasable.

Vern Kiebler Learning Center - provides housing for the domestic animals, administrative offices and a multi-purpose education room.

Oldest Barn in Wheaton - built in 1862, the barn was moved to Cosley Farm in 1974; contains a display of antique farm equipment

Train Depot - built in 1887, the depot was moved to its current site in 1910 and served as Mr. Cosley's country residence

Caboose - this historic, 1880 railroad car originally served on the Chicago, Burlington & Quincy Railroad

**Future Plans:** Cosley Farm plans to renovate its wildlife area with naturalized exhibits; the $1.2 million project will begin in the fall of 1993.

## SEASONAL FESTIVALS & PROGRAMS

Farm Day - second Saturday in June

Fall Festival - October

Winter Wonderland: Festival of Lights & Christmas Tree Sale - day after Thanksgiving through December 23

## FOR MORE INFORMATION

Cosley Animal Farm and Museum, 1356 Gary Avenue, Wheaton, Illinois 60187; 708-665-5534; Manager: Jerry Douglas

# 79     PEORIA'S GLEN OAK ZOO
## Peoria, Illinois

Peoria's Glen Oak Zoo, founded in 1955, covers 7 acres. The Zoo is committed to public education, to participation in local, state and national conservation programs and to providing quality, family-oriented recreation.

## VISITOR INFORMATION

**Directions:** From Interstate 74, take the War Memorial Drive Exit (Route 150). Drive east on War Memorial Drive to Prospect Road. Turn south on Prospect, to the Zoo.

**Open to the Public:** 10 AM-8 PM, Memorial Day to Labor Day; 10 AM-4:30 PM the remainder of the year

**Closed:** Thanksgiving, Christmas and New Years Day

**Admission (1993):** Adult: $3.00     Child: $1.00     Senior: $2.70

**Parking Fee:** None

**Children's Zoo:** Yes     **Separate Admission:** No

**Annual Membership:** Individual: $20     Family: $30

**Programs & Tours:** The Zoo offers a variety of educational programs including tours, seminars, lectures, workshops and outreach programs.

**AAZPA Member:** Yes

## COLLECTIONS & EXHIBITS

**Collection:** The Zoo's current collection includes the following number of species:
Mammals: 32        Birds: 25        Reptiles: 34
Amphibians: 5      Fish: 16         Invertebrates: 5

**Special Exhibits** at Peoria's Glen Oak Zoo include:
Lions Trace - this new outdoor African Lion habitat opened in 1992

## SEASONAL FESTIVALS & PROGRAMS

Conservation Day - early June
McZoo Day - mid July
HallZooWeen - late October

## FOR MORE INFORMATION

Peoria's Glen Oak Zoo, 2218 N. Prospect Road, Peoria, Illinois 61603; 309-686-3365;
Director: Jan Schweitzer

*Zebra*
*(photo courtesy Glen Oak Zoo)*

# 80         MILLER PARK ZOO
## Bloomington, Illinois

Owned and operated by the city of Bloomington, the Miller Park Zoo was first opened in 1891. The facility now encompasses 12 acres.

## VISITOR INFORMATION

**Directions:** From Interstate 74, take the Veterans Parkway Exit. Turn left on Morris Avenue, proceed ¼ mile and turn right into the park.

**Open to the Public:** 10 AM-6 PM Memorial Day weekend through Labor Day; 10 AM-4:30 PM remainder of year

**Closed:** Christmas Day

**Admission (1993):** Adult: $1.50     Child: $1.00     Senior: $1.00

**Parking Fee:** None

**Children's Zoo:** Yes     **Separate Admission:** No

**Annual Membership:** Individual: $10     Family: $20     Senior: $5

**AAZPA Member:** Yes

## COLLECTIONS & EXHIBITS

**Collection:** The Zoo's current collection includes the following number of species:
| | | |
|---|---|---|
| Mammals: 22 | Birds: 31 | Reptiles: 26 |
| Amphibians: 5 | Mollusks: 5 | Fish: 2 |

**Special Exhibits** at the Miller Park Zoo include:
Rainforest Exhibit
Sumatran Tiger Exhibit
New Guinea Singing Dogs Exhibit

**Future Plans:** A Red Wolf Exhibit is scheduled to open in June, 1993.

## FOR MORE INFORMATION

The Miller Park Zoo, 1020 S. Morris Avenue, Bloomington, Illinois 61701; 309-823-4250; Director: John Tobias

# 81 HENSON ROBINSON ZOO
## Springfield, Illinois

Situated in a beautiful park on the east shore of Lake Springfield, the Henson Robinson Zoo covers 14 acres. The Zoo, established in 1970, recently added an Illinois Wetlands display, funded by the state's non-game checkoff program.

## VISITOR INFORMATION

**Directions:** The Zoo is located in southeastern Springfield. From Interstate 55, take Exit #94 and drive east on East Lake Drive. Proceed approximately 3 miles and watch for signs directing you to the Zoo.

**Open to the Public:** Early April to early November, 10 AM-5 PM

**Closed:** Early November to early April

**Admission (1993):** Adult: $2.00    Child: $.75    Senior: $1.00

**Parking Fee:** None

**Children's Zoo:** Yes    **Separate Admission:** No

**Annual Membership:** Individual: $15    Family: $30

**Programs & Tours:** Group Education Programs (call 529-2097)

**AAZPA Member:** Yes

## COLLECTIONS & EXHIBITS

**Collection:** The Zoo's current collection includes the following number of species:
    Mammals: 35         Birds: 32         Reptiles: 18
    Amphibians: 4       Insects: 3

**Special Exhibits** at the Henson Robinson Zoo include:
    Lemur Breeding Complex - home to Emperor & Golden lion tamarins
    Otter/Beaver Exhibit
    New Cougar Exhibit
    New Cheetah Exhibit
    Nocturnal Building - includes Fat-tailed dwarf lemurs and Coquerel's mouse lemurs
    Penguin Exhibit
    Illinois Wetlands Display

**Future Plans:** Multiple exhibits are scheduled for completion in 1993. These include a Red Wolf Exhibit, a Rainforest Exhibit, a Himalayan Black Bear Exhibit, a Gibbon Exhibit and an Animal Hospital/Food Preparation Complex.

*Penguin Habitat, Henson Robinson Zoo*
*(photo courtesy Michael J. Janis, Director)*

### CAPTIVE BREEDING & RESEARCH

The Henson Robinson Zoo has had special **breeding** success with the following species:

Red ruffed lemurs
Black lemurs
Binturongs - leads all North American zoos in the captive breeding of this species

### SEASONAL FESTIVALS & PROGRAMS

Dr. Doolittle Day - Saturday before Mother's Day
Fur Feather Fin Fall Fling - early October
Zoolie Ghoulie Safe Halloween - late October

### FOR MORE INFORMATION

Henson Robinson Zoo, 1100 East Lake Drive, Springfield, Illinois 62707; 217-529-2097; Director: Michael J. Janis

# 82

## SCOVILL CHILDREN'S ZOO
### Decatur, Illinois

This 15-acre Zoo, founded in 1967, is part of Scoville Park, a 62-acre preserve that stretches along the east shore of Lake Decatur. The Park also features the Robert Leathers Playground, botanical gardens, picnic areas and a miniature train ride which circles the Zoo. The train's engine, built in 1962, is a ¼ scale replica of the 1863 C.P. Huntington steam engine.

## VISITOR INFORMATION

**Directions:** Follow U.S. 36 to the east edge of Decatur; cross Lake Decatur, take a right at the first traffic signal (S. Country Club Road) and proceed another .5 mile to the Zoo, on your right.

**Open to the Public:** 10 AM-6:30 PM daily, Memorial Day to Labor Day; 10 AM-4 PM weekdays, 10 AM-6:30 PM weekends, mid April to Memorial Day and Labor Day to mid October

**Closed:** mid October to mid April (except special events)

**Admission (1993):** Adult: $1.50    Child: $1.00    Senior: $1.25

**Parking Fee:** None

**Annual Membership:** Individual: $15    Family: $30

**Programs & Tours:** The Zoo offers a variety of educational programs including the "Mobile Zoo" and "Zoo Crew." The latter provides "hands-on" experience for 5th-8th grade students. Tours are available; reservations required.

**AAZPA Member:** No

## COLLECTIONS & EXHIBITS

**Collection:** The Zoo's current collection includes the following number of species:
Mammals: 23          Birds: 16          Reptiles: 18
Amphibians: 5          Fish: 27          Insects: 1
Other Invertebrates: 2

**Special Exhibits** at the Scovill Children's Zoo include:
Parrot Island
Herpaquarium - salt and fresh water species
Primate Center - features ring-tailed lemurs, spider monkeys and the endangered golden lion tamarin

**Future Plans:** A Domestic Animal Petting Zoo will be completed in 1993, an Illinois Wildlife Exhibit is slated for 1994 and a South American Exhibit will open in 1995.

## SEASONAL FESTIVALS & PROGRAMS

Zippy Zoo Days - early to mid May
Turtle Races - August
Fall Festival - mid September; includes "The Great Train Robbery"
Boo-at-the-Zoo - late October
Christmastime at the Zoo - last half of December

## FOR MORE INFORMATION

Scovill Children's Zoo, 71 S. Country Club Road, Decatur, Illinois 62521-4470; 217-421-7435; Director: Mike Borders

# 83     FORT WAYNE CHILDREN'S ZOO
## Fort Wayne, Indiana

One of the few zoos in the United States that are completely self-supporting, the Fort Wayne Children's Zoo was founded in 1965. The 38-acre Zoo was the 11th American zoo to be accredited by the AAZPA and has been recognized for its elegant design and its attention to the needs of children and families.

On a per capita basis, the Fort Wayne Children's Zoo is one of the best attended facilities in the country. Convinced that their visitors want to do more than look at animals, the Zoo offers many interactive, educational displays.

## VISITOR INFORMATION

**Directions:** From I-69, take Exit 109-A and follow the signs to the Zoo. The Children's Zoo is north of the downtown area.

**Open to the Public:** Open late April to mid October, 9 AM-5 PM Mon.-Sat., 9 AM-6 PM Sunday; also open 6-9 PM on 10 days preceding Halloween and 5-9 PM on 20 days before Christmas

**Closed:** Mid October to late April, except for Halloween and Christmas seasons, as noted above.

**Admission (1993):** Adult: $3.50     Child: $2.00 (under 2 free)

**Parking Fee:** None

**Annual Membership:** Individual: $23     Family: $35     Grandparent: $35

**Programs & Tours:** The Zoo offers many interactive displays including rides, graphics and discovery centers. A Zoomobile visits local elementary schools.

**AAZPA Member:** Yes

## COLLECTIONS & EXHIBITS

**Collection:** The Zoo's current collection includes the following number of species:

| | | |
|---|---|---|
| Mammals: 49 | Birds: 66 | Reptiles: 11 |
| Amphibians: 6 | Fish: 36 | Mollusks: 3 |
| Other Invertebrates: 17 | | |

**Special Exhibits** at the Fort Wayne Children's Zoo include:

Australian Adventure - this 4.5 acre, $2.75 million exhibit is the "largest Australian exhibit outside of Australia;" it features a walk-through kangaroo display and a 20,000 gallon Great Barrier Reef Aquarium.

African Veldt - in this 22-acre savannah the animals roam free while human visitors are confined to safari jeeps

**Future Plans:** A $4 million Indonesian Rainforest is scheduled to open in June, 1994. New Great Ape and Sumatran Tiger Exhibits are also planned (projected to open in 1995 and 1996, respectively).

## CAPTIVE BREEDING & RESEARCH

The Fort Wayne Children's Zoo has had special **breeding** success with the following species:

| | |
|---|---|
| European white storks | Eastern grey kangaroos |
| Giraffes | Black-footed penguins |
| Colobus monkeys | White-throated capuchin monkeys |

The Zoo participates in the Species Survival Plan of the AAZPA and coordinates a primate conservation project for the Mentawai Islands, where the Zoo is working to establish a new National Park.

**Research** based at the Fort Wayne Children's Zoo includes:
- Studies on the metabolism of sea anemones

## SEASONAL FESTIVALS & PROGRAMS

Working for Wildlife Day - early June
Behind-the-Scenes Day - late June
Run Wild! 4-Mile Race - July 4th
ZooLoo Au - early August
Great Zoo Halloween - October
Christmas at the Zoo - December

## FOR MORE INFORMATION

Fort Wayne Children's Zoo, 3411 Sherman Blvd., Fort Wayne, Indiana 46808; 219-482-4610; Director: Earl Wells

# 84

## THE INDIANAPOLIS ZOO
### Indianapolis, Indiana

Founded in 1964, the Indianapolis Zoo moved to the west bank of the White River in 1988. The new facility, covering 64 acres, has three times the space of the old zoo and is characterized by natural habitats of earth's major biomes.

The new Indianapolis Zoo also features the world's largest totally-enclosed, environmentally controlled Whale and Dolphin Pavilion and is home to Indiana's first major aquarium.

## VISITOR INFORMATION

**Directions:** The Indianapolis Zoo is just west of the downtown area on the west bank of the White River. From I-65, take Exit 114; drive south on Dr. Martin Luther King Street/West Street to Washington Street. Turn west on Washington Street and proceed 1 mile to the Zoo.

From I-70, take Exit 79A; drive north on West Street/Missouri Street to Washington Street. Turn west on Washington Street and proceed 1 mile to the Zoo.

**Open to the Public:** 365 days per year, 7 days per week; hours vary with the seasons

**Admission (1993):** Adult: $8.50    Child: $5.00    Senior: $6.00

**Parking Fee:** $2.00

**Children's Zoo:** Yes    **Separate Admission:** No

**Annual Membership:** Individual: $35    Family: $50

**AAZPA Member:** Yes

## COLLECTIONS & EXHIBITS

**Collection:** The Zoo's current collection includes the following number of specimens:

| | |
|---|---|
| Mammals: 280 specimens | Birds: 275 specimens |
| Reptiles: 270 specimens | Amphibians: 15 specimens |
| Fish: 1175 specimens | Invertebrates: 340 specimens |

**Special Exhibits** at the Indianapolis Zoo include:

Whale and Dolphin Pavilion - 74,000 square-foot complex; this is the largest totally-enclosed, environmentally controlled marine mammal complex in the world.

Aquarium Complex - features over 200 species of aquatic life (both fresh and salt water species); includes puffin, penguin, polar bear and sea lion exhibits; habitats include open ocean (sharks), mangrove mudflat, Indiana pond, rift lake and coral reef.

Amazon Exhibit - this walk-through exhibit begins at the River's surface and descends to the depths of this tropical waterway; inhabitants include aquatic turtles, caimans, anacondas, piranha, pacu and armored catfish.

Deserts Conservatory - created within an 80-ft.-diameter domed building; features lizards, free-flying birds and desert flora.

Japanese Snow Macaques - this naturalized exhibit of the most northernly living primate (other than man) includes a simulated hot spring, a feature characteristic of the macques' homeland.

Kodiak Bear Exhibit - naturalized with streams, waterfalls and rockwork, this exhibit is home to earth's largest land carnivore.

African Elephant Exhibit - part of the Plains Biome, this exhibit includes a 10-foot deep swimming hole.

Siberian Tiger Exhibit - home to earth's largest feline, this exhibit uses a mesh covering which allows the large cats to climb on trees and rockwork in the habitat.

*Polar Bear*
*(photo by Mike Fender, Indianapolis News, courtesy Indianapolis Zoo)*

## CAPTIVE BREEDING & RESEARCH

The Indianapolis Zoo has had special **breeding** success with the following species:

Ricord iguana                    Siberian tiger
Tufted puffin                    Collared lemur
Radiated tortoise

**Research** projects based at the Zoo include:
- Reproductive physiology and artificial insemination in African elephants
- Study of the relationship between diet and molting in captive penguins
- Study of basking temperature preference in caimans
- Study of electric organ discharge in skates to deter predation by sharks
- Research on visitor perceptions of natural habitat exhibits
- Study of nocturnal behavior and sleep patterns in African Elephants
- Study of reconciliation behavior in Japanese macaques
- Investigation of Pouch Migration in Tammar wallabies
- Study of growth patterns in Tammar and Bennett Wallabies

## SEASONAL FESTIVALS & PROGRAMS

Kroger Arctic Survival Days - January and February
Ground Hog Day - February 2
St. Patrick's Day Celebration - mid March
Bloomfest - mid April to mid May
Baboon Easter Egg Hunt - Easter weekend
Wild 'n Woolly Weekend - mid April
ZooFest - late April
Zoopolis "500" Tortoise Race - late April
Country Fair Spring Holidays - early May
Spring Senior Expo - early May
Spring Senior Safari Days and Grandparent's Weekend - mid May
Zoo's Birthday Celebration - mid June
Teddy Bear Affair - mid July
Indiana Bell's "Animals & All That Jazz" - August concert series
Elephant Awareness Month - September
Disability Awareness Week - early October
Zoo Boo! Days - late October
Kroger Halloween Zoobilee - late October
Christmas at the Zoo - late November to December 23

## FOR MORE INFORMATION

Indianapolis Zoo, 1200 West Washington, Indianapolis, Indiana 46222; 317-630-2001; President & CEO: Roy A. Shea

# 85

## MESKER PARK ZOO
### Evansville, Indiana

The Mesker Park Zoo, founded in 1928, is the oldest and largest (by area) zoo in Indiana. Located within a valley, the 67-acre Zoo offers fine views of the southern Indiana countryside. Peddle boat rides are available on the park's 6-acre lake which is stocked with fish, turtles and waterfowl.

## VISITOR INFORMATION

**Directions:** Take U.S. 41 South from I-64; proceed 17 miles to Route 66 West. Take 66 West 3.6 miles to St. Joe. Turn left on St. Joe and proceed 2 blocks to Bement Avenue.

From Kentucky, take U.S. 41 North across the Ohio River to 62 West. Follow 62 West for 4 miles to St. Joe. Turn right and proceed 1.5 miles to Bement Avenue.

**Open to the Public:** 365 days per year; 9 AM-7 PM June through September; 9 AM-4 PM October through May

**Admission (1993):** Adult: $3.00    Child: $2.00    Senior: $2.00

**Parking Fee:** None

**Children's Zoo:** Yes    **Separate Admission:** No

**Annual Membership:** Individual: $25    Family: $35    Senior: $15

**AAZPA Member:** Yes

## COLLECTIONS & EXHIBITS

**Collection:** The Zoo's current collection includes the following number of species:
  Mammals: 83          Birds: 120        Reptiles: 45
  Amphibians: 1        Fish: 3           Insects: 1
  Other Invertebrates: 3

**Special Exhibits** at the Mesker Park Zoo include:
  Spacious, grassy hoofstock exhibits
  Giraffe Exhibit - permits contact with this tallest mammal
  "Blue Bears" - the only pair in captivity
  Australian Outback Exhibit - a collection of unique species from "down under"
  African Panorama Exhibit - viewed from two large decks

**Future Plans:** A Discovery Center Education/Rainforest Complex will open in 1993.

## CAPTIVE BREEDING & RESEARCH

The Mesker Park Zoo has had special **breeding** success with the following species:

African hedgehog                    Blue-crowned motmot
Lion-tailed macaque                 Sitatunga antelope
Spurwing lapwing                    Dourocouli

The Zoo is studying the use of primate birth control implants (currently used in the Park's macaque colony).

## SEASONAL FESTIVALS & PROGRAMS

Easter at the Zoo - Saturday before Easter
Zooday - second Saturday in June
Winter Carnival - second Saturday in August
Children's Art Fair - third Saturday in September
Boo at the Zoo - weekend before Halloween
Christmas at the Zoo - first ten days in December

## FOR MORE INFORMATION

The Mesker Park Zoo, 2421 Bement Avenue, Evansville, Indiana 47720-5500; 812-428-0715; Director: Ronald A. Young

# 86

## THE TOLEDO ZOO
### Toledo, Ohio

Recognized as one of the most complete zoos in America, the Toledo Zoo, founded in 1899, exhibits over 2500 specimens, representing almost 500 species. Though many of its buildings date from the WPA Era, the 30-acre Zoo has naturalized its habitats and will open a new, outdoor gorilla exhibit in 1993.

Perhaps best known for its Hippoquarium, the Toledo Zoo also boasts one of the largest fresh and saltwater aquariums in the country.

## VISITOR INFORMATION

**Directions:**    From I-75, take Exit 201-A. Head southwest on Route 25 to the Zoo.

From the Ohio Turnpike, take Exit 4. Proceed north on Reynolds Road (U.S. 20) and then east on Glendale Avenue to the Zoo.

**Open to the Public:**  10 AM-5 PM, April through September; 10 AM-4 PM, October through March

**Closed:** Thanksgiving, Christmas and New Years Day

**Admission (1993):** Adult: $4.00     Child: $2.00     Senior: $2.00

**Parking Fee:** $2.00

**Children's Zoo:** Yes     **Separate Admission:** No

**Annual Membership:** Individual: $20     Family: $30     Grandparent: $25

**AAZPA Member:** Yes

## COLLECTIONS & EXHIBITS

**Collection:**  The Zoo's current collection includes over 2500 specimens, representing almost 500 species.

**Special Exhibits** at the Toledo Zoo include:
Hippoquarium - the world's only filtered hippo pool with underwater viewing; the pool holds 360,000 gallons
Aquarium - one of the largest fresh and saltwater aquariums in the country
African Savanna - large, mixed-species habitats
Koala Exhibit
"Diversity of Life" - a hands-on exhibit in the Museum of Science

**Future Plans:**  Gorilla Meadows, a large outdoor, naturalistic habitat, will open in 1993.

*Toledo Zoo's Hippoquarium*
*(photo courtesy the Toledo Zoo)*

## CAPTIVE BREEDING & RESEARCH

The Toledo Zoo has had special **breeding** success with the following species:

| | |
|---|---|
| Cheetahs | Polar bears |
| Lowland gorillas | Virgin Island boa |
| Snow leopards | Penguin species |

**Research** projects based at the Toledo Zoo include:
- Participation in 18 Species Survival Plans
- Studies on the Virgin Island boa and the Aruba Island rattlesnake

## SEASONAL FESTIVALS & PROGRAMS

Conservation Carnival - July
Pumpkin Path - Halloween Night
Lights Before Christmas - day after Thanksgiving to January

## FOR MORE INFORMATION

The Toledo Zoo, 2700 Broadway, Toledo, Ohio 43609; 419-385-5721; Director: Bill Dennler

# 87     CLEVELAND METROPARKS ZOOLOGICAL PARK
### Cleveland, Ohio

Spreading across 165 acres of rolling, wooded terrain, the Cleveland Metroparks Zoo was founded in 1882. As part of its transformation to naturalized, mixed-species exhibits, the Zoo opened its new Rainforest habitat in November, 1992, which features over 600 animals and 7000 plants.

One of few U.S. zoos to display Francois monkeys, the Cleveland Metroparks Zoo is actively involved in the Species Survival Plans of the AAZPA, an inter-zoo program to protect, breed and re-introduce endangered species.

## VISITOR INFORMATION

**Directions:** The Metroparks Zoo is southwest of downtown Cleveland. From I-71, take the Fulton Road/W. 25th St. Exit and follow the signs (the Zoo is south of the Interstate). Alternatively, from I-480, take the State Road North Exit and follow signs to the Zoo.

**Open to the Public:** 9 AM-5 PM Mon.-Fri. and 9 AM-7 PM Sat.-Sun., Memorial Day through Labor Day; 9 AM-5 PM remainder of the year. Buildings open at 10 AM and close 15 minutes before the grounds close.

**Closed:** Christmas and New Years Day

**Admission (1993):** Adult: $7.00 Zoo + Rainforest, $5.00 Zoo only
Child: $4.00 Zoo + Rainforest, $3.00 Zoo only (under 2 free)

**Parking Fee:** None

**Children's Zoo:** Yes     **Separate Admission:** No

**Annual Membership:** Individual: $25     Family: $40     Senior: $17 ($30 Couple)

**Programs & Tours:** The "Get Close Program" involves live demonstrations and mobile exhibits throughout the Zoo. The Zoo's "Adventure Series" offers entertaining classes and travel programs. The Outback Railroad takes visitors through the Australian habitats and the Children's Farm.

**AAZPA Member:** Yes

## COLLECTIONS & EXHIBITS

**Collection:** The Zoo's current collection includes the following number of species:
Mammals: 86          Birds: 154          Reptiles: 39
Amphibians: 9          Fish: 107          Invertebrates: 87

**Special Exhibits** at the Cleveland Metroparks Zoo include:
The Rainforest - an 87,000 square-foot exhibit featuring over 600 tropical animals and 7000 plants
Rhino/Cheetah Exhibit - white rhinos and cheetahs share the same habitat (the only U.S. zoo to combine these species in one exhibit)
African Plains Exhibit - this large, mixed-species enclosure simulates conditions on the African plains
Bear Habitats - the Zoo boasts a large bear collection
African Bongo Exhibit
Greenhouse - seasonal displays of over 300 plants

**Future Plans:** An Outdoor Gorilla Habitat is scheduled to open in 1993. The Administration/Education Complex was recently expanded.

## CAPTIVE BREEDING & RESEARCH

The Cleveland Metroparks Zoo has had special **breeding** success with the following species:

| | |
|---|---|
| Cheetahs | Francois Langurs |
| Spectacled Bears | Masai Giraffes |
| Sloth Bears | Spur-winged Geese |
| Polar Bears | White Storks |
| Lesser Pandas | Abdom Storks |
| Clouded Leopards | Waterbucks |

As mentioned above, the Zoo participates in many of the Species Survival Plans administered by the AAZPA.

*Cheetah*
*(photo courtesy Cleveland Metroparks Zoological Park)*

## SEASONAL FESTIVALS & PROGRAMS

EarthFest - April
Zippity Zoo Doo (Fundraiser) - June
Senior Celebration - September
Boo at the Zoo - October
Holiday Lights - December

## FOR MORE INFORMATION

Cleveland Metroparks Zoological Park, 3900 Brookside Park Drive, Cleveland, Ohio
44109; 216-661-7511; Director: Steve H. Taylor

# 88

## SEA WORLD OF OHIO
## Aurora, Ohio

Located on a scenic, glacial lake in the rolling hills of northeast Ohio, this 90-acre Park is far from any seashore. Nevertheless, its twenty attractions and exhibits introduce visitors to the wonders of the sea, bringing sharks, killer whales, dolphins and other marine species to the heart of the Midwest.

Opened in 1970, Sea World of Ohio is owned by Anheuser-Busch Companies, Inc. The Park operates from late May through mid September.

## VISITOR INFORMATION

**Directions:**   The Park is off Ohio 43, northwest of Aurora, Ohio. From I-480 between I-271 and the Ohio Turnpike, exit to Twinsburg and head east on Ohio 82. Drive almost 5 miles and turn left onto Ohio 43.

**Open to the Public:**   Daily, late May through mid September (call for specific dates); opens 10 AM; closing time varies.

**Closed:**  Mid September to late May

**Admission (1993):**  Subject to change.
    Adult: $20.95       Child: $16.95 (under 3 free)

**Parking Fee:** $3.00

**Annual Membership:**  Subject to change.
    Adult: $44.95      Child: $39.95

    $5.00 off each pass when four or more persons from same household purchase season passes at the same time.

**Programs & Tours:**  Daily animal shows, demonstrations and on-site educational exhibits.

**AAZPA Member:** Yes

## COLLECTIONS & EXHIBITS

**Collection:**  Sea World of Ohio harbors over 2500 specimens of marine life, representing more than 375 species.

**Special Exhibits** at Sea World of Ohio include:
    Penguin Encounter - home to more than 120 polar penguins; also features the only blue-eyed shags on exhibit in the eastern U.S. Simulating polar conditions, the exhibit is characterized by an icy, 45,000 gallon pool, daily snowfalls and realistic lighting.
    World of the Sea Aquarium - features 20 geographically-themed aquariums depicting aquatic habitats and creatures from around the globe.

"Total Access - A Landscape for All" - this unique garden debuted at "Ameriflora" in Columbus, Ohio, in 1992. Designed in cooperation with Yardmaster, Inc., the garden features a "sensory walk" which accommodates handicapped visitors.

Birds of the World - this free-flight aviary is home to a variety of exotic birds from around the world.

Seal & Sea Lion Exhibit - visitors are permitted to feed these marine mammals at their naturalized, community pool.

**Future Plans:** "Shark Encounter" opens in 1993. This educational exhibit will feature the largest collection of sharks in the Midwest, representing five species. The 340,000 gallon tank will also house moray eels, pilot fish, tangs and sawfish.

## SEASONAL FESTIVALS & PROGRAMS

Summer Nights - after dark entertainment, mid June through late August and weekends into early September

Autumn Arts & Crafts Show - weekends, late September and early October (call for information)

## FOR MORE INFORMATION

Sea World of Ohio, 1100 Sea World Drive, Aurora, Ohio 44202-8700; 216-995-2121, 800-63-SHAMU, Public Relations: 216-995-2110; Director: Brad Andrews

*"Shark Encounter," a brand new 340,000 gallon exhibit housing five species of sharks, opened in May, 1993.*
*(®1993, Sea World, Inc. Reproduced by permission.)*

# 89      AKRON ZOOLOGICAL PARK
### Akron, Ohio

The Akron Zoological Park, established in 1950, covers 25 wooded acres. Committed to public education and wildlife conservation, the Zoo directs 1% of all admission fees to its Conservation Endowment Fund.

## VISITOR INFORMATION

**Directions:**    The Zoo is west of downtown Akron. From I-76/I-77, take Exit 21C and follow to Downtown/Cedar Exit. Turn left on Exchange St. and then left on Maple St. Pass 2 lights and turn left on Edgewood Avenue to the Zoo.

**Open to the Public:**    Daily, mid April to mid October; 10 AM-5 PM, weekdays; 10 AM-6 PM weekends & holidays; open until 8 PM on Thursdays, June through August.

**Closed:** Mid October to mid April (except holiday programs)

**Admission (1993):** Adult: $4.00    Child: $2.50    Senior: $3.00

**Parking Fee:** None

**Children's Zoo:** Yes    **Separate Admission:** No

**Annual Membership:** Individual: $25    Family: $35    Grandparents: $35

**Programs & Tours:** The Zoo offers a variety of educational programs including a Zoomobile.

**AAZPA Member:** Yes

## COLLECTIONS & EXHIBITS

**Collection:** The Zoo's current collection includes the following number of species:
Mammals: 24        Birds: 49        Reptiles: 20

**Special Exhibits** at the Akron Zoological Park include:
Walk-through Aviary
Lemur Exhibit - home to black & white ruffed lemurs
River Otter Exhibit - features underwater viewing
Ohio Farmyard - permits close encounters with domestic stock

**Future Plans:** The Ohio Farmyard will be renovated by 1995.

## CAPTIVE BREEDING & RESEARCH

The Akron Zoological Park has had special **breeding** success with the following species:
Cotton-top tamarin
Bighorn sheep

*Black and white ruffed lemur*
*(photo by Lori Mavrigian; courtesy Akron Zoological Park)*

## SEASONAL FESTIVALS & PROGRAMS

Opening Day/Spring Fling - mid April
Earth Day - May
ZooCamp - June
Zoorific Birthday Parties - May to September
Recycle Day - early June
Zoobilation - late June
Reptile Day - mid July
Nocturnal Golf Classic - early August
Member's Night - early September
Boo at the Zoo! - late October
Holiday Lights Celebration - late November to early January

## FOR MORE INFORMATION

Akron Zoological Park, 500 Edgewood Ave., Akron, Ohio 44307; 216-434-8645;
Info line: 216-434-9567; Director: L. Patricia Simmons

# 90

## COLUMBUS ZOO
### Columbus, Ohio

The Columbus Zoo, founded in 1927, is home to "Colo," the first gorilla born in captivity. The Zoo is also one of only four U.S. facilities to house bonobos and one of the few to display moose.

Located northwest of downtown Columbus, the Zoo is part of a 404 acre complex that includes an amusement/water park and an 18-hole golf course (there is a separate admission charge to these other attractions).

## VISITOR INFORMATION

**Directions:**    The Columbus Zoo is located in the Scioto River Valley, northwest of the downtown area. Take the Sawmill Road Exit (Exit #20) from the I-270 Beltway and follow the signs to the Zoo.

**Open to the Public:**   365 days per year; 9 AM-6 PM Memorial Day to Labor Day; 9 AM-5 PM the remainder of the year.

**Admission (1993):**  Adult: $5.00    Child: $3.00 (under 2 free)    Senior: $3.00

**Parking Fee:**  $2.00

**Children's Zoo:**  Yes    **Separate Admission:**  No

**Annual Membership:**  Individual: $35    Family: $45

**AAZPA Member:**  Yes

## COLLECTIONS & EXHIBITS

**Collection:**  The Zoo's current collection includes the following number of species:
   Mammals: 95          Birds: 83          Reptiles: 238
   Amphibians: 28       Fish: 359          Insects: 99

**Special Exhibits** at the Columbus Zoo include:
   North America - this fine collection of naturalized exhibits features bison, black and grizzly bears, moose, eagles, wolverines, bobcats, cougars, otters and rare Mexican wolves
   Australia - includes koalas, Bennett's wallabies, red kangaroos and emus
   Tiger Exhibits - naturalized homes for Sumatran and White Bengal Tigers
   Great Apes Exhibits - gorilla families (including "Colo," the first gorilla born in captivity) and bonobos
   Reptile House - a superb collection of snakes, lizards and turtles
   Cheetah Exhibit - an elevated boardwalk and gazebo overlooks this large, grassy habitat

**Future Plans**   Expansion of the Aquarium (to include a 100,000 gallon coral reef tank), a new North American Wetlands Exhibit and enlargement of the Great Apes Complex are all scheduled for 1993.

## CAPTIVE BREEDING & RESEARCH

The Columbus Zoo has had special **breeding** success with the following species:

| | |
|---|---|
| Lowland Gorillas | Colobus Monkeys |
| Cheetahs | Bongos |
| Bald Eagles | Black-footed Penguins |
| Lake Victoria Cichlids | Baird's Tapir |
| Red Pandas | Wart Hogs |
| Snow Leopards | |

**Research** based at the Columbus Zoo includes:
- Reproductive biology of the Australian Salamander fish
- Characterization of a unique isolate of Feline Immuno-deficiency Virus from nondomestic felids
- Standardized data collection for the analysis of growth of hand-raised zoo animals

## SEASONAL FESTIVALS & PROGRAMS

Great Eggspectations - weekend before Easter
Cycling Safari - first Saturday in May
Zoofari (Fundraiser) - last Saturday in June
Pioneer Days - last weekend in September
Boo at the Zoo - week before Halloween
Wildlight Wonderland - Thanksgiving weekend to New Years

## FOR MORE INFORMATION

Columbus Zoo, 9990 Riverside Drive, P.O. Box 400, Powell, Ohio 43065-0400; 614-645-3550; Director: Jack Hanna

# 91 CINCINNATI ZOO & BOTANICAL GARDEN
## Cincinnati, Ohio

Consistently ranked as one of the top ten zoos in the country, the Cincinnati Zoo & Botanical Garden is home to almost 100 species of endangered plants and animals from across the globe. The grounds are adorned with 2000 species of plants, ranging from hardy bamboos to rare shrubs, wildflowers and 200-year old trees.

Founded in 1875, this 67-acre Zoo also boasts three buildings that are listed on the National Register of Historic Landmarks: the Elephant House, the Reptile House and the Passenger Pigeon Memorial. The latter pays tribute to "Martha," the last passenger pigeon on earth, which died at the Cincinnati Zoo in 1914.

The Zoo's Fleischmann Aquarium is one of the largest inland aquariums in the country and the fabulous Insect World exhibit, which opened in 1978, is the largest display of live insects in the U.S.

## VISITOR INFORMATION

**Directions:** The Cincinnati Zoo & Botanical Garden is located north of the downtown area between I-75 and I-71. From I-75, take Exit #6 (Mitchell Avenue), head east and follow the signs to the Zoo.

From I-71, take Exit #5 (Dana Ave.), head west and follow the signs to the Zoo. The auto entrance is on Dury Avenue.

**Open to the Public:** 365 days per year; 9 AM-6 PM Memorial Day to Labor Day; 9 AM-5 PM remainder of year; grounds close at 8 PM in summer, at dusk the remainder of the year.

**Admission (1993):** Adult: $6.50    Child: $3.75    Senior: $4.25

**Parking Fee:** $4.00

**Children's Zoo:** Yes    **Separate Admission:** $.75 (non-members)

**Annual Membership:** Individual: $33.00    Family: $51.00

**Programs & Tours:** The Zoo offers a wide variety of educational programs through-out the year, including the RC Cola Wildlife Theater during the summer. The Zoo staff has also produced a series of television programs, aimed at school children, which air on Public TV stations across the country.

**AAZPA Member:** Yes

## COLLECTIONS & EXHIBITS

**Collection:** The Zoo's current collection includes the following number of species:
Mammals: 139    Birds: 201    Reptiles: 116
Amphibians: 94    Fish: 58    Insects: 123

**Special Exhibits** at the Cincinnati Zoo & Botanical Garden include:

Insect World - largest display of live insects in the country; also features naked mole rats (the only mammal with an insect-like social structure)

Komodo Dragon Exhibit - one of only two zoos in U.S. to display the world's largest lizard; the pair in Cincinnati was donated by the Government of Indonesia.

Cat House - hailed as the "most comprehensive collection of wild cats on earth." This facility has bred more species of small cats than any other zoo in the world. The component exhibits were recently renovated to mimic the natural habitat of these species.

Wildlife Canyon - features some of the rarest animals in the Zoo: Mhorr gazelles, zebra duikers, takins and Sumatran rhinos.

Walrus Exhibit - includes underwater viewing of these marine mammals.

Gorilla World - this lush, outdoor exhibit is home to two lowland gorilla families, the largest social group on display in the country.

**Future Plans:** Jungle Trails, a simulated 2-acre rain forest, will open in 1993; the exhibit will feature orangutans, bonobos and other small primates from the tropical forests of Asia and Africa.

*Scene at African Veldt Exhibit*
*(photo by Darcy Folzenlogen)*

## CAPTIVE BREEDING & RESEARCH

The Cincinnati Zoo & Botanical Garden has had special **breeding** success with the following species:
Lowland gorillas - world leader in captive gorilla births
Small cat species - more births than any other zoo in the world
Black rhino - more births than any other zoo in the world
White Bengal tigers - the Zoo has bred over half of the world's total population

The Zoo is home to the Carl H. Lindner, Jr. Family Center for Reproduction of Endangered Wildlife. This facility is a world leader in assisted reproduction techniques, including in vitro fertilization, artificial insemination, cryopreservation and embryo transfer.

## SEASONAL FESTIVALS & PROGRAMS

Spring Floral Festival - April & May
Zoo Babies - June
Jazzoo (summer concert series) - June through August
Summer Blockbuster Event (new theme each year) - mid July/mid August
Wildlife Weekend - late August
Halloween Happening - late October
Festival of Lights - mid November through New Years

## FOR MORE INFORMATION

Cincinnati Zoo & Botanical Garden, 3400 Vine St., Cincinnati, Ohio 45220-1399; 513-281-4700; Director: Edward J. Maruska

# IV. NORTH CENTRAL REGION

92. **Roosevelt Park Zoo** (Minot, North Dakota)

93. **Dakota Zoo** (Bismarck, North Dakota)

94. **Bramble Park Zoo** (Watertown, South Dakota)

95. **Great Plains Zoo & Delbridge Museum** (Sioux Falls, South Dakota)

96. **St. Paul's Como Zoo** (St. Paul, Minnesota)

97. **The Minnesota Zoo** (Apple Valley, Minnesota)

98. **Heritage Zoo** (Grand Island, Nebraska)

99. **Folsom Children's Zoo & Botanical Gardens** (Lincoln, Nebraska)

100. **Omaha's Henry Doorly Zoo** (Omaha, Nebraska)

101. **Blank Park Zoo of Des Moines** (Des Moines, Iowa)

102. **Sunset Zoological Park** (Manhattan, Kansas)

103. **Topeka Zoological Park** (Topeka, Kansas)

104. **Emporia Zoo** (Emporia, Kansas)

105. **Lee Richardson Zoo** (Garden City, Kansas)

106. **Sedgwick County Zoo & Botanical Garden** (Wichita, Kansas)

107. **Kansas City Zoological Garden** (Kansas City, Missouri)

108. **Saint Louis Zoo** (St. Louis, Missouri)

109. **Dickerson Park Zoo** (Springfield, Missouri)

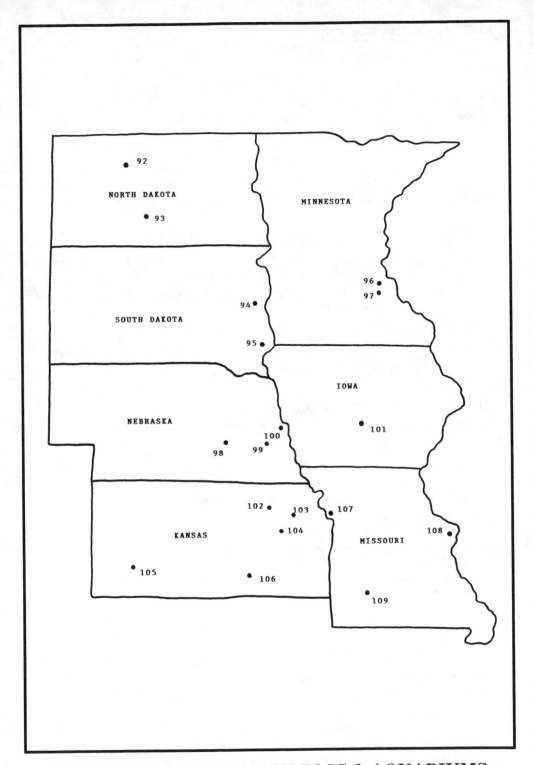

# NORTH CENTRAL REGION ZOOS & AQUARIUMS

# 92

## ROOSEVELT PARK ZOO
### Minot, North Dakota

The Roosevelt Park Zoo, established in 1920, is home to more than 100 mammals, birds and reptiles. Located in the Mouse River Valley, the Zoo covers 20 acres.

## VISITOR INFORMATION

**Directions:** The Zoo is on the eastern edge of Minot. Proceed 15 blocks east from the intersection of Broadway and Burdick.

**Open to the Public:** 10 AM-8 PM May through September; 8 AM-4 PM October through April

**Admission:** Free October through April
Under 6 Free all year
May through September:
   Adult: $2.00    Child: $1.00 (6-12)

**Parking Fee:** None

**Children's Zoo:** Yes    **Separate Admission:** No

**Annual Membership:** Individual: $15    Family: $25    Senior: $5

**AAZPA Member:** Yes

## COLLECTIONS & EXHIBITS

**Collection:** The Zoo's current collection includes the following number of specimens:
   Mammals: 84 specimens    Birds: 30 specimens
   Reptiles: 5 specimens

**Special Exhibits** at the Roosevelt Park Zoo include:
   Zoo Education Center
   Kangaroo Exhibit
   Giraffe Exhibit
   North American Exhibit

**Future Plans:** A Primate Building is scheduled for completion in 1995.

## SEASONAL FESTIVALS & PROGRAMS

Zoo Camp for Children - June through August
Zoofari (Annual Fundraiser) - July

## FOR MORE INFORMATION

Roosevelt Park Zoo, 1219 Burdick Expressway E., Minot, North Dakota 58701; 701-852-2751; Director: Donald Fricke

# 93

## DAKOTA ZOO
### Bismarck, North Dakota

With a collection of over 500 animals and a potential land coverage of 100 acres, the Dakota Zoo is the largest zoo in North Dakota. Founded in 1961, the Zoo stretches along the east bank of the Missouri River. Self-supporting, the Dakota Zoo receives no direct tax revenues.

## VISITOR INFORMATION

**Directions:** The Dakota Zoo is at the southwest edge of Bismarck in Sertoma Park, along the east bank of the Missouri River.

**Open to the Public:** 10 AM-8 PM May through September; Noon to 5 PM weekends in October

**Closed:** November through April

**Admission:** Adult: $3.00    Child: $1.00    Senior: $3.00

**Parking Fee:** None

**Children's Zoo:** Yes    **Separate Admission:** No

**Annual Membership:** Individual: $15    Family: $25

**AAZPA Member:** Yes

## COLLECTIONS & EXHIBITS

**Collection:** The Zoo's current collection includes the following number of species:
Mammals: 41        Birds: 48        Reptiles: 18
Insects: 1

**Special Exhibits** at the Dakota Zoo include:
Naturalistic River Otter Exhibit
Naturalistic Alaskan Brown Bear Exhibit

**Future Plans:** New wolf, coyote, arctic fox, red fox, swift fox, raccoon and coati exhibits are scheduled to open in 1993. A prairie dog exhibit will also open in 1993. A pheasant aviary is scheduled for completion in June, 1994, and a new exhibit for North American hoofstock will open in 1995.

## CAPTIVE BREEDING & RESEARCH

The Dakota Zoo has had special **breeding** success with the following species:
Double-wattled cassowary        Bactrian camel
American elk        Reeve's muntjac

Current **research** at the Dakota Zoo includes:
- Study of indirect carriers of internal parasites
- Study of the underwater vocalizations of otters

## SEASONAL FESTIVALS & PROGRAMS
Wednesday Night Programs - May through September
Children's Day - late June
Members' Picnic - middle of July
Zoo Flea Market - mid August
Zoofest - late August

## FOR MORE INFORMATION
The Dakota Zoo, P.O. Box 711, Bismarck, North Dakota 58502; 701-223-7543;
Director: Terry K. Lincoln

*The Dakota Zoo Otter Exhibit*
*(photo by Terry Lincoln; courtesy Dakota Zoo)*

# 94

## BRAMBLE PARK ZOO
### Watertown, South Dakota


Home to one of the largest collections of waterfowl and pheasants in the country, the
Bramble Park Zoo was established in 1912. The 17-acre facility features over 400
specimens of mammals, reptiles and birds.

## VISITOR INFORMATION

**Directions:**  The Zoo is located along South Dakota Highway 20 in northwest Watertown. Directional signs are spaced along Interstate 29, U.S. Highway 212 and Highway 20.

**Open to the Public:**  10 AM-9 PM (or dusk), March 15 to November 30; 10 AM-5 PM, December 1 to March 14

**Closed:**  Thanksgiving and Christmas Day

**Admission (1993):**  Adult: $2.00    Child: $1.00 (under 5 free)

**Parking Fee:**  None

**Children's Zoo:**  Yes    **Separate Admission:**  No

**Annual Membership:**  Individual: $25    Family: $25

**Programs & Tours:**  The Zoo emphasizes education through the use of displays, tours and demonstrations.

**AAZPA Member:**  No

## COLLECTIONS & EXHIBITS

**Collection:** The Zoo's current collection includes the following number of species:
Mammals: 36          Birds: 60          Reptiles: 5
Invertebrates: 1

**Special Exhibits** at the Bramble Park Zoo include:
Free flight aviary with Pheasant World - one of the largest collections of pheasants in North America
Great Plains Exhibit - this naturalistic habitat features bison, pronghorns and other animals native to the North American plains.

**Future Plans:**  An exhibit of small, tropical animals will open in 1993.

## CAPTIVE BREEDING & RESEARCH

The Bramble Park Zoo has had special **breeding** success with the following species:
Black lemurs

## SEASONAL FESTIVALS & PROGRAMS

Conservation Day - June
Education Series for Children - June & July

## FOR MORE INFORMATION

Bramble Park Zoo, P.O. Box 910, Watertown, South Dakota 57201; 605-882-3464; Director: Dan D. Miller

# 95 GREAT PLAINS ZOO & DELBRIDGE MUSEUM
## Sioux Falls, South Dakota

Founded in 1963, this 50-acre park includes both a zoo and a natural history museum. The Delbridge Museum houses one of the largest collections of mounted animals in the world.

## VISITOR INFORMATION

**Directions:** From Highway 29, exit onto 12th St. and drive east. Turn south on Kiwanas Avenue and proceed .25 mile to the Zoo & Museum.

**Open to the Public:** 9 AM-6 PM Summer; 10 AM-4 PM Winter

**Closed: Thanksgiving, Christmas, New Years Day**

**Admission (1993):** Adult: $4.75    Child: $2.50    Senior: $3.75

**Parking Fee:** None

**Children's Zoo:** Yes    **Separate Admission:** No

**Annual Membership:** Individual: $25    Family: $50

**AAZPA Member:** Yes

## COLLECTIONS & EXHIBITS

**Collection:** The Zoo's current collection includes the following number of species:
Mammals: 37              Birds: 28              Reptiles: 4

**Special Exhibits** at the Great Plains Zoo include:
Penguin Exhibit - black-footed penguins
North American Plains Exhibit - includes bison, elk, deer
Wild Dogs of America Exhibit - features red wolves, gray wolves, fox, coyote
Birds of Prey Exhibit
Australian Outback Exhibit
Grizzly Bear Den
Primate Building

**Future Plans:** An Asian Cat Exhibit (Siberian tigers and snow leopards) will open in 1994. The African Savannah (featuring giraffes, zebra, antelope) is scheduled for completion in 1995.

## CAPTIVE BREEDING & RESEARCH

The Great Plains Zoo has had special **breeding** success with the following species:
Siberian tigers - well adapted to the climate extremes of South Dakota
Snow leopards
Black-footed penguins

The Zoo participates is special survival plans for several endangered species: Snow leopards, Siberian tigers, Red wolves, Lemurs & Red pandas.

## SEASONAL FESTIVALS & PROGRAMS

Zoo & Aquarium Month - June
Zoofest - July
Zippity Zoo Day - August
Halloween Zoo Boo - October
Breakfast with Santa - December

## FOR MORE INFORMATION

Great Plains Zoo & Delbridge Museum, 805 S. Kiwanis Avenue, Sioux Falls, South
Dakota 57104; 605-339-7059; Director: Edward D. Asper

*Black-footed Penguins*
*(photo courtesy Great Plains Zoo & Delbridge Museum)*

# 96

## ST. PAUL'S COMO ZOO
### St. Paul, Minnesota

Located in a regional park, St. Paul's Como Zoo is free to the public. The 11.5 acre facility, established in 1903, is currently the only zoo in Minnesota to display gorillas, orangutans and giraffes. The Zoo is owned and managed by the City of St. Paul.

## VISITOR INFORMATION

**Directions:**     The Zoo is 8 miles northwest of downtown St. Paul; follow Como Avenue to the Park.

Alternatively, take Exit #239 from I-94. Drive north for 2.5 miles on this parkway to the Zoo.

**Open to the Public:**   Grounds 8 AM-8 PM, Buildings 10 AM-6 PM, April to September; Grounds 8 AM-5 PM, Buildings 10 AM-4 PM, October to March. Open 365 days per year.

**Admission (1993):** Free

**Parking Fee:** None

**Children's Zoo:** No

**Annual Membership:** Individual: $15    Family: $25

**AAZPA Member:** Yes

## COLLECTIONS & EXHIBITS

**Collection:** The Zoo's current collection includes the following number of species:

| | | |
|---|---|---|
| Mammals: 34 | Birds: 41 | Reptiles: 14 |
| Amphibians: 1 | Fish: 27 | |

**Special Exhibits** at St. Paul Como Zoo include:
Gorilla Exhibit - one of two all male socialization groups in North America; only gorillas displayed in Minnesota
Orangutan Exhibit - only display of this species in the State
Giraffe Exhibit - only giraffes on exhibit in Minnesota

## CAPTIVE BREEDING & RESEARCH

St. Paul's Como Zoo has had special **breeding** success with the following species:

| | |
|---|---|
| Orangutan | Snow leopard |
| Black-footed penguin | Siberian tiger |

"Science Teens," a cooperative program with neighborhood high schools, provides animal behavior research opportunities for 11th & 12th grade students.

## SEASONAL FESTIVALS & PROGRAMS

Zoo Boo - several days prior to Halloween
Holiday Kingdom Light Festival - last half of December

## FOR MORE INFORMATION

St. Paul's Como Zoo, Midway Parkway and Kaufman Drive, St. Paul, Minnesota 55103; 612-488-4041; Director: Victor L. Camp


# 97      THE MINNESOTA ZOO
### Apple Valley, Minnesota

The Minnesota Zoo, founded in 1978, is renowned for its large, naturalized habitats which are grouped into five geographic regions. Visitors wander along five corresponding trails to view the exhibits and can board the Skytrail monorail to gain a treetop perspective of the Northern Hemisphere habitats.

This 485-acre facility is strongly committed to public education and international conservation. Its "World of Birds" show introduces visitors to a wide variety of avian species and highlights their natural talents. Active in many international breeding and conservation programs, the Minnesota Zoo has adopted Ujung Kulon International Park, in Java, Indonesia, in an effort to protect the endangered Java rhino.

## VISITOR INFORMATION

**Directions:**    The Zoo is located 20 minutes south of downtown St. Paul. Head south on I-35E and exit onto Cedar Avenue (Highway 77). Turn left (south), and proceed to Zoo Boulevard. Follow signs to the Zoo.

**Open to the Public:**   Daily; opens at 9 AM; closing time varies with the seasons.

**Closed:** Christmas Day

**Admission (1993):** Adult: $6.00     Child: $2.50     Senior: $4.00

**Parking Fee:** None

**Children's Zoo:** Yes     **Separate Admission:** No

**Annual Membership:** Individual: $30     Family: $45

**Programs & Tours:**   The Zoo has an extensive education network including guided tours, workshops, classes for children and adults, field trips, outreach programs, zoolab and on-site exhibits.

**AAZPA Member:** Yes

*Southeast Asian Sun Bear*
*(photo courtesy Minnesota Zoo)*

## COLLECTIONS & EXHIBITS

**Collection:** The Zoo's current collection includes the following number of species:

| | | |
|---|---|---|
| Mammals: 62 | Birds: 129 | Reptiles: 23 |
| Amphibians: 1 | Fish: 191 | Invertebrates: 33 |

**Special Exhibits** at the Minnesota Zoo include:

Coral Reef - an ocean fish and shark exhibit, featuring a simulated coral reef, underwater viewing and daily feedings.

Southeast Asian Sun Bear Exhibit - located along the Tropics Trail

Takin Exhibit - only 25 of these rare animals are on display outside of its native China

Minnesota Trail - highlights species native to the State; features otter, beaver, cougars and trumpeter swans.

Northern Trail - home to animals of the Northern Hemisphere, including moose, musk oxen, wild horses, Bactrian camels and timber wolves; may be viewed from the Skytrail monorail which provides a treetop, guided tour.

Discovery Trail - leads through the Children's Zoo and into the Zoolab.

World of Birds Show - presented at the new Weesner Family Amphitheater.

**Future Plans:** An indoor, 1000-seat Dolphinarium is planned.

## CAPTIVE BREEDING & RESEARCH

The Minnesota Zoo has had special **breeding** success with the following species:

Bottlenose dolphins          Trumpeter swans
Asian small-clawed otter      Przewalski's horse
Gibbon species               Asian tigers
Siberian tigers              Bali mynah
Clouded leopards

**Research projects** based at the Minnesota Zoo include:
- Tiger Reproductive Research Project; a cooperative effort with the National Zoo and Omaha's Henry Doorly Zoo
- Coordination of and Participation in Taxon Advisory Groups
- Administrates SSPs for Siberian tiger and White-cheeked gibbon
- Participates in many international conservation programs

## SEASONAL FESTIVALS & PROGRAMS

Ski the Zoo - Cross Country Skiing on Zoo grounds; November to March
Summer Concert Series - May to August
Beastly Ball (fundraiser) - October
Spooktacular - October
Holiday of Lights - November to December
ZooYear's Eve - December

## FOR MORE INFORMATION

The Minnesota Zoo, 13000 Zoo Boulevard, Apple Valley, Minnesota 55124-8199; 612-432-9000; Director: Katheryn Roberts

# 98

## HERITAGE ZOO
### Grand Island, Nebraska

Founded in 1981, the Heritage Zoo specializes in the protection, display and propagation of native Nebraska species. In fact, this 7.5 acre facility has the largest collection of Nebraska animals of any zoo in the country.

## VISITOR INFORMATION

**Directions:** From I-80, exit onto Highway 281 north. Turn right (east) on Stolley Park Road; the Zoo will be 1.5 miles ahead, in Stolley State Park.

**Open to the Public:** Daily, 10 AM-6 PM, May 1 to October 10; Open weekends only, 10 AM-6 PM, March 20-April 30.

**Closed:** mid October through mid March (except Halloween event)

**Admission (1993):** Adult: $3.00     Child: $1.75

**Parking Fee:** None
**Children's Zoo:** Yes     **Separate Admission:** No

**Annual Membership:** Individual: $21.20     Family: $31.80

**AAZPA Member:** No

## COLLECTIONS & EXHIBITS

**Collection:** The Zoo's current collection includes the following number of species:
   Mammals: 30          Birds: 35          Reptiles: 15
   Amphibians: 2          Insects: 1          Other Invertebrates: 1

**Special Exhibits** at the Heritage Zoo include:
   Nebraska species - largest collection of any zoo

**Future Plans:** The Omaha World Herald Herpetarium will open in the summer of 1993 and will be completed in 1994. A Flight Cage for bald and golden eagles and a Monogolian Wolf Exhibit are slated for 1993-1994. A Northern Eurasian Small Cat Exhibit is scheduled for construction (1993-1995).

## CAPTIVE BREEDING & RESEARCH

The Heritage Zoo has had special **breeding** success with the following species:
   Florida sandhill cranes
   Ring-tailed lemurs

The Director of the Heritage Zoo is the Research Librarian for the IUCN Cat Specialist Group and this library is located on the Zoo grounds.

## SEASONAL FESTIVALS & PROGRAMS

May Day Free Day - May 1
Zippidy Zoo Dah Days Spring Festival - mid May
Zoo Conservation Day - early June
Children's Carnival - early August
Heritage Hay Days (Craft Fair) - late September
Boo at the Zoo - late October

## FOR MORE INFORMATION

Heritage Zoo, 2103 W. Stolley Park Rd., Grand Island, Nebraska 68801; 308-381-5416; Director: Gail E. Foreman, Ph.D.

# 99 FOLSOM CHILDREN'S ZOO & BOTANICAL GARDENS
## Lincoln, Nebraska

This small, intimate Zoo, founded in 1965, offers many interactive displays. Adorned with a wide variety of plants, it is the only zoo that is a member of the Nebraska Statewide Arboretum.

## VISITOR INFORMATION

**Directions:** From I-80, take Exit 401 (9th Street). Proceed east to 27th Street and turn south. Cross Capitol Parkway and continue another block to the Zoo.

**Open to the Public:** Daily, last weekend in April until last weekend in September, 10 AM-5 PM; open until 8 PM on Thursdays and Sundays, June through August.

**Closed:** Last weekend in September until last weekend in April (except holdiay programs)

**Admission (1993):** Adult: $3.50    Child: $1.50    Senior: $3.00

**Parking Fee:** None

**Annual Membership:** Individual: $27    Family: $38

**AAZPA Member:** Yes

## COLLECTIONS & EXHIBITS

**Collection:** The Zoo's current collection includes the following number of species:

| | | |
|---|---|---|
| Mammals: 28 | Birds: 27 | Reptiles: 18 |
| Amphibians: 2 | Fish: 4 | Insects: 1 |
| Mollusks: 1 | Other Invertebrates: 7 | |

**Special Exhibits** at the Folsom Children's Zoo & Botanical Gardens include:
Rainforest Exhibits
Eagle's Nest - for children to explore
Marmoset & Tamarin Displays - specialty of the Zoo

**Future Plans:** A Grasslands Biome Exhibit will open in 1994; this 3-acre complex will focus on grasslands of the world and will feature baboons, emus, wallabies and a Conservatory.

## CAPTIVE BREEDING & RESEARCH

The Folsom Children's Zoo & Botanical Gardens has had special **breeding** success with the following species:

| | |
|---|---|
| Golden lion tamarins | Rodrigues fruit bats |
| Golden-headed lion tamarins | Blue & Yellow macaws |
| Pygmy marmosets | Geoffroy's cat |

The Zoo has published a fruit bat husbandry manual.

## SEASONAL FESTIVALS & PROGRAMS
ZooMusic with Lincoln Symphony - mid May
Zootime Jamboree - July 4th
Members Only Bash - mid July
Halloween Hullabaloo - late October
Winter Lights - first three weekends in December

## FOR MORE INFORMATION
Folsom Children's Zoo & Botanical Gardens, 1222 South 27th Street, Lincoln, Nebraska 68502; 402-475-6741; Director: John P. Chapo

# 100 OMAHA'S HENRY DOORLY ZOO
## Omaha, Nebraska

The new "Lied Jungle," at Omaha's Henry Doorly Zoo, is the world's largest indoor rainforest. Hailed "architecturally stupendous and zoologically thrilling" by Time Magazine, the exhibit was ranked as one of the best design achievements of 1992.

The 130 acre Zoo, founded in 1965, also boasts the world's largest aviary and the largest Cat Complex in North America.

## VISITOR INFORMATION
**Directions:** From Interstate 80, exit onto 13th St. South and follow signs to the Zoo.
**Open to the Public:** Daily, 9:30 AM-5 PM
**Closed:** Thanksgiving, Christmas and New Years Day
**Admission (1993):** Adult: $6.00    Child: $3.00 (under 5 free)    Senior: $4.50
**Parking Fee:** None
**Children's Zoo:** Yes    **Separate Admission:** No
**Annual Membership:** Family: $50
**AAZPA Member:** Yes

## COLLECTIONS & EXHIBITS
**Collection:** The Zoo's current collection includes the following number of species:

| | | |
|---|---|---|
| Mammals: 92 | Birds: 195 | Reptiles: 47 |
| Amphibians: 21 | Fish: 88 | Insects: 10 |
| Other Invertebrates: 32 | | |

**Special Exhibits** at Omaha's Henry Doorly Zoo include:

The Lied Jungle - the world's largest indoor rainforest is home to over 125 species of animals and over 2000 plants from the tropical forests of Asia, Africa and South America. Covered by an 8-story-high dome, the 1.5 acre exhibit is accessed by a .5-mile network of trails.

The Aviary - largest in the world; features ducks, egrets, storks, flamingos, ibis, cranes and pheasants

Bear Canyon - home to grizzlies, polar bears and sun bears

Cat Complex - the largest cat facility in North America; features Sumatran and Siberian tigers, African lions, snow leopards, cougars and jaguars

Steam Train - offers a 2.5 mile, panoramic tour of the Zoo

**Future Plans:**    A Zebra Exhibit will open in 1993 and a new Aquarium is scheduled for completion in 1995.

*The Lied Jungle Exhibit*
*(photo courtesy Omaha's Henry Doorly Zoo)*

## CAPTIVE BREEDING & RESEARCH

Omaha's Henry Doorly Zoo has had special **breeding** success with the following species:

| | |
|---|---|
| Black-footed ferrets | Crane species |
| Wild gaur | Nile lechwe |
| Big Cat species | Gazelles |

**Research projects** based at the Zoo include:
- Genetic screening of wild gaurs
- Field research on wild gaurs and Asian bears
- Reproductive research, including artificial insemination in cranes, big cats and black-footed ferrets

## SEASONAL FESTIVALS & PROGRAMS

Conservation Day - June
Zoo Bike Ride - July
Zoo Run - October
Halloween Party - October
Holiday Lights - December

## FOR MORE INFORMATION

Omaha's Henry Doorly Zoo, 3701 South 10th Street, Omaha, Nebraska 68107; 402-733-8401; Director: Dr. Lee G. Simmons

# 101 BLANK PARK ZOO OF DES MOINES
### Des Moines, Iowa

Originally established in 1965, the new Blank Park Zoo opened in 1986. This 22 acre facility, characterized by large, naturally landscaped exhibits, typifies the modern zoo.

## VISITOR INFORMATION

**Directions:** The Zoo is 7 miles south of the downtown area. Follow SW 9th St. south to the Zoo. Alternatively, from I-35, exit onto State Route 5 and drive east for 9 miles to SW 9th St. Turn right (south) to the Zoo entrance.

**Open to the Public**: 10 AM-5 PM, May 1 through October 15

**Closed**: October 16 through April 30

**Admission (1993)**: Adult: $3.00    Child: $1.50    Senior: $2.00

**Parking Fee**: None

**Children's Zoo**: Yes    **Separate Admission**: No

**Annual Membership**: Individual: $15    Family: $30    Senior: $10

**AAZPA Member**: Yes

## COLLECTIONS & EXHIBITS

**Collection**: The Zoo's current collection includes the following number of species:

| | | |
|---|---|---|
| Mammals: 16 | Birds: 46 | Reptiles: 7 |
| Amphibians: 4 | Fish: 7 | Insects: 2 |
| Mollusks: 1 | Other Invertebrates: 5 | |

**Special Exhibits** at the Blank Park Zoo include:
Otter Exhibit - includes underwater viewing
African Boardwalk
Australian Walkabout
Walk through Aviary
Farm Animal Contact Area

## CAPTIVE BREEDING & RESEARCH

The Blank Park Zoo has had special **breeding** success with the following species:

| | |
|---|---|
| Reticulated giraffe | Red wallaby |
| Sea lion | Emu |
| Harbor seal | Parrot species |
| Siberian tiger | Macaws |
| Ring-tailed lemur | Waterfowl species |
| Japanese macaque | Red-tailed boas |

## SEASONAL FESTIVALS & PROGRAMS

"Night Eyes" Halloween Event - late October

## FOR MORE INFORMATION

Blank Park Zoo of Des Moines, 7401 SW 9th Street, Des Moines, Iowa 50315; 515-285-4722; Director: David Allen

# 102     SUNSET ZOOLOGICAL PARK
### Manhattan, Kansas

Owned and managed by the City of Manhattan, this 26 acre Zoo was established in 1933. It is the only zoo in Kansas to display snow leopards, red pandas and cheetahs. Though located within a relatively small city, the Sunset Zoological Park receives excellent support from the community and has witnessed the completion of more than two dozen project since 1990.

## VISITOR INFORMATION

**Directions:** Follow Kansas 177 north from Interstate 70 into Manhattan. Turn left (west) on Ft. Riley Blvd., right on Westwood and then left on Oak St. into the Zoo. From within the City, signs direct you to the Sunset Zoological Park.

**Open to the Public:** 10 AM-6 PM, March to November; open until 9 PM on Thursdays, June to August; from December to February, 10 AM-6 PM weekends, Noon-4 PM weekdays.

**Closed:** New Years Day, Thanksgiving, Christmas Day

**Admission (1993):** Adult: $2.00    Child: $1.00 (under 5 free)

**Parking Fee:** None

**Children's Zoo:** Yes    **Separate Admission:** No

**Annual Membership:** Individual: $15    Family: $25    Senior: $10

**Programs & Tours:** The Zoo's Education Department has been recognized for its diverse range of programs, including Zoo tours, summer classes, Junior Zoo Keepers, Zoo Management Internships and Winter Education Programs.

**AAZPA Member:** Yes

## COLLECTIONS & EXHIBITS

**Collection:** The Zoo's current collection includes the following number of species:
    Mammals: 35     Birds: 37     Reptiles: 14
    Amphibians: 1     Insects: 1     Other Invertebrates: 2

**Special Exhibits** at the Sunset Zoological Park include:
    Hurst Majors Children's Zoo - features a petting farm, a nursery and tropical bird exhibits
    Primate Building - designed to provide unrestricted viewing of chimps and other primates
    Asian Forest Preserve - home to Bengal tigers and Indian sloth bears; each exhibit is a naturalized, ¼ acre enclosure
    Australian Habitat - this open, mixed species exhibit features emus, wallabies, black swans and Cormo (domestic Australian sheep)
    Top Tier Exhibits - home to arctic fox, the Indonesian bear cat and North American bobcats
    Snow Leopards of Tibet Exhibit - only snow leopards on display in Kansas

**Future Plans:** The Steven & Migette Kaup Cheetah Country exhibit will open in the near future. A Primate Conservation Center is scheduled for completion in 1994.

## CAPTIVE BREEDING & RESEARCH

The Sunset Zoological Park has had special **breeding** success with the following species:

Andean Condor

Cotton-topped Tamarin

Chimpanzee

Rare domestic breeds - the Zoo is a member of the American Minor Breeds Conservancy, an organization dedicated to preserving rare domestic animals, such as Longhorn Cattle and Jacob Sheep.

**Research** at the Sunset Zoological Park includes:
- Semen analysis in Asian & South American bears
- Study of horsefly distribution and preferences

## SEASONAL FESTIVALS & PROGRAMS

Earth Day - mid April

ZOObilation - Memorial Day Weekend; Arts & Crafts Fair

Thursday Night Wild - extended hours (until 9 PM) Thursday evenings in June, July and August

Cool Cats Jazz Festival - Labor Day

SPOOKtacular - Halloween

## FOR MORE INFORMATION

Sunset Zoological Park, 2333 Oak St., Manhattan, Kansas 66502; 913-587-APES; Director: Donald W. Wixom

*Snow Leopard*
*(photo by Scott Traylor; courtesy Sunset Zoo)*

# 103 TOPEKA ZOOLOGICAL PARK
## Topeka, Kansas

Founded in 1933, this 30-acre Zoo boasts a superb Rainforest Exhibit and is home to the world's first walk-through gorilla enclosure.

## VISITOR INFORMATION

**Directions:** The Zoo is one quarter mile south of Interstate 70 at the Gage Blvd. Exit. Enter the Zoo parking lot via the Zoo Parkway which is accessed from either 6th St. or 10th St.

**Open to the Public:** Daily, 9 AM-4:30 PM

**Closed:** Christmas Day

**Admission (1993):** Adult: $3.00    Child: $1.50    Senior: $1.50

**Parking Fee:** None

**Children's Zoo:** Yes    **Separate Admission:** No

**Annual Membership:** Individual: $15    Family: $25    Senior: $10

**AAZPA Member:** Yes

## COLLECTIONS & EXHIBITS

**Collection:** The Zoo's current collection includes the following number of species:

| | | |
|---|---|---|
| Mammals: 42 | Birds: 52 | Reptiles: 34 |
| Amphibians: 5 | Fish: 1 | Invertebrates: 3 |

**Special Exhibits** at the Topeka Zoological Park include:

Security Benefit Children's Zoo - includes a petting zoo for children and a shaded gazebo for adults

Tropical Rainforest - climate-controlled building with over 150 species of tropical plants and a wide variety of animals

Discovering Apes Exhibit - visitors view orangutans from an Indonesian tree house and enter the world's first walk-through gorilla enclosure via a glass tunnel

Lion's Pride Exhibit - African lions are viewed from the Simba Trail (which is lined with tall adrenalin grass), from the Kopje rock station or from the bush camp

## CAPTIVE BREEDING & RESEARCH

The Topeka Zoological Park has had special **breeding** success with the following species:

| | |
|---|---|
| Bali mynah | Nicobar pigeon |
| Mexican porcupine | Fairy bluebird |
| Bornean orangutan | Giant Indian fruit bat |
| Golden eagle | Reeve's muntjac |
| Trumpeter swan | Cotton-topped tamarin |
| Blue-crowned pigeon | |

The Zoo has a Scientific Studies Committee which reviews all **research** projects and ensures the health and well-being of all study subjects.

## SEASONAL FESTIVALS & PROGRAMS

Teddy Bear Fair - early June
Ice Day - mid August
Senior Citizens' Day - October
Boo at the Zoo - late October
Zooluminations - early December

## FOR MORE INFORMATION

The Topeka Zoological Park, 635 SW Gage Blvd., Topeka, Kansas 66606-2066; 913-272-5821; Director: Hugh Quinn, Ph.D.

# 104

## EMPORIA ZOO
### Emporia, Kansas

This 8-acre zoo, founded in 1934, is in Soden's Grove Park on the north bank of the Cottonwood River. The Zoo has both walk-through and drive-through areas.

## VISITOR INFORMATION

**Directions:** From the Intersection of U.S. 50 and Kansas Route 99 (6th & Commercial in downtown Emporia), drive south on Kansas 99 for 3 miles to Soden's Grove Park; the Zoo is in the Park, on Soden's Road.

**Open to the Public:** Walk-through area is open 10 AM-4:30 PM daily; hours extended to 8 PM on Sundays & Wednesdays in summer; drive-through area open dawn to dusk.

**Closed:** Christmas Day

**Admission (1993):** Free

**Parking Fee:** None

**Children's Zoo:** No

**Annual Membership:** Individual: $10     Family: $20

**AAZPA Member:** Yes

## COLLECTIONS & EXHIBITS

**Collection:** The Zoo's current collection includes the following number of species:
Mammals: 17          Birds: 51          Reptiles: 4

The Emporia Zoo boasts a comprehensive collection of native waterfowl.

**Future Plans:**   Toucan & Monitor Exhibits will open in 1993. An American Alligator Exhibit is scheduled for completion in 1996.

## CAPTIVE BREEDING & RESEARCH

The Emporia Zoo has had special **breeding** success with the following species:
| | |
|---|---|
| Golden eagle | Ruddy ducks |
| Mule deer | Hooded mergansers |
| Canvasback | Nene |

**Research** at the Zoo, in cooperation with Emporia State University, includes:
- Behavior studies of waterfowl
- Study of binturong behavior

## SEASONAL FESTIVALS & PROGRAMS

Annual Members Social - Spring
Annual Open House - first Sunday in October
Zoo Lighting Ceremony - last Sunday in November

## FOR MORE INFORMATION

The Emporia Zoo, P.O. Box 928, Emporia, Kansas 66801-0928; 316-342-5101; Director: David P. Traylor

# 105   LEE RICHARDSON ZOO
### Garden City, Kansas

Located within Finnup Park, this 47-acre zoo was established in 1929. The facility may be toured by automobile or on foot.

## VISITOR INFORMATION

**Directions:**   The Zoo is at the south end of 4th St. From the intersection of U.S. 83 and U.S. 50, proceed east on U.S. 50 and then south on 4th St.

**Open to the Public:**  Daily, 8 AM to ½ hour before sunset;
Winter hours are 8 AM-4:30 PM (December through February)

**Closed:**  New Years Day, Thanksgiving, Christmas Day

**Admission:** $1.00 per vehicle; free for walkers

**Parking Fee:** None

**Children's Zoo:** No

**Annual Membership:**  Contact Friends of the Lee Richardson Zoo at P.O. Box 1638, Garden City, Kansas 67846; 316-276-6243

**AAZPA Member:** Yes

## COLLECTIONS & EXHIBITS

**Collection:** The Zoo's current collection includes the following number of specimens:
Mammals: 76 specimens
Reptiles: 9 specimens
Birds: 157 specimens
Fish: 75 specimens

**Special Exhibits** at the Lee Richardson Zoo:
A Walk-through Aviary

**Future Plans:**  A Wild Asia Exhibit is scheduled to open in July, 1994.

## CAPTIVE BREEDING & RESEARCH

The Lee Richardson Zoo has had special **breeding** success with the following species:
Bali Mynah
Reticulated Giraffe
Red-billed Hornbills

## SEASONAL FESTIVALS & PROGRAMS

Conservation Day - first Saturday in June
Zoobalee - July 4th
Elephant Swim - at municipal pool, late August

## FOR MORE INFORMATION

Lee Richardson Zoo, South 4th Street, Finnup Park, Garden City, Kansas 67846; 316-276-1250; Director: Daniel A. Baffa

# 106

## SEDGWICK COUNTY ZOO
## & BOTANICAL GARDEN
### Wichita, Kansas

This beautiful, "master-planned" zoo incorporates naturalistic exhibits in a pastoral, horticultural setting. The 212 acre facility opened in 1971.

## VISITOR INFORMATION

**Directions:** The Zoo is located at Exit #10 (Zoo Blvd.) from Interstate 235, northwest of downtown Wichita.

**Open to the Public:** 365 days per year; 9 AM-5 PM April through October; 10 AM-5 PM November through March

**Admission:** Adult: $4.00    Child: $2.00 (4 & under free)

**Parking Fee:** None

**Children's Zoo:** Yes    **Separate Admission:** No

**Annual Membership:** Individual: $30 (1+1)    Family: $40    Senior: $25 (couple)

**AAZPA Member:** Yes

## COLLECTIONS & EXHIBITS

**Collection:** The Zoo's current collection includes the following number of species:
Mammals: 52          Birds: 131          Reptiles: 61
Amphibians: 15        Fish: 10

**Special Exhibits** at the Sedgwick County Zoo and Botanical Garden include:
A Jungle Exhibit
Three Continental Farms
A Walk-through Pampas/Outback
A Unique Herpetarium

**Future Plans:** A North American Prairie Exhibit is scheduled to open in 1993.

## CAPTIVE BREEDING & RESEARCH

The Sedgwick County Zoo & Botanical Garden has had special **breeding** success with the following species:
Golden lion tamarins          Green tree pythons
Chimpanzee                    Monitors
Orangutans                    Arrow poison frogs

The Zoo is a primary participant in Chimpanzoo, chimpanzee research in collaboration with the Jane Goodall Institute.

*African Elephant*
*(photo by Jim Marlett; courtesy Sedgwick County Zoo and Botanical Garden)*

## SEASONAL FESTIVALS & PROGRAMS
Easter Event - Saturday before Easter
Free Zoo Day - late May (on Riverfest Day)
Night of the Living Zoo (at Halloween)

## FOR MORE INFORMATION
The Sedgwick County Zoo & Botanical Garden, 5555 Zoo Blvd., Wichita, Kansas 67212; 316-942-2212 (recording); 316-942-2213 (office); Director: Mark C. Reed

# 107 KANSAS CITY ZOOLOGICAL GARDEN
### Kansas City, Missouri

The Kansas City Zoological Garden opened in 1909. This 170 acre facility, owned by the City, is currently in the midst of a $65 million expansion and renovation project.

## VISITOR INFORMATION
**Directions:** The Zoo is southeast of the downtown area. From I-70, head south on I-435. Exit onto 63rd Street and head west for 2 miles to the Zoo.
**Open to the Public:** 9 AM-5 PM Summer; 9 AM-4 PM the remainder of the year.
**Closed:** Christmas and New Years Day

**Admission (1993):** Adult: $3.00     Child: Under 12 Free
**Parking Fee:** None
**Children's Zoo:** Yes     **Separate Admission:** No
**Annual Membership:** Individual: $20     Family: $30
**AAZPA Member:** Yes

## COLLECTIONS & EXHIBITS

**Collection:** The Zoo's current collection includes the following number of species:
Mammals: 40          Birds: 116          Reptiles: 18
Amphibians: 1        Fish: 1            Insects: 1
Other Invertebrates: 1

**Future Plans:**   An Australian Exhibit will open in 1993. A new Domestic Animal Exhibit and an Elephant Compound are scheduled for completion in 1994. African Plains, Forest and Island Habitats are slated for 1995.

## CAPTIVE BREEDING & RESEARCH

The Kansas City Zoological Garden has had special **breeding** success with the following species:

Chimpanzees                    Victoria crowned pigeons
Orangutans                     Maned wolves
Roseate spoonbills             Red pandas

## FOR MORE INFORMATION

The Kansas City Zoological Garden, 6700 Zoo Drive, Kansas City, Missouri 64132; 816-333-7406; Director: Dr. Mark K. Wourms

# 108       SAINT LOUIS ZOO
### St. Louis, Missouri

Soon after Forest Park was set aside for public use in 1875, local citizens began donating animals for exhibition. The Smithsonian Institution erected a large Flight Cage in the Park for the 1904 World's Fair and the Zoo was formally established in 1913. Three years later, voters approved a tax levy to provide public funding of the facility.

Now recognized as one of the finest zoos in the world, the Saint Louis Zoo covers 83 acres and was one of the first to use open, moated enclosures and molded rock grottos to naturalize their exhibits.

## VISITOR INFORMATION

**Directions:**   Forest Park is west of the downtown area and can be reached via Interstate 64 (U.S. 40) or via Forest Park Parkway. Take the Hampton Avenue Exit from Interstate 64 and proceed north to the Zoo.

**Open to the Public:** Daily, 9 AM-5 PM; open until 8 PM on Tuesdays from Memorial Day to Labor Day

**Closed:** Christmas and New Years Day

**Admission (1993):** Free; one of the few large zoos in the world that do not charge admission. The Zoo is supported by city taxes and by private donations.

**Parking Fee:** $3.00

**Children's Zoo:** Yes    **Separate Admission:** $.50 Summer; $.75 Winter

**Annual Membership:** Individual: $40    Family: $40    Senior: $30

**Programs & Tours:** The Educational Department provides over 3000 programs to more than 450,000 individuals each year. Among the innovative programs are Classroom of the Future (16 stations with teacher-controlled console) and the Interactive Multimedia Resources Interface (a computer-laser disc juke box-VCR-printer) which allows teachers to produce custom-designed "courseware".

**AAZPA Member:** Yes

## COLLECTIONS & EXHIBITS

**Collection:** The Zoo's current collection includes the following number of species:

| | | |
|---|---|---|
| Mammals: 97 | Birds: 216 | Reptiles: 196 |
| Amphibians: 39 | Mollusks: 110 | Insects: 13 |
| Fish: 102 | Other Invertebrates: 77 | |

**Special Exhibits** at the Saint Louis Zoo include:

Jungle of the Apes - groups of chimps, orangutans and gorillas live in naturalistic habitats

Big Cat Country - includes 35 species

Cheetah Survival Center - over 30 cubs born here since 1974

The Living World - education center combining high technology and 150 living species

Bear Pits - the rock walls, constructed in the 1920s, were cast from molds of limestone bluffs along the Mississippi River; this technique served as a model for other zoos.

Flight Cage - historic structure built by Smithsonian Institution for 1904 World's Fair

Primate House - renovated in 1977 to allow animals to live in natural, social groupings; to be expanded in 1993.

Waterfowl lakes - 5 acres of wetland with 75 species of waterfowl

Birdhouse - spacious exhibits with rocky pools and living plants; nearly invisible steel wire strands used to confine the birds.

**Future Plans:** A Birds of Prey Exhibit and expansion of the Primate House are both scheduled for 1993. Other plans include an Endangered Species Research Center & Hospital, a new Elephant House, renovation of the Children's Zoo, a new Small Mammal House and reconstruction of the Central Plaza.

## CAPTIVE BREEDING & RESEARCH

The Saint Louis Zoo has had special **breeding** success with the following species:
Speke's Gazelle - first successful artificial insemination (1979)

| | |
|---|---|
| Black Lemur | Chinese Giant Salamander |
| Black Rhino | Amur Leopard |
| Snow Leopard | Lesser Kudu |
| Banteng | Guam Kingfisher |
| Malayan Tapir | Batleur Eagle |
| Cheetah | Arabian Oryx |

**Research Projects** based at the Saint Louis Zoo include:
- Cross matching of blood in black rhinos
- Telemetry of basal body temperature in cheetahs
- Semen collection in Crane species
- Behavioral studies of lion-tailed macaques

## SEASONAL FESTIVALS & PROGRAMS

Zoo & Aquarium Conservation Day - early June
"Boo at the Zoo" - late October
"Holiday Zoobilation" - mid December
Other annual events include a Wildlife Art Walk, a Photo Contest and a
5K Run for the Apes

## FOR MORE INFORMATION

The Saint Louis Zoo, Forest Park, St. Louis, Missouri 63110; 314-781-0900;
Director: Charles H. Hoessle

# 109 DICKERSON PARK ZOO
### Springfield, Missouri

Established in 1923, the Dickerson Park Zoo encompasses 70 acres. The facility is known for its research on the captive breeding of Asian elephants.

## VISITOR INFORMATION

**Directions:** The Zoo is on the northern edge of Springfield, just northeast of the intersection of Interstate 44 and the Kansas Expressway (Highway 13).

**Open to the Public:** 10 AM-6 PM, April to September;
10 AM-4:30 PM, October to March

**Closed:** Thanksgiving, Christmas and New Years Day; also closed during periods of inclement weather (October-March)

**Admission (1993):** Adult: $3.00    Child: $1.75

**Parking Fee:** None

**Children's Zoo:** Yes (new in 1993)    **Separate Admission:** No

**Annual Membership:** Individual: $15    Family: $25

**AAZPA Member:** Yes

## COLLECTIONS & EXHIBITS

**Collection:** The Zoo's current collection includes the following number of species:

Mammals: 32          Birds: 49          Reptiles: 34
Amphibians: 3        Invertebrates: 2

**Special Exhibits** at the Dickerson Park Zoo include:
Missouri Habitats - features animals native to Missouri
African Plains Exhibit
Asian Elephants - breeding program based at the Zoo

**Future Plans:** A Petting Zoo and a River Otter Exhibit will both be completed in 1993.

*Asian Elephant with baby born July, 1991*
*(photo courtesy Dickerson Park Zoo)*

## CAPTIVE BREEDING & RESEARCH

The Dickerson Park Zoo has had special **breeding** success with the following species:

Asian elephant          Cheetah          Maned wolf

An Asian Elephant Breeding Program is based at the Dickerson Park Zoo. **Research** includes artificial insemination in this species.

## SEASONAL FESTIVALS & PROGRAMS

Teddy Bear Rally - late April
Zoolympics - August
Halloween Spooktacular - late October

## FOR MORE INFORMATION

Dickerson Park Zoo, 3043 North Fort, Springfield, Missouri 65803; 417-833-1570; Director: Mike Crocker

# V. SOUTH CENTRAL REGION

110. **Oklahoma City Zoological Park** (Oklahoma City, Oklahoma)

111. **Tulsa Zoo & Living Museum** (Tulsa, Oklahoma)

112. **Little Rock Zoological Gardens** (Little Rock, Arkansas)

113. **Abilene Zoological Gardens** (Abilene, Texas)

114. **Fossil Rim Wildlife Center** (Glen Rose, Texas)

115. **Fort Worth Zoological Park** (Fort Worth, Texas)

116. **Dallas Zoo** (Dallas, Texas)

117. **Dallas Aquarium** (Dallas, Texas)

118. **Caldwell Zoo** (Tyler, Texas)

119. **Cameron Park Zoo** (Waco, Texas)

120. **Ellen Trout Zoo** (Lufkin, Texas)

121. **El Paso Zoo** (El Paso, Texas)

122. **San Antonio Zoo** (San Antonio, Texas)

123. **Sea World of Texas** (San Antonio, Texas)

124. **Houston Zoological Gardens** (Houston, Texas)

125. **Gladys Porter Zoo** (Brownsville, Texas)

126. **Louisiana Purchase Gardens & Zoo** (Monroe, Louisiana)

127. **Zoo of Acadiana** (Broussard, Louisiana)

128. **Greater Baton Rouge Zoo** (Baker, Louisiana)

129. **Audubon Zoological Garden** (New Orleans, Louisiana)

130. **Aquarium of the Americas** (New Orleans, Louisiana)

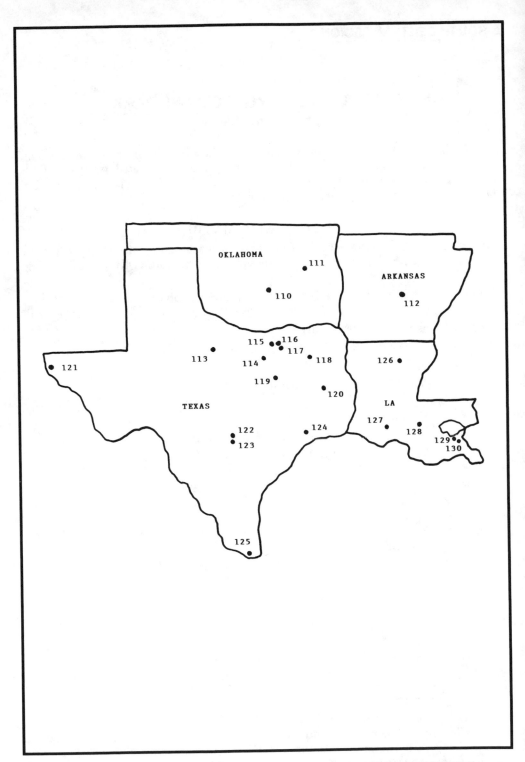

# SOUTH CENTRAL REGION ZOOS & AQUARIUMS

# 110 OKLAHOMA CITY ZOOLOGICAL PARK
## Oklahoma City, Oklahoma

Established in 1904, the Oklahoma City Zoo is the oldest zoo in the southwest. The Zoo also operates the Zoo Amphitheater which was constructed by the civilian conservation corps in 1933; the renovated amphitheater, designated an historical site, hosts outdoor concerts throughout the summer.

## VISITOR INFORMATION

**Directions:** The Zoo is northeast of the downtown area. Access is via the N.E. 50th St. Exit from Interstate 35 or via the Martin Luther King Blvd. Exit off Interstate 44.

**Open to the Public:** Daily, 9 AM-6 PM April to September;
9 AM-5 PM October to March

**Closed:** Christmas and New Years Day

**Admission (1993):** Adult: $4.00    Child: $2.00    Senior: $2.00

**Parking Fee:** None

**Children's Zoo:** Yes    **Separate Admission:** No

**Annual Membership:** Individual (Adult): $25    Family: $40    Grandparent: $40

## COLLECTIONS & EXHIBITS

**Collection:** The Zoo's current collection includes the following number of species:
| | | |
|---|---|---|
| Mammals: 91 | Birds: 132 | Reptiles: 110 |
| Amphibians: 24 | Fish: 111 | Invertebrates: 68 |

**Special Exhibits** at the Oklahoma City Zoo include the following:
The Noble Aquatic Center: Marinelife from around the world
Island Life Exhibit - features Galapagos tortoises and flamingos; highlights the diversity of island life

**Future Plans:** The Great EscApe (three great ape species in a tropical forest habitat) will open in June, 1993. Bear Trek is scheduled for completion in 1995.

## CAPTIVE BREEDING & RESEARCH

The Oklahoma City Zoo is participating in Species Survival Plans for several endangered species; the Zoo has had excellent **breeding** success with:
| | |
|---|---|
| Western Lowland Gorillas | Galapagos Tortoises |
| Spectacled Bears | Oustalet's Chameleon |
| Snow Leopards | |

Current **research** at the Oklahoma City Zoo includes:
- The study of gorilla reproduction
- Cooperative research with the Henry Doorly Zoo (Omaha, Nebraska) on bear reproduction

## SEASONAL FESTIVALS & PROGRAMS

Zoo Run - early May
Animal Crackers Ball - mid September
Haunt the Zoo for Halloween - late October
Zoo Lights! - late November through New Years Day

## FOR MORE INFORMATION

The Oklahoma City Zoological Park, 2101 N.E. 50, Oklahoma City, Oklahoma 73111-7199; 405-424-3344; Director: Stephen R. Wylie

# 111  TULSA ZOO & LIVING MUSEUM
## Tulsa, Oklahoma

Founded in 1927, the Tulsa Zoo & Living Museum covers 70 acres. The Living Museum combines live and static displays to trace the natural history of North America.

## VISITOR INFORMATION

**Directions:**  The Zoo is reached by taking Sheridan North off I-244 or by heading east on 36th St. North off Highway 75.

**Open to the Public:**  Open daily at 10 AM; closing time varies with the season.

**Closed:** Christmas Day

**Admission (1993):** Adult: $4.00    Child: $2.00 (under 5 Free)    Senior: $3.00

**Parking Fee:** None

**Children's Zoo:** No

**Annual Membership:** for information call 918-834-9453

**AAZPA Member:** Yes

## COLLECTIONS & EXHIBITS

**Collection:** The Zoo's current collection includes the following number of species:

| | | |
|---|---|---|
| Mammals: 50 | Birds: 61 | Reptiles: 43 |
| Amphibians: 11 | Fish: 77 | Mollusks: 3 |
| Insects: 1 | Other Invertebrates: 34 | |

**Special Exhibits** at the Tulsa Zoo include:
  The Living Museum - combines live and static displays to trace the natural history of North America

**Future Plans:**   An Aldabran tortoise exhibit will open in 1993. Elephant Encounter will be completed by 1994 and a Tropical American Rain Forest is scheduled to open in 1995.

## CAPTIVE BREEDING & RESEARCH

The Tulsa Zoo & Living Museum has had special **breeding** success with the following species:

| | |
|---|---|
| Chimpanzee | Pancake Tortoise |
| Mandrill | Green Basilisk Lizard |
| Siamang | Green Tree Python |
| Snow Leopard | Spadefish |

The Zoo conducts studies on Chimpanzee reproductive physiology and is a participant in Chimpanzoo.

## SEASONAL FESTIVALS & PROGRAMS

Docent Training Programs - January & February
Waltz-at-the-Zoo - Black-tie event in June
Summer Workshops (Children) - June and July
Summer Zoofari - July to August
Dinosaurs Alive! - September to November
Hallowzooeen - October
Zoolightful - December

## FOR MORE INFORMATION

Tulsa Zoo & Living Museum, 5701 E. 36th St. N., Tulsa, Oklahoma 74115; 918-596-2401; Director: David G. Zucconi

# 112 LITTLE ROCK ZOOLOGICAL GARDENS
## Little Rock, Arkansas

The Little Rock Zoological Gardens features a mix of old and new exhibits on 42 acres in War Memorial Park. Founded in 1925, the Zoo's WPA Era buildings contrast with modern, naturalized habitats.

## VISITOR INFORMATION

**Directions:** The Zoo is west of the downtown area. Take I-630 to Exit 4 (Fair Park Blvd.), turn north and follow signs to the Zoo.

**Open to the Public:** 9 AM-5 PM, April to September; 9:30 AM-4:30 PM, October to March

**Closed:** Thanksgiving, Christmas and New Years Day

**Admission (1993):** Adult: $2.50    Child: $1.00

**Parking Fee:** None

**Children's Zoo:** Yes    **Separate Admission:** No

**Annual Membership:** Individual: $20    Family: $30

**AAZPA Member:** Yes

## COLLECTIONS & EXHIBITS

**Collection:** The Zoo's current collection includes the following number of species:

| | | |
|---|---|---|
| Mammals: 76 | Birds: 53 | Reptiles: 58 |
| Amphibians: 9 | Fish: 1 | Insects: 8 |

**Special Exhibits** at the Little Rock Zoological Gardens include:

Big Cat Display - completed in 1981, the large, outdoor exhibits feature jaguars and Bengal tigers

Great Ape Display - home to lowland gorillas, chimpanzees and orangutans, these large, landscaped exhibits opened in 1988.

**Future Plans:** A new Children's Discovery Area, new Front Entry Complex, Administration Building and Food Storage Area are scheduled for completion by 1994.

## CAPTIVE BREEDING & RESEARCH

The Little Rock Zoological Gardens has had special **breeding** success with the following species:

| | |
|---|---|
| Scimitar horned oryx | Siamang |
| Giant anteater | White-handed gibbon |
| Pronghorn antelope | Wart Hog |
| Kings Island wallaby | Cotton-eared marmoset |
| Chimpanzee | Serval cats |
| Reticulated giraffe | Ocelot |
| Siberian lynx | |

## SEASONAL FESTIVALS & PROGRAMS

Kids Day - April
Conservation Days/Zoo & Aquarium Month - June
"Zoo Days" - August; features silent auction, Dinamation Exhibit, evening party, arts & crafts, etc.
"Boo at the Zoo" - October

## FOR MORE INFORMATION

Little Rock Zoological Gardens, #1 Jonesboro Drive, Little Rock, Arkansas 72205; 501-666-2406; Director: David G. Westbrook

# 113    ABILENE ZOOLOGICAL GARDENS
## Abilene, Texas

The Abilene Zoo was founded in 1919 and moved to its present, 60-acre site in 1966. Though relatively small, the Zoo boasts an impressive record in the captive breeding of reptiles and is the southernmost zoo in North America to successfully breed a polar bear.

## VISITOR INFORMATION

**Directions:**   The Zoo is located on the east side of Abilene, in the Nelson Park Complex, at State Highway 36 and Loop 322 (the Jake Roberts Freeway); the Zoo is across from the West Texas Fairgrounds and the Taylor County Coliseum.

**Open to the Public:**   9 AM-5 PM, Mon.-Fri., and 9 AM-7 PM Sat.-Sun., Memorial Day to Labor Day; 9 AM-5 PM remainder of the year.

**Closed:** Thanksgiving, Christmas and New Years Day

**Admission (1993):** Adult: $2.00    Child: $1.00    Senior: $1.00

**Parking Fee:** None

**Children's Zoo:** No

**Annual Membership:** Individual: $10    Family: $25

**AAZPA Member:** Yes

## COLLECTIONS & EXHIBITS

**Collection:** The Zoo's current collection includes the following number of species:

| | | |
|---|---|---|
| Mammals: 23 | Birds: 64 | Reptiles: 61 |
| Amphibians: 17 | Fish: 49 | Invertebrates: 35 |

**Special Exhibits** at the Abilene Zoological Gardens include:

The Discovery Center - compares the ecosystems of Southwestern U.S. and Central America with the Plains of Africa and the Island of Madagascar

Giraffe & Hornbill Exhibit - viewed from an elevated walkway

## CAPTIVE BREEDING & RESEARCH

The Abilene Zoological Gardens has had special **breeding** success with the following species:

Polar bear - most southernly bred polar bear in North America
Mottled rattlesnake - first captive breeding
Storr's Dwarf Monitor - first captive breeding
African bush viper - first captive breeding
Wirot's viper - first captive breeding
March's palm viper - first captive breeding
Angolan Colobus monkey
Moustached Guenon monkey
Secretary birds

## SEASONAL FESTIVALS & PROGRAMS

Wildflower Day - May
Conservation Day - early June
ZooFest - September/October (for Society Members only)
Boo at the Zoo - late October

## FOR MORE INFORMATION

Abilene Zoological Gardens, P.O. Box 60, Abilene, Texas 79604; 915-676-6085; Director: Jim Fleshman

# 114    FOSSIL RIM WILDLIFE CENTER
## Glen Rose, Texas

Established in 1987, Fossil Rim Wildlife Center is a for-profit conservation center, dedicated to involving the public and private sectors in the business of cost-effective conservation. Using this 3000 acre Center as a model, the Corporation plans to demonstrate that global conservation projects can be approached as socially respon- sible business ventures. The Center itself will soon become a self-sustaining, investor- owned conservation facility.

Most animals at the Wildlife Center are free to roam within natural habitats of up to 400 acres in size. Such conditions encourage instinctive behavior, augmenting the Center's success with captive breeding of threatened and endangered species.

## VISITOR INFORMATION

**Directions:** From Glen Rose (which is 1 hour southwest of Dallas-Fort Worth), proceed southwest on Highway 67 to County Road 2008. Turn onto 2008 and continue one mile to the Wildlife Center.

**Open to the Public:** Daily, 9 AM until 2 hours before sunset.

**Closed:** Thanksgiving and Christmas Day

**Admission (1993):** Adult: $9.95 + tax    Child: $6.95 + tax    Senior: $8.95 + tax

**Parking Fee:** None

**Children's Zoo:** Yes    **Separate Admission:** No

**Annual Membership:** Individual: $30    Family: $100

**AAZPA Member:** Yes

## COLLECTIONS & EXHIBITS

**Collection:** The Center's current collection includes the following number of species:
    Mammals: 39        Birds: 16        Reptiles: 5

**Special Exhibits** at Fossil Rim Wildlife Center include:
    Most animals at the center roam in large, mixed-species, natural habitats. Visitors drive through these areas to view the animals.

**Future Plans:** Mexican wolves were added in 1992 and okapis are scheduled to arrive in 1993. Various native Texan species, to be exhibited along the Nature Trail, will also join the Center in 1993.

## CAPTIVE BREEDING & RESEARCH

Fossil Rim Wildlife Center has had special **breeding** success with the following species:

| | |
|---|---|
| Cheetah | Addax |
| Red wolf | Grevy's zebra |
| Dama gazelle | Reticulated giraffe |
| Arabian oryx | Scimitar horned oryx |

**Research projects** based at the Wildlife Center include:
- Reproductive research - endocrinology, artificial insemination, in vitro fertilization and embryo transfer) in cheetahs, addax and white rhinos.
- Behavioral and genetic studies on antelope species
- Research on immobilization techniques

## SEASONAL FESTIVALS & PROGRAMS

Earth Day Celebration - April
Conservation Day - June
Owl Prowl - Halloween
Holiday on the Rim - December

## FOR MORE INFORMATION

Fossil Rim Wildlife Center, P.O. Box 2189, Glen Rose, Texas 76043; 817-897-2960; Chair of the Board: M. Christine Jurzykowski; President: James R. Jackson

*Foothills Safari Camp: Jeep tours are led by wildlife experts.*
*(photo by Greg Logan; courtesy Fossil Rim Wildlife Center)*

# 115 FORT WORTH ZOOLOGICAL PARK
## Fort Worth, Texas

Established in 1909, this is the oldest, continuously operating zoo in Texas. The 60-acre facility is the only zoo in the U.S. to display representatives of all the Great Ape species and boasts one of the five largest reptile/amphibian collections in the country. In addition, the Fort Worth Zoological Park is one of only three zoos in the world to display white, black and one-horned rhinos.

## VISITOR INFORMATION

**Directions:** From Interstate 30, exit South on University Drive and turn left on Colonial Parkway.

**Open to the Public:** 365 days per year: 10 AM-5 PM; longer hours from June through August; open noon-5 PM on New Years Day, Thanksgiving and Christmas.

**Admission (1993):** Adult: $5.00    Child: $2.50    Senior: $2.50
Admission fee is ½ price every Wednesday.

**Parking Fee:** None

**Children's Zoo:** No

**Annual Membership:** Individual: $35    Family: $49    Senior: $25

**AAZPA Member:** Yes

## COLLECTIONS & EXHIBITS

**Collection:** The Zoo's current collection includes the following number of species:

| | | |
|---|---|---|
| Mammals: 63 | Birds: 120 | Reptiles: 214 |
| Amphibians: 26 | Fish: 300 | Insects: 20 |
| Other Invertebrates: 35 | | |

**Special Exhibits** at the Fort Worth Zoological Park include:
World of Primates - this 2.5 acre rainforest habitat is home to lowland gorillas, orangutans, bonobos, chimps, colobus monkeys and free-flying tropical birds
Asian Falls Exhibit - features Sumatran tigers, white tigers, Malayan sun bears, Asian rhinos and eastern Sarus cranes; a 40-foot waterfall graces the exhibit
Texas! Exhibit - displays native Texan wildlife; includes a prairie dog village and a petting barnyard
African Savannah - features black and white rhinos, giraffes and African birds
Herpetarium - one of the five largest collections of reptile and amphibians in the country

**Future Plans:** New Asian rhino and Birds of Prey Exhibits are scheduled to open in 1993. An Education Complex and an Amphitheatre will be completed in 1994.

*The Fort Worth Zoo's new "World of Primates" exhibit*
*(photo by Barbara Love Logan; courtesy Fort Worth Zoo)*

## CAPTIVE BREEDING & RESEARCH

The Fort Worth Zoological Park has had special **breeding** success with the following species:

| | |
|---|---|
| Golden Lion Tamarin | Dumeril's Ground Boa |
| Black Rhino | Louisiana Pine Snake |
| Chimpanzee | Roseate Spoonbill |

**Research** on the Louisiana Pine Snake, the Asian Elephant and the Panther Chameleon are among the projects based at the Fort Worth Zoological Park.

## SEASONAL FESTIVALS & PROGRAMS

Teddy Bear Picnic - early June
Sunset Safari Special - June through August
Boo! at the Zoo - late October
Zoo Festival of Lights - December

## FOR MORE INFORMATION

Fort Worth Zoological Park, 1989 Colonial Parkway, Fort Worth, Texas 76110; 817-871-7050; Director: Ted A. Beattie

# 116

## DALLAS ZOO
### Dallas, Texas

The Dallas Zoo, founded in 1888, is proud of its commitment to research, exemplified by its award-winning Gorilla Conservation Research Center. This latter facility is part of the Zoo's 25-acre "Wilds of Africa," a collection of six naturalized exhibits that recreate African habitats on the plains of Texas.

The 70-acre Zoo, owned by the City of Dallas, is currently drawing up a Masterplan for future renovation and development; construction will begin in 1994.

## VISITOR INFORMATION

**Directions:** The Zoo is located 3 miles south of downtown Dallas. Head south on I-35 to the Ewing Avenue Exit and follow the signs; the Zoo is just east of the Interstate.

**Open to the Public:** Daily, 9 AM-5 PM

**Closed:** Christmas Day

**Admission (1993):** Adult: $5.00    Child: $2.50    Senior: $4.00

**Parking Fee:** $2.00

**Children's Zoo:** Yes (summer only)    **Separate Admission:** No

**Annual Membership** (includes membership to Dallas Aquarium):
    Individual: $30        Family: $45

**AAZPA Member:** Yes

## COLLECTIONS & EXHIBITS

**Collection:** The Zoo's current collection includes the following number of species:
    Mammals: 73            Birds: 136
    Reptiles: 112          Amphibians: 11

**Special Exhibits** at the Dallas Zoo include:
    "Wilds of Africa" - this 25-acre exhibit is a composite of six African habitats (Forest, Bush, Woodland, River, Desert and Mountain). The exhibit may be toured by taking a 1-mile monorail ride or by walking the 1500-foot Nature Trail. A free-flight Aviary and the Gorilla Conservation Research Center are also located in this exhibit.

**Future Plans:** The Zoo's Masterplan calls for renovation of older exhibits and a 30-acre addition. Expansion of the Wilds of Africa will include a Chimpanzee Exhibit and several new habitats: Savanna, Water Hole, Swamp and Lake. Completion dates are pending.

## CAPTIVE BREEDING & RESEARCH

The Dallas Zoo has had special **breeding** success with the following species:

| | |
|---|---|
| Dik-dik | Goliath heron |
| Suni antelope | Angolan python |
| Okapi | Speckled pit viper |
| Bushmaster snake | Collared sunbird |
| Bismarck ringed python | Roseate spoonbill |
| Kori bustard | |

**Research projects** based at the Dallas Zoo include:
- Study of okapi mother-infant interactions
- Study of estrus in Gunther's dik-dik
- Research on ocelot reproduction, parental behavior and thermal regulation
- Field studies and captive management of bushmaster snake
- Propagation and behavior of black-capped and white-eyed vireos
- Studies on the natural history of Texas rat snakes
- At least 50 other research projects
- Award-winning Gorilla Conservation Research Center

## SEASONAL FESTIVALS & PROGRAMS

African Heritage Weekend - April
TV 39 Family Day - May
Conservation Day - June
Big Cat Day - August
Zoo-to-do Gala - August
Hispanic Heritage Weekend - September

## FOR MORE INFORMATION

Dallas Zoo, 621 East Clarendon Drive, Dallas, Texas 75203; 214-946-5154;
Director: Richard W. Buickerood

*Monorail ride through "Wilds of Africa" exhibit*
*(photo by Robert Cabello; courtesy Dallas Zoo)*

# 117         DALLAS AQUARIUM
## Dallas, Texas

Located in Fair Park, the Dallas Aquarium opened in 1936 to coincide with the Texas Centennial Celebration. The Aquarium is an historic, Art Deco structure, one of many in the Park; indeed, Fair Park contains one of the largest collections of Art Deco buildings in the world.

The Dallas Zoo took over management and operation of the Aquarium in 1989 and, since that time, has added many new exhibits while renovating the older displays. Much of the funding for this revitalization was provided by the Meadows Foundation, a private, philanthropic organization.

## VISITOR INFORMATION

**Directions:** From downtown Dallas, take I-30 East to the 2nd Avenue Exit. Curve right on R.B. Cullum Blvd. to the Martin Luther King Blvd. entrance to Fair Park. The Aquarium is in Fair Park, near the giant ferris wheel.

**Open to the Public:** Daily, 9 AM-4:30 PM; hours extended during Texas State Fair, in October.

**Closed:** Thanksgiving and Christmas Day

**Admission (1993):** Adult: $1.00     Child: $1.00     Senior: $1.00

**Parking Fee:** None

**Annual Membership** (to Dallas Zoo & Aquarium):
Individual: $30     Family: $45

**AAZPA Member:** Yes

## COLLECTIONS & EXHIBITS

**Collection:** The Aquarium's current collection includes the following number of species:

Reptiles: 10      Fish: 356        Amphibians: 3
Mollusks: 1      Other Invertebrates: 15

**Special Exhibits** at the Dallas Aquarium include:
World of Aquatic Diversity - 25 displays highlight unusual and bizarre adaptations of marine and fresh water species; this largest addition to the Aquarium opened in October, 1992.
Alligator Snapping Turtle Display
Electric Eel Exhibit
Shark Exhibit - feeding at 2:30 PM, Wed., Fri. & Sun.
Piranha Exhibit - feeding at 2:30 PM, Tues., Thur. & Sat.

*Piranha Exhibit at Dallas Aquarium*
*(photo by Robert Cabello; courtesy Dallas Aquarium)*

**Future Plans:** The Aquarium plans a 1200 square-foot addition in 1994; this will include handicapped accessible restrooms, an expanded gift shop, two new exhibits, educational displays and a breeding lab for rare and endangered species.

## CAPTIVE BREEDING & RESEARCH

The Dallas Aquarium has had special **breeding** success with the following species:
Desert pupfish (5 species) - endangered species
Comal Springs salamander - an endangered native of Texas
Fountain darter - an endangered species

**Research projects** based at the Dallas Aquarium include:
- Breeding project and field research on Comal Springs salamander
- Captive breeding and behavioral research on desert pupfish; the Dallas Aquarium is leading an international effort to save these endangered fish
- Husbandry and parasitology studies of batfish

## FOR MORE INFORMATION

Dallas Aquarium, P.O. Box 150113, Juanita Craft Station, Dallas, Texas 75315-0113; 214-670-8443; Director: Richard W. Buickerood

# 118

## CALDWELL ZOO
### Tyler, Texas

Originating as an animal menagerie at the Caldwell Playschool, the Caldwell Zoo was founded by Mr. and Mrs. D.K. Caldwell and opened to the public in 1952. The 50-acre facility is still owned and managed by Caldwell Schools, Inc., which perpetuates the goals of the Zoo's founders: wildlife preservation and visitor education.

## VISITOR INFORMATION

**Directions:** From Interstate 20, enter Tyler on U.S. 69 or U.S. 271. Cross Loop 323. The Zoo is on Martin Luther King Blvd., just south of the Loop and just east of U.S. 69.

**Open to the Public:** 9:30 AM-6 PM, April through September; 9:30 AM-4:30 PM, October through March

**Closed:** Thanksgiving, Christmas and New Years Day

**Admission:** Free

**Parking Fee:** None

**Children's Zoo:** No

**Annual Membership:** not available

**AAZPA Member:** Yes

## COLLECTIONS & EXHIBITS

**Collection:** The Zoo's current collection includes the following number of species:

| | | |
|---|---|---|
| Mammals: 46 | Birds: 91 | Reptiles: 74 |
| Amphibians: 12 | Fish: 46 | Invertebrates: 7 |

**Special Exhibits** at the Caldwell Zoo include:
East African Exhibit
South American Exhibit
Native Texas Area

**Future Plans:** The Zoo is currently in the process of updating its Masterplan for development.

## CAPTIVE BREEDING & RESEARCH

The Caldwell Zoo has had special **breeding** success with the following species:

| | |
|---|---|
| Hyancinth macaws | Chilean flamingos |
| Crowned cranes | Grevy's zebras |

**Research projects** based at the Zoo include:
- Artificial insemination in cheetahs; this project produced a cheetah cub in September, 1991.
- Study of Vitamin E levels in elephants

## FOR MORE INFORMATION

Caldwell Zoo, 2203 Martin Luther King Blvd., Tyler, Texas 75702; 903-593-0121; Director: Hayes Caldwell

# 119

### CAMERON PARK ZOO
### Waco, Texas

Founded in 1955, the Cameron Park Zoo opens a new, 51 acre facility in August, 1993. The new Zoo features spacious, naturalized habitats and was designed to enhance the beauty of Cameron Park, a 400 acre wooded preserve on the scenic Brazos River.

## VISITOR INFORMATION

**Directions:**  From Interstate 35, take the 4th Street S. Exit and head west for 1 miles to the Zoo.

**Open to the Public** (Zoo opens August, 1993):
9 AM-6 PM weekdays, 9 AM-7 PM weekends, Summer;
9 AM-5 PM weekdays, 9 AM-6 PM weekends, remainder of year

**Closed:** Christmas and New Years Day

**Admission (1993):** Adult: $3.50    Child: $2.00

**Parking Fee:** None

**Children's Zoo:** No

**Annual Membership:** Individual: $20    Family: $35    Senior: $10

**AAZPA Member:** No (new facility)

## COLLECTIONS & EXHIBITS

**Collection:** The Zoo's current collection includes the following number of species:
Mammals: 16              Birds: 17              Reptiles: 2

**Special Exhibits** at the Cameron Park Zoo include:
Gibbon Island - viewed from a deck and landscaped with a large waterfall
African Savannah - features zebra, giraffe, antelope, rhinos, elephants and other African species; viewed from the African Treetops deck which harbors a restaurant, gift shop and outdoor cafe
Sumatran Tiger Exhibit - viewed from a jungle path

**Future Plans:** This new Zoo will open in August, 1993.

## CAPTIVE BREEDING & RESEARCH

The Cameron Park Zoo has had special **breeding** success with the following species:
Binturong                  King vultures
Tigers                     Bald Eagles
Leopards                   Gibbons

## FOR MORE INFORMATION
Cameron Park Zoo, P.O. Box 2570, Waco, Texas 76703; 817-750-5976; Director: Tim Jones

*Sumatran Tiger Habitat at the Cameron Park Zoo*
*(photo courtesy Tim Jones, Director)*

# 120     ELLEN TROUT ZOO
### Lufkin, Texas

Having received a hippo as a gag gift, local industrialist Walter Trout donated the animal to the city of Lufkin in 1965, setting in motion the creation of the Ellen Trout Zoo two years later. Today, this 13-acre facility is praised as one of the finest small city zoos in America, harboring a fine collection of reptiles, small mammals, large cats, waterfowl, parrots and birds of prey. Adjacent to the Zoo is the Z.O. & O. Miniature Railroad which offers rides through Ellen Trout Park.

## VISITOR INFORMATION
**Directions:**    The Zoo is located approximately .5 mile west of U.S. Highway 59 on North Loop 287 in Ellen Trout Park.

**Open to the Public:** Daily; 9 AM-6 PM Summer; 9 AM-5 PM Winter; hours change with daylight savings time; indoor exhibits open 1 hour later and close 1 hour earlier

**Admission:** Adult: $2.00    Child: $1.00

**Parking Fee:** None

**Children's Zoo:** No

**Annual Membership:** Individual: $15    Family: $25

**Programs & Tours:** Reservations by calling 634-6313

**AAZPA Member:** Yes

## COLLECTIONS & EXHIBITS

**Collection:** The Zoo's current collection includes the following number of species:
Mammals: 32          Birds: 62          Reptiles: 65
Amphibians: 5        Fish: 3            Invertebrates: 3

**Special Exhibits** at the Ellen Trout Zoo include:
Tropical Asia Exhibit - features Asian species, many of which are endangered, in a naturalized setting of tropical flora
Large Cat Exhibit - includes jaguars and an authentic replica of a Mayan temple

## CAPTIVE BREEDING & RESEARCH

The Ellen Trout Zoo has had special **breeding** success with the following species:
West African crowned cranes          Jaguars
King vultures                        Bay duikers
Emu                                  Black & white ruffed lemurs
Blackbuck antelope                   Louisiana pine snakes

The Zoo is currently conducting **research** on the propagation of Louisiana pine snakes and on captive breeding of West African crowned cranes.

## SEASONAL FESTIVALS & PROGRAMS

Earth Day - April
Friends of Ellen Trout Zoo Members Gala - early October
Halloween "Zoo Boo" - late October
Dinamations Exhibit (Robotic Dinosaurs) - planned for April 1 through July 4, 1993

## FOR MORE INFORMATION

The Ellen Trout Zoo, 402 Zoo Circle, Lufkin, Texas 75901; 409-633-0399; Director: Gordon B. Henley, Jr.

# 121
## EL PASO ZOO
### El Paso, Texas

Established in 1940, the El Paso Zoo covers 10 acres. The Zoo is owned and managed by the City of El Paso.

## VISITOR INFORMATION

**Directions:** From I-10 East, take the Juarez Exit to Paisano Drive, far left lane, turn left on Gateway North; proceed 1 block to Findley, turn right.

From I-10 West, take Reynolds Exit; turn right (west) on Alameda; proceed to and turn left on Boone Street; drive approximately ¼ mile to the Zoo.

**Open to the Public:** 9:30 AM-4 PM, Winter; 9:30-5 PM Spring through Fall

**Closed:** Thanksgiving, Christmas and New Years Day

**Admission (1993):** Adult: $2.00    Child: $1.00    Senior: $1.00

**Parking Fee:** None

**Children's Zoo:** Scheduled for completion in August, 1993

**Annual Membership:** For information contact the El Paso Zoological Society at 915-532-8156.

**AAZPA Member:** Yes

## COLLECTIONS & EXHIBITS

**Collection:** The Zoo's current collection includes the following number of species:
Mammals: 29          Birds: 40          Reptiles: 45
Amphibians: 2          Fish: 22          Invertebrates: 7

**Special Exhibits** at the El Paso Zoo include:
South American Pavilion - all vertebrate classes are represented; a highlight of the exhibit is the golden lion tamarin, an SSP species
American Biome - contrasts Central American forest and Chihuahuan desert with use of diurnal/nocturnal exhibits

**Future Plans:** Several projects are scheduled for completion in 1993; these include America's Aviary, Paraje (Children's Zoo), a Conservation/Education Center, and Asia, a 5-acre expansion.

## SEASONAL FESTIVALS & EXHIBITS

Sweetheart Day - mid February
Swing into Spring - late March
Easter Bunny - mid April
Conservation Day - late June
Society Members' Night - late July
Library Day - early August
Mona the Elephant's Birthday - early October
Winter Holiday Party - mid December

**FOR MORE INFORMATION**

El Paso Zoo, 4001 East Paisano Drive, El Paso, Texas 79905-4223; 915-521-1850; Director: Lea Hutchinson V.M.D.

*Gibbon Exhibit
(photo by M. Quinn;
courtesy El Paso Zoo)*

# 122         SAN ANTONIO ZOO
## San Antonio, Texas

Home to one of the largest and most varied collections of African antelopes in the world, the San Antonio Zoo was founded in 1914. This 29-acre facility, situated at the headwaters of the San Antonio River, is ideally suited to display animals from a wide variety of natural habitats. Moist, semi-tropical conditions are found along the River while semi-arid hillsides and limestone cliffs surround the lowlands.

With over 3000 animals, representing more than 700 species, the San Antonio Zoo boasts one of the largest collections in North America. It is the only zoo in the south-central U.S. to display koalas.

**VISITOR INFORMATION**

**Directions:**    The San Antonio Zoo is located in Brackenridge Park along U.S. 281, halfway between the Airport and the downtown area. Call 210-734-7184 for specific directions.

**Open to the Public:**   365 days per year; 9:30 AM-6:30 PM April to October;
9:30 AM-5 PM November to March

**Admission (1993):** Adult: $5.00    Child: $3.00    Senior: $3.50

**Parking Fee:** None

**Children's Zoo:** Yes    **Separate Admission:** No

**Annual Membership:** Individual: $25    Family: $45    Senior: $20/$30 Couple

**Programs & Tours:**   A variety of educational programs are offered by the Zoo
including guided tours, animal demonstrations, community
outreach programs and on-site exhibits.

**AAZPA Member:** Yes

## COLLECTIONS & EXHIBITS

**Collection:**   The Zoo's current collection includes over 3000 animals, representing
over 700 species.

**Special Exhibits** at the San Antonio Zoo include:
  Africa's Rift Valley Exhibit
  Amazonia - this rainforest habitat features jaguars, giant anteaters, macaws,
    capuchin monkeys, spider monkeys, tamarins and marmosets
  Australian Walkabout - includes the only koalas on exhibit in the south-central
    U.S.; also features kangaroos, wallabies, wombats, New Guinea singing dogs and
    a variety of Australian birds
  Children's Zoo - includes "The Tropical Tour," a boat ride and a nursery
  Hixon Bird House - one of the finest bird collections in the country
  Whooping Crane exhibit
  Friedrich and Barrier Reef Aquariums

**Future Plans:**   Development plans include an American Wetlands Exhibit and a
new Zoo Plaza (visitor facilities); completion dates are still pending.

## CAPTIVE BREEDING & RESEARCH

The San Antonio Zoo has had special **breeding** success with the following species:
  Southern white rhinoceros - first captive birth of this species in the United States
  Caribbean flamingo - one of the first zoos to hatch and rear these birds
  Snow leopard
  African antelope species - the Zoo maintains off-exhibit breeding facilities for
    these animals; received a significant achievement award from the AAZPA for
    captive propagation of Jackson's hartebeest

The San Antonio Zoo participates in 25 of the 53 Species Survival Plans coordinated
by the AAZPA.

## SEASONAL FESTIVALS & PROGRAMS
Zoo Fiesta Art Show - April
Zoo Family Picnic - May
Summer Camp for Kids - June through August
Zoo Boo Halloween Party - October 31
Zoobilation - November

## FOR MORE INFORMATION
San Antonio Zoo, 3903 N. St. Mary's St., San Antonio, Texas 78212; 210-734-7184; Director: Louis R. Di Sabato

# 123 SEA WORLD OF TEXAS
### San Antonio, Texas

Opened in 1988, Sea World of Texas offers more than 25 attractions, shows and exhibits. This 250-acre Park, one of nine Anheuser-Busch theme parks, is home to the world's largest captive population of beluga whales. It also features "Cypress Gardens West," a 16-acre botanical garden landscaped with waterways, fountains, bridges and over 200,000 flowering plants.

## VISITOR INFORMATION
**Directions:** The Park is 16 miles northwest of downtown San Antonio at the intersection of Westover Hills and Ellison Boulevard, just off State Highway 151. Numerous directional signs guide visitors to the Park.

**Open to the Public:** Daily in Summer; weekends and some holidays, Spring and Fall; call 512-523-3611 for hours.

**Closed:** November through February

**Admission (1993):** Subject to change.   Adult: $23.95 + tax   Child: $15.95 + tax

**Parking:** $3.00 per day, per vehicle

**Children's Zoo:** No

**Annual Membership:** Subject to change.
Adult: $69.95    Child: $49.95    Senior: $49.95

**Programs & Tours:** Educational programs include behind-the-scenes tours, summer courses (Camp Sea World) and state-certified workshops. For information call 512-523-3608.

**AAZPA Member:** Yes

## COLLECTIONS & EXHIBITS

**Collection:** The Park's current animal collection includes the following number of species:

|              |          |
|--------------|----------|
| Mammals: 10  | Birds: 64 |
| Reptiles: 3  | Fish: 110 |

**Special Exhibits** at Sea World of Texas include:

Wet Wild & Wonderful - this show, new in 1992, features the world's largest oceanarium population of beluga whales; Pacific white-sided dolphins also take part in this educational and entertaining presentation.

The Legend of Shamu - a spectacular killer whale show

Sharks & The Coral Reef - this 4-aquarium exhibit introduces visitors to species that inhabit the depths of tropical seas; features sharks, moray eels, tropical fish and a re-created coral reef.

Penguin Exhibit - home to more than 200 penguins; also features educational displays and an exhibit of alcids.

Seal & Sea Lion Community - a mixed community of seals, sea lions and otter; visitors are permitted to feed the residents.

Avian Exhibits - features waterfowl, flamingos and other exotic birds.

Cypress Gardens West - 16-acre botanical garden landscaped with waterways, fountains, bridges and over 200,000 flowering plants.

**Future Plans:** A spacious walk-through Aviary, an Alligator Exhibit and a new Water Park will all open in 1993.

*Feeding time at the Reef.*
*(© 1993, Sea World of Texas)*

## CAPTIVE BREEDING & RESEARCH

Sea World of Texas has had special **breeding** success with the following species:

| | |
|---|---|
| Killer whales | Gentoo penguins |
| Beluga whales | Epaulette sharks |
| Atlantic bottlenose dolphins | Chilean flamingos |
| California sea lions | Common puffins |
| Harbor seals | Common murres |
| King penguins | |

**Research** based at Sea World of Texas includes:
- Studies of killer whale communication and object identification
- General cetacean husbandry including breeding and training
- Research on penguins in re-created sub-Antarctic habitat

## SEASONAL FESTIVALS & PROGRAMS

Concert Series - throughout the year
"Small Wonders" - this 1993 program introduces children to marine animal babies
"Summer Night Magic" - special after-dark program featuring entertainment and a laser/fireworks show; nightly from late June through mid August

## FOR MORE INFORMATION

Sea World of Texas, 10500 Sea World Drive, San Antonio, Texas 78251; 210-523-3000; info line: 210-523-3611; General Manager: Ms. Robin D. Carson


# 124 HOUSTON ZOOLOGICAL GARDENS
### Houston, Texas

The Houston Zoological Gardens, owned and operated by the City of Houston, was established in 1922. The 50-acre facility offers a variety of educational programs throughout the year.

## VISITOR INFORMATION

**Directions:** From Highway 288, exit onto MacGregor Avenue and head west. Proceed to Golf Course Drive; the Zoo lot will be on your left.

**Open to the Public:** 365 days per year, 10 AM-6 PM

**Admission (1993):** Adult: $2.50    Child: $.50    Senior: $2.00

**Parking Fee:** None

**Children's Zoo:** Yes    **Separate Admission:** No

**Annual Membership:** Individual: $25    Family: $40

**Programs & Tours:** The Education Department offers a variety of programs throughout the year. These include lectures, film/slide presentations, workshops and outreach programs. Call 713-525-3362.

**AAZPA Member:** Yes

## COLLECTIONS & EXHIBITS

**Collection:** The Zoo's current collection includes the following number of species:

Mammals: 108        Birds: 199        Reptiles: 116
Amphibians: 14      Insects: 7        Fish: 117

**Future Plans:**   Renovation of the Small Mammal House will be completed in 1993. The Wortham World of Primates, featuring naturalized exhibits, will also open in 1993.

## CAPTIVE BREEDING & RESEARCH

The Houston Zoological Gardens has had special **breeding** success with the following species:

Spectacled bears        Elephants
Snow leopards           Primate species

## SEASONAL FESTIVALS & PROGRAMS

Earth Day - April
Conservation Day/Zoo Month - June
Zoo Boo - October
Beastly Feast - November
Caroling to Animals - December

## FOR MORE INFORMATION

Houston Zoological Gardens, 1513 N. MacGregor, Houston, Texas 77030; 713-525-3300; Assistant Zoo Manager: M. Bowerman

# 125        GLADYS PORTER ZOO
### Brownsville, Texas

Built, stocked and donated to the city of Brownsville by Earl C. Sams, former president and chairman of the J.C. Penney Company, this Zoo opened to the public in September, 1971, and is named for Mr. Sams' daughter, a dedicated conservationist. Though relatively small in area (31 acres), the Zoo's subtropical setting, naturalistic exhibits and attention to the nuances of animal behavior have resulted in a remarkable record of captive breeding, including many worldwide "firsts."

## VISITOR INFORMATION

**Directions:**   Take the 6th Street Exit off 77 South. Turn right on Ringgold; the Zoo entrance is at 6th & Ringgold.

**Open to the Public:**   365 days per year; 9 AM-5 PM with extended summer & daylight savings hours; visitors may remain on the grounds until dusk.

**Admission:** Adult: $4.75   Child: $2.50   Senior: 20% Discount with AARP or AAA

*Jentink's duiker was first bred in captivity at the
Gladys Porter Zoo. The Zoo is home to nine of only
eleven captive individuals in the world.*
*(photo courtesy Gladys Porter Zoo)*

**Parking Fee:** $1.00

**Children's Zoo:** Yes    **Separate Admission:** No

**Annual Membership:** Individual: $17.50    Family: $35

**Programs & Tours:** Educational classes, spring thru fall

**AAZPA Member:** Yes

### COLLECTIONS & EXHIBITS

**Collection:** The Zoo's current collection includes the following number of species:

| | | |
|---|---|---|
| Mammals: 88 | Birds: 150 | Reptiles: 79 |
| Amphibians: 11 | Fish: 47 | Invertebrates: 30 |

The Gladys Porter Zoo is laid out in four zoogeographic areas: Tropical America, Indoaustralia, Asia and Africa. Most exhibits are naturalistic displays, surrounded only by waterways known as resacas, and the park is adorned with a superb collection of tropical plants.

**Special Exhibits** at the Zoo include the following:
Hunter's Hartebeest - this is the only zoo in the world to display this species and it was the first to breed this animal in captivity (1974)
Herpetarium
Aquarium - both marine and freshwater
Children's Zoo with nursery

**Future Plans:** A new Sea Lion Exhibit will open in 1993 and renovation of the gorilla, chimpanzee and orangutan complex will be completed by 1997.

## CAPTIVE BREEDING & RESEARCH

The Gladys Porter Zoo has had special **breeding** success with the following species:
Jentink's duiker - including the first captive birth (1970)
Orangutans - including the first successful caesarean section of this species (1970)
Lowland gorillas
Malagasy radiated tortoise - including the first hatched in an American zoo (1973)
Arabian oryx
Mindoro crocodile - including the first hatched outside of the Philippines (1989)

The Zoo is involved in many **research projects** including:
- the study of Jentink's duiker reproduction
- research on Hunter's hartebeest reproduction
- administration of the Kemp's Ridley Sea Turtle Recovery Program
- research on gibbon reproduction
- the study of Galapagos tortoises

## SEASONAL FESTIVALS & PROGRAMS

Zoobilee - late April or early May
Conservation Day - June
National Zoo & Aquarium Day - June
Zoofari - first Saturday in October
Boo at the Zoo - October 30 & 31
Fiesta of Lights - Saturday & Sunday evenings in December
Winter in Texas - Wednesdays, November through March

## FOR MORE INFORMATION

The Gladys Porter Zoo, 500 Ringgold, Brownsville, Texas 78520; 512-546-7187; Director: Don D. Farst, DVM

# 126 LOUISIANA PURCHASE GARDENS & ZOO
### Monroe, Louisiana

Covering 80 acres, the Louisiana Purchase Gardens and Zoo was founded in 1923. Sixty years later, the Louisiana Purchase Zoological Society, a non-profit corporation of volunteers and local citizens, was established to promote and support the facility.

Much of the Zoo can be viewed from a coal-burning, steam-powered train that runs through the park or from boats that ply the lagoon waterways.

## VISITOR INFORMATION

**Directions:** From Interstate 20, exit onto Highway 165 and drive south toward Columbia. Proceed to the fifth stoplight and turn right on Ticheli Road. Go through the first stoplight and follow this road to the Zoo entrance.

**Open to the Public:** 10 AM-6 PM summer; 10 AM-5 PM winter

**Closed:** Thanksgiving and Christmas Day

**Admission (1993):** Adult: $3.25    Child: $2.00 (under 3 free)    Senior: $2.00

**Parking Fee:** None

**Children's Zoo:** No

**Annual Membership:** Individual: $25    Family: $35    Senior: $15

**AAZPA Member:** No

## COLLECTIONS & EXHIBITS

**Collection:** The Zoo's current collection includes the following number of specimens:
Mammals: 313 specimens    Reptiles: 125 specimens    Birds: 33 specimens

**Special Exhibits** at the Louisiana Purchase Gardens & Zoo include:
White Tiger Exhibit
Primate/Guenon Collection

**Future Plans:** A new Tiger Exhibit is scheduled to open in spring of 1994.

## CAPTIVE BREEDING & RESEARCH

The Louisiana Purchase Gardens & Zoo has had special **breeding** success with the following species:

Sri Lanka tree viper
Sthulmann's guenon
Spot-nose guenon
Debrazza guenon
Lion-tailed macaque
Siamangs

Grevy's zebra
Fishing cat
Snow leopard
Black & white colobus
Addax
Gibbon species

**Research** based at the Louisiana Purchase Gardens and Zoo includes:
  - Behavioral studies of siamangs, conducted by Northeast Louisiana University,
    Monroe, Louisiana

## SEASONAL FESTIVALS & PROGRAMS

Easter Program
Mother's Day Program
Zoobilation - May
Rhythm & Zoo's Concert Series - summer
Edzoocation Programs - summer
Boo at the Zoo - late October
Cookies & Cocoa with Santa - December

## FOR MORE INFORMATION

The Louisiana Purchase Gardens & Zoo, P.O. Box 123, Monroe, Louisiana 71210;
318-329-2400; Director: Jake Yelverton


# 127     ZOO OF ACADIANA
### Broussard, Louisiana


Home of the largest walk-through aviary in the South, the Zoo of Acadiana opened in
1992. This 25 acre facility boasts large, naturalized habitats, accessed by screened
boardwalks which bring visitors face to face with the wild inhabitants.

## VISITOR INFORMATION

**Directions:**   The Zoo is a few minutes south of Lafayette on Highway 182, 1 mile east
of Highway 90. From Interstate 10, take Exit 103A; go 10 miles through
Lafayette and take the Cade Exit. Turn left onto Highway 182 and
proceed 1 mile to the Zoo (on your right).

**Open to the Public:**   9 AM-7 PM Memorial Day to Labor Day;
9 AM-5 PM remainder of the year

**Closed:** Christmas Day

**Admission (1993):** Adult: $5.00     Child: $2.50     Senior: $4.00

**Parking Fee:** None

**Children's Zoo:** Yes     **Separate Admission:** No

**Annual Membership:** Individual: $20     Family: $40     Senior: $35 (Grandparent)

**AAZPA Member:** No; application planned

## COLLECTIONS & EXHIBITS

**Collection:** The Zoo's current collection includes the following number of species:

Mammals: 31          Birds: 50          Reptiles: 3

**Special Exhibits** at the Zoo of Acadiana include:

Aviary - the largest walk-through aviary in the South; features exotic parrots and waterfowl

Leopard tortoises - the only display of this species in Louisiana

Alligator Exhibit

Hoofed Mammal Exhibit - a spacious, hillside enclosure

Cat Habitats - include jaguars and Bengal tigers

Primate Collection - excellent variety of primates

**Future Plans:**   Future development of the Zoo will adhere to a theme of large, naturalized habitats which encourage natural behavior of the animals.

## SEASONAL FESTIVALS & PROGRAMS

Since the Zoo of Acadiana is less than a year old, these seasonal events are still in the planning stage.

## FOR MORE INFORMATION

Zoo of Acadiana, 116 Lakeview Drive, Broussard, Louisiana 70518; 318-837-4325; Director: Mr. Cable Prejean (Owner)

# 128      GREATER BATON ROUGE ZOO
### Baker, Louisiana

Encompassing 145 acres, the Greater Baton Rouge Zoo was founded in 1970. The facility harbors one of the finest collections of African hoofstock, big and small cats and primates of any medium-sized zoo in the country.

## VISITOR INFORMATION

**Directions:**   Take I-110 North to Exit #8; exit to the right and proceed to the second traffic light; turn right and drive another .5 miles to the entrance.

**Open to the Public:**  Daily, January 2 through December 23;
Daylight Savings Hours: 10 AM-6 PM;
Non-Daylight Hours: 10 AM-5 PM

**Closed:** December 24 through January 1

**Admission:** Adult: $2.00    Child: $1.00    Senior: $2.00

**Parking Fee:** None

**Children's Zoo:** Yes    **Separate Admission:** No

**Annual Membership:** Individual: $15    Family: $20    Senior: $15

**AAZPA Member:** Yes

## COLLECTIONS & EXHIBITS

**Collection:** The Zoo's current collection includes the following number of species:

| | | |
|---|---|---|
| Mammals: 81 | Birds: 126 | Reptiles: 6 |
| Amphibians: 1 | Fish: 1 | |

**Special Exhibits** at the Greater Baton Rouge Zoo include the following:

African Hoofstock Exhibits
Big & Small Cat Species
Primate Complex
Children's Zoo - includes a play area

**Future Plans:**  A new entrance complex, herpetarium, new primate complex and new psittacine exhibit are all scheduled for completion in 1993.

## CAPTIVE BREEDING & RESEARCH

The Greater Baton Rouge Zoo has had special **breeding** success with the following species:

Snow leopards                    Palm cockatoos
Clouded leopards                 Eclectus parrots
Maned wolves                     African antelope species
Red wolves                       Gibbon species

## SEASONAL FESTIVALS & PROGRAMS

Zoobilation - September

## FOR MORE INFORMATION

The Greater Baton Rouge Zoo, P.O. Box 60, Baker, Louisiana 70704; 504-775-3877; Director: G.R. Felton, Jr.

# 129 AUDUBON ZOOLOGICAL GARDEN
### New Orleans, Louisiana

The origin of the Audubon Zoological Garden dates back to the World's Industrial & Cotton Centennial of 1884. After this event drew to a close, its Horticultural Hall retained a collection of plants, macaws, monkeys and songbirds. Other animals were added to this menagerie over the following decades but the entire exhibit succumbed to a hurricane in 1915.

Formation of a zoological society, in 1919, marked the rebirth of the zoo and WPA buildings, erected in the 1930s, formed a nucleus for the growing facility. Since that time, the Audubon Zoological Garden has matured into one of the finest zoos in the country, characterized by spacious natural exhibits.

The Audubon Zoological Garden is now operated by the Audubon Institute, a non-profit organization that also manages the Aquarium of the Americas, Audubon Park, Woldenberg Riverfront Park, the Freeport-McMoRan Audubon Species Survival Center, the Audubon Center for Research on Endangered Species and the Audubon Kingdom of Insects. The Institute, which began as the Friends of the Zoo, in 1974, has established a mission to preserve Earth's resources through public education, research and conservation.

*Drill Baboon,
a resident of
the Audubon Zoo's
World of Primates.*
(photo courtesy
Audubon Zoological
Park)

*Rare white alligators are found in the Audubon Zoo's*
*Louisiana Swamp Exhibit.*
*(photo courtesy Audubon Zoological Garden)*

## VISITOR INFORMATION

**Directions:** The Zoo is located in Audubon Park on the Mississippi River. From Interstate 10, exit onto Carrollton Avenue and head southwest. Nearing the River, turn left on St. Charles, right on Broadway and left on Magazine Street to the Park and Zoo.

Alternatively, from the downtown area, catch the Magazine Street bus or the St. Charles Avenue streetcar to Audubon Park; a shuttle takes visitors to the Zoo from St. Charles Avenue. Or catch the John James Audubon riverboat at the foot of Canal Street (call 504-586-8777).

**Open to the Public:** 9:30 AM-5:30 PM, April through September;
9:30 AM-4:30 PM, October through March

**Close:** Mardi Gras Day, the first Friday in May, Thanksgiving Day
and Christmas Day

**Admission (1993):** Adult: $7.50    Child: $3.50    Senior: $3.50

**Parking Fee:** None

**Children's Zoo:** Yes

**Annual Membership:** Individual: $30    Family: $49    Senior: $15

**Programs & Tours:** The Education Department offers a variety of programs
including summer camp, workshops, lectures and Zoomobile.

**AAZPA Member:** Yes

## COLLECTIONS & EXHIBITS

**Collection:** The Audubon Zoological Garden is home to 1800 animal specimens and
over 1000 varieties of ornamental plants.

**Special Exhibits** at the Audubon Zoological Park include:

Reptile Encounter - a collection of the world's most dangerous reptiles and
amphibians

Pathways to the Past - a hands-on exhibit and computerized dinosaur display that
explores the evolutionary link between reptiles and birds

Tropical Bird House - this rainforest is home to exotic plants and colorful birds

Asian Domain - graced by an Indian Temple, this area features sun bears, white
Bengal tigers, Asian elephants, leopards and sarus cranes

World of Primates - naturalized homes for lowland gorillas, drill baboons, lemurs,
tamarins, siamangs, orangutans and other primates

African Savannah - the open habitats in this area feature white rhinos, giraffe,
zebras, antelope, ostriches, hippos, storks and other African natives

North American Grasslands - residents include tule elk, red wolves, collared
peccaries, American bison and sandhill cranes

South American Pampas - home to tapirs, capybaras, rheas, guanacos, flamingos
and macaws

Louisiana Swamp Exhibit - features black bears, nutrias, raccoons, cougars, otters,
water birds and rare white alligators

Wisner Discovery Village - introduces children to the wonders of nature while
emphasizing respect for wildlife; includes a petting zoo and nocturnal exhibits.

California Sea Lion Exhibit - newly remodeled

Heymann Conservatory - cultivates plantlife for the other zoo exhibits and for
Audubon Park.

**Future Plans:** Wilderness Park will be a natural area devoted to native Louisiana wildlife. Nature trails will provide access and the site will be used for releasing wild birds rehabilitated at the Zoo. Completion date pending.

## CAPTIVE BREEDING & RESEARCH

The Freeport-McMoRan Audubon Species Survival Center, a cooperative project with the other Louisiana Zoos, opened in 1992. This 1200 acre facility will concentrate on **breeding** endangered species such as rhinos, red wolves, tapirs, gorillas, tigers and tropical storks. Breeding programs will be conducted in cooperation with the AAZPA and the International Union for the Conservation of Nature.

The Audubon Center for Research on Endangered Species, to open in 1993, will conduct **research** on captive breeding, embryo implantation, animal behavior, animal nutrition and reintroduction techniques.

## FOR MORE INFORMATION

Audubon Zoological Garden, P.O. Box 4327, New Orleans, Louisiana 70178; 504-861-2537; President/CEO: Ronald Forman

# 130 AQUARIUM OF THE AMERICAS
### New Orleans, Louisiana

The Aquarium of the Americas, established in 1990, is dedicated to conservation of aquatic life through visitor education and recreation. Located adjacent to the French Quarter on the banks of the Mississippi, the Aquarium houses 7500 specimens, representing 400 species. Its 60 exhibits introduce the visitor to the varied aquatic life of the Western Hemisphere by replicating marine and fresh water habitats of North and South America.

## VISITOR INFORMATION

**Directions:** The Aquarium is located at Canal Street and the Mississippi River, in Woldenberg Riverfront Park. You can cruise to the Aquarium on the John James Audubon River Cruise (call 504-586-8777 for information).

**Open to the Public:** 9:30 AM-6 PM Sun.-Wed., 9:30 AM-9 PM Thurs., 9:30 AM-7 PM Fri.-Sat.

**Closed:** Christmas Day & Mardi Gras Day

**Admission (1993):** Subject to change   Adult: $8.00   Child: $4.25   Senior: $6.25

**Parking Fee:** None

**Annual Membership:** Individual: $35   Family: $59   Senior: $25

**AAZPA Member:** No (new facility)

*Mississippi River
Delta Exhibit*
(photo by Jackson Hill;
courtesy Aquarium
of the Americas)

## COLLECTIONS & EXHIBITS

**Collection:**   The Aquarium of the Americas houses 7500 specimens, representing 400 species of marine and fresh water life.

**Special Exhibits** at the Aquarium include:

Caribbean Reef Exhibit - this 132,000 gallon display is viewed from a 30-foot acrylic tunnel; features angelfish, parrotfish and cownose rays.

Mississippi River Delta - a collection of species and habitats that typify the lower Mississippi; includes paddlefish, longnose gar, endangered lake sturgeon and rare white alligators.

Amazon Rain Forest - home to red-bellied piranhas, macaws, poison arrow frogs and the giant anaconda; landscaped with waterfalls, rare orchids and other tropical plants.

Gulf of Mexico Exhibit - this 500,000 gallon tank features sharks, stingrays, giant grouper, tarpon and an artificial reef induced by a ¼ scale oil rig.

**Future Plans:**   An Imax Theater and a new 6,000 square-foot exhibit hall are planned.

## CAPTIVE BREEDING & RESEARCH

The Aquarium of the Americas has had special **breeding** success with the following species:

| | |
|---|---|
| Southern stingray | Red Terror |
| Black-footed penguins | Parrot cichlids |
| Quail | Uaru |
| Brazilian cardinals | Reticulated poison dart frogs |
| Candy-striped plecostomas | Red swamp crawfish |
| Four-eyed fish | |

*Gulf of Mexico Exhibit*
*(photo by Jackson Hill; courtesy Aquarium of the Americas)*

**Research projects** based at the Aquarium of the Americas include:

- Joint research with U.S. Army Corps of Engineers to reduce injuries to loggerhead sea turtles during dredging operations
- Aspergillosis monitoring and treatment in black-footed penguins
- Nutritional and physiological monitoring of sea turtles
- Survey of whale shark distribution in northern Gulf of Mexico
- Captive husbandry and breeding of black-footed penguins
- Reproductive studies on poison arrow frogs
- Research on hard and soft coral growth and reproduction
- Monitoring and dosing of ozone gas sterilization of closed-system artificial sea-water systems
- Experimental administration of medications to fish via a gelatin diet
- Studies on fish pathology and parasitology
- Ultrasonic monitoring of sea turtle reproductive state and physiology

## SEASONAL FESTIVALS & PROGRAMS

Reggae Riddums Festival Preview - June
Father's Day Celebration - June
Go Fourth on the River - July 4th
Aquarium Birthday Celebration - Labor Day weekend

## FOR MORE INFORMATION

Aquarium of the Americas, 1 Canal Street (at Mississippi River), New Orleans, Louisiana 70130; 504-861-2537; Director: Ron Forman

131. **Olympic Game Farm** (Sequim, Washington)

132. **Woodland Park Zoological Gardens** (Seattle, Washington)

133. **The Seattle Aquarium** (Seattle, Washington)

134. **Point Defiance Zoo & Aquarium** (Tacoma, Washington)

135. **Northwest Trek Wildlife Park** (Eatonville, Washington)

136. **Walk in the Wild** (Spokane, Washington)

137. **Metro Washington Park Zoo** (Portland, Oregon)

138. **Oregon Coast Aquarium, Inc.** (Newport, Oregon)

139. **Wildlife Safari** (Winston, Oregon)

140. **Zoo Boise** (Boise, Idaho)

141. **Tautphaus Park Zoo** (Idaho Falls, Idaho)

142. **Zoo Montana, Inc.** (Billings, Montana)

143. **Honolulu Zoo** (Honolulu, Hawaii)

144. **Waikiki Aquarium** (Honolulu, Hawaii)

145. **Sea Life Park Hawaii** (Waimanalo, Hawaii)

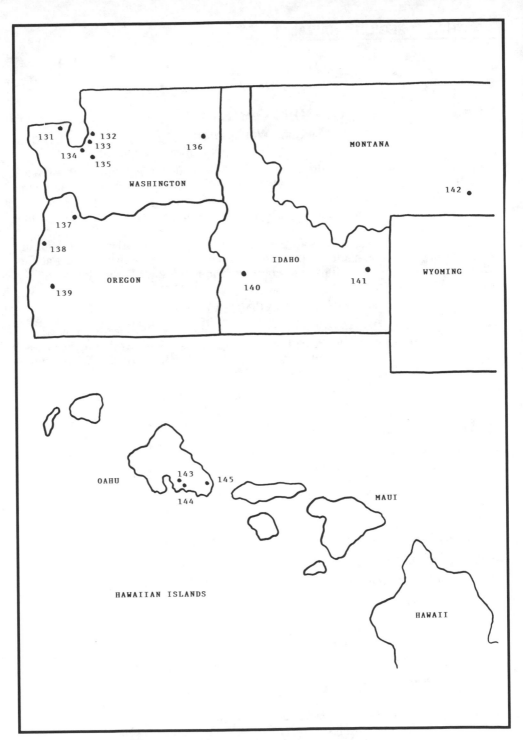

**NORTHWEST REGION & HAWAII
ZOOS & AQUARIUMS**

# 131

## OLYMPIC GAME FARM
### Sequim, Washington

Located on the north coast of the beautiful Olympic Peninsula, Olympic Game Farm opened in 1961. The 93-acre facility is viewed by a 3-mile drive-through tour and/or a 1-mile walking tour. The drive-through area features large, mixed-species habitats, while the walking tour introduces visitors to predators such as bears, big cats, lynx and wolves.

The Olympic Game Farm leads all U.S. wildlife parks in the captive propagation of grizzly bears. Its Aquarium features seven species of fish native to the Pacific Northwest and the Farm's film-set has been used in many Walt Disney Productions.

## VISITOR INFORMATION

**Directions:** From U.S. 10 in Sequim (17 miles east of Port Angeles), turn north on the Sequim/Dungeness Way. Drive approximately 2 miles to Woodcock Road, turn left and proceed another 2 miles to Ward Road. Turn right and drive 1 mile to the Game Farm.

**Open to the Public:** Daily, 9 AM; closing hours vary with seasons. Driving tour open all year. Walking tour open May 15 to September 15.

**Closed:** Thanksgiving, Christmas and New Years Day

**Admission Fee (1993):**
Walk or Drive Tour: Adult: $5.00     Child: $4.00     Senior: $4.00
Walk and Drive Tours: Adult: $7.00     Child: $5.00     Senior: $5.00
Group rates available (scheduled tours; 10 or more persons)

**Parking Fee:** None

**Children's Zoo:** No (however, they do have a petting farm)

**Annual Membership:** Not available

**Programs & Tours:** Guided walking tours are offered in the spring and summer.

**AAZPA Member:** No

## COLLECTIONS & EXHIBITS

**Collection:** The Game Farm's current collection includes the following number of species:
Mammals: 41          Birds: 8          Fish: 7

**Special Exhibits** at the Olympic Game Farm include:
Aquarium - features seven species of fish native to the Pacific Northwest
Hoofed Mammals - free-ranging herds of zebra, fallow deer, elk, bison, black-tailed deer, mouflon sheep and other species

Trout Pond - stocked with Camloops rainbow trout
Predator Collection - includes grizzly bears, wolverines, lynx, arctic fox, wolves,
jaguars, cougars and other species

### CAPTIVE BREEDING & RESEARCH

The Olympic Game Farm has had special **breeding** success with the following
species:

| | |
|---|---|
| Grizzly bear | Fallow deer |
| Cougar | Yak |
| Bison | Mouflon sheep |

### FOR MORE INFORMATION

Olympic Game Farm, 1423 Ward Road, Sequim, Washington 98382; 206-683-4295;
Director: Rick Dallmus

# 132 WOODLAND PARK ZOOLOGICAL GARDENS
### Seattle, Washington

Long recognized for its commitment to naturalistic exhibits, the Woodland Park
Zoo, founded in 1900, is in the midst of a major redevelopment project. By 1997, this
92-acre Zoo will be transformed into eight bioclimatic exhibit zones: African Savanna,
Tropical Rain Forest, Tropical Asia, Temperate Forest, Australasia, Northern Trail,
Steppe and Desert. Funds for this transformation were raised primarily through the
passage of a $31.5 million bond issue in 1985. An additional $10 million, needed to
release the bond issue funds, is being raised by the Woodland Park Zoological Society.

### VISITOR INFORMATION

**Directions:** Woodland Park is north of the downtown area and north of Seattle
Center. From Interstate 5, exit onto 50th Avenue N.W. and drive west
for approximately 2.5 miles to the south entrance of the Zoo.

**Open to the Public:** 365 days per year; 9:30 AM-6 PM March 15 to October 14;
9:30 AM-5 PM October 15 to March 14

**Admission (1993):** Adult: $5.00    Child: $2.75    Senior: $3.75

**Parking Fee:** $2.00 for 4 hours

**Children's Zoo:** Yes    **Separate Admission:** No

**Annual Membership:** Individual: $21    Family: $39

**AAZPA Member:** Yes

*Red-billed Toucans in the Tropical Rainforest Exhibit*
*(photo by Ian Dewar; courtesy Woodland Park Zoo)*

## COLLECTIONS & EXHIBITS

**Collection:** The Zoo's current collection includes the following number of species:

| | | |
|---|---|---|
| Mammals: 84 | Birds: 100 | Reptiles: 53 |
| Amphibians: 7 | Insects: 3 | Fish: 1 |
| Other Invertebrates: 10 | | |

**Special Exhibits** at the Woodland Park Zoological Gardens include:
Asian Elephant Forest
Lowland Gorilla Exhibit
Tropical Rainforest - enclosed within a 2-story glass dome
African Savanna
Marsh & Swamp Exhibit
Education Center - includes a hands-on Discovery Room

**Future Plans:** The Zoo's masterplan is discussed in the introduction. Renovation of the Family Farm (Children's petting zoo) and completion of the Northern Trail Exhibit are both scheduled for 1994.

## CAPTIVE BREEDING & RESEARCH

The Woodland Park Zoological Gardens has had special **breeding** success with the following species:

| | |
|---|---|
| Snow Leopards | Malayan Sun Bears |
| Maned Wolves | Lowland Gorillas |
| Humboldt Penguins | Solomen Leaf Frogs |

The Zoo participates in several Species Survival Plans administered through the AAZPA. **Research projects** based at the facility include:
- Study of African elephants in Tanzania
- Animal Behavioral Workshops

## SEASONAL FESTIVALS & PROGRAMS

Endangered Species Month - March
Wildlife Weekend - March
Conservation Day - June
Whoop-de-Zoo - June
Jungle Party - July
Summer Concert Series - July and August
Zoo Parent Family Reunion - August
Wildlife Weekend - August
Fair in the Farm - September

## FOR MORE INFORMATION

Woodland Park Zoological Gardens, 5500 Phinney Ave. N., Seattle, Washington 98103; 206-684-4880; Director: David L. Towne

# 133    THE SEATTLE AQUARIUM
### Seattle, Washington

The Seattle Aquarium, founded in 1977, focuses primarily on sealife of the Pacific Northwest. Most of the Aquarium's specimens were collected from Washington coastal areas and the facility's tanks are filled with saltwater pumped directly from Puget Sound.

## VISITOR INFORMATION

**Directions:** From Interstate 5, take the Mercer Exit. Follow signs to the Waterfront/Ferries by taking Broad St. west (past Seattle Center) and then Alaskan Way south to Pier 59. Pay lots and metered parking is available near the Aquarium.

**Open to the Public:** 365 days per year; 10 AM-5 PM Labor Day to Memorial Day; 10 AM-7 PM Memorial Day to Labor Day.

**Closed:** Christmas morning (open Noon-5 PM Christmas Day)

**Admission (1993):** Adult: $6.00    Child: $3.50 (3-5, $1.00)    Senior: $3.50

**Parking Fee:** No on-site parking; pay lots and metered parking available in area

**Annual Membership:** Individual: $29    Family: $39

**Programs & Tours:** Educational programs throughout the year. Over 40,000 school children learn about wildlife conservation and water quality issues at the Aquarium each year.

**AAZPA Member:** Yes

## COLLECTIONS & EXHIBITS

**Collection:** The Aquarium's current collection includes the following number of species:

Mammals: 3          Birds: 12          Reptiles: 1
Invertebrates: 164    Fish: 213

*A view from the Underwater Dome*
(photo by Leo J. Shaw; courtesy Seattle Aquarium)

**Special Exhibits** at the Seattle Aquarium include:

Underwater Dome - this 400,000 gallon tank highlights the marine life of Puget Sound, including octopus, halibut, ling cod, salmon, sea stars, wolf eels, perch, rockfish and anemones. A diver feeds the inhabitants each day at 1:30 PM.

Pacific Coral Reef - this 23,000 gallon tank exhibits marine life found on and near Pacific coral reefs

Principles of Survival Exhibit - features lionfish, leaffish, seahorses and lungfish

Otters and Seals Exhibit

Delicate Balance Exhibit - educates visitors about the interrelationship of nature, politics and pollution along Puget Sound

Salmon and People Exhibit - includes the world's only Aquarium-based salmon run

Coconut Crab Exhibit

Puget Sound Fishes Exhibit - home to tiger rockfish, wolf eels and rat fish

Touch Tank

Birds & Shores Exhibit - watch puffins "fly" underwater

**Future Plans:** A Tidepool Exhibit and Discovery Lab will open in 1993.

## CAPTIVE BREEDING & RESEARCH

The Seattle Aquarium has had special **breeding** success with the following species:

| | |
|---|---|
| Sea Otter | Pacific Spiny Lumpsucker |
| Northern Fur Seal | Coho Salmon |
| Harbor Seal | Giant Pacific Octopus |

A tropical sea turtle rehabilitation program is based at the Seattle Aquarium; stranded turtles are rehabilitated and then released in warmer waters off San Diego.

## SEASONAL FESTIVALS & PROGRAMS

Maritime Week - mid May
Beach Sweep - June
Elliott Bay Cleanup - Summer
Salmon Homecoming - October
Santa Dives in the Dome - December

## FOR MORE INFORMATION

The Seattle Aquarium, 1483 Alaskan Way, Pier 59, Seattle, Washington 98101; 206-386-4300; 206-386-4320 (recording); Director: Cynthia A. Shiota

# 134 POINT DEFIANCE ZOO & AQUARIUM
## Tacoma, Washington

The unique collection at the Point Defiance Zoo and Aquarium represents species from countries that border the Pacific Ocean. Though relatively small in size (29 acres), the Zoo lays claim to many "firsts," including the first zoo to hatch rare octopus leioderma eggs, the first to hand-rear an infant harbor porpoise to maturity and the first zoo to display tiger quolls in the U.S. Founded in 1960, this facility has also been instrumental in the captive breeding of red wolves, bringing that species back from near extinction.

## VISITOR INFORMATION

**Directions:** From I-5, take Exit #132 and follow the signs to Bremerton/Highway 16. Take the 6th Avenue Exit and turn left onto Pearl Street which leads into Point Defiance Park.

**Open to the Public:** Daily; 10 AM-4 PM Labor Day to Memorial Day; 10 AM-7 PM Memorial Day to Labor Day

**Closed:** Thanksgiving, Christmas Day

**Admission:** Adult: $6.25   Child: $4.50   Senior: $5.75

**Parking Fee:** None

**Children's Zoo:** Yes   **Separate Admission:** No

**Annual Membership:** Individual: $30   Family: $45   Senior: $45 (grandparent)

**AAZPA Member:** Yes

## COLLECTIONS & EXHIBITS

**Collection:** The Zoo & Aquarium's current collection includes the following number of species:

| | | |
|---|---|---|
| Mammals: 36 | Birds: 54 | Reptiles: 19 |
| Amphibians: 3 | Fish: 155 | Insects: 2 |
| Other Invertebrates: 76 | | |

**Special Exhibits** at Point Defiance Zoo & Aquarium include:
Rocky Shores - a marine mammal exhibit
Discovery Reef Aquarium - a display of sharks and tropical fish
Polar Bear Complex - surface and underwater viewing
Elephant Barn - a state-of-the-art facility

**Future Plans:** A masterplan through the year 2000 calls for expansion of the Southeast Asia Exhibit (to include sun bears, orangutans and tigers) and conversion of the "World of Adaptations" into an environmental learning center.

## CAPTIVE BREEDING & RESEARCH

The Point Defiance Zoo & Aquarium has had special **breeding** success with the following species:

| | |
|---|---|
| Red wolves | Dogfish |
| Emerald tree boas | Beluga whales |
| Gila monsters | Pygmy marmosets |
| Leaf-nosed fruit bats | |

**Research** at Point Defiance includes the study of beluga whale vocalizations and research on bat contraception.

## SEASONAL FESTIVALS & PROGRAMS

Zoosounds Children's Concerts - June
Zoobilee (black tie fundraiser) - July
Zoolights (holiday light display) - December

## FOR MORE INFORMATION

The Point Defiance Zoo & Aquarium, 5400 North Pearl St., Tacoma, Washington 98407; 206-591-5337; Director: Tom Otten

# 135 NORTHWEST TREK WILDLIFE PARK
### Eatonville, Washington

Thanks to the generosity of Dr. and Mrs. David T. Hellyer, the Metropolitan Park District of Tacoma opened Northwest Trek Wildlife Park in 1975. The 635-acre Preserve, located in the foothills of Mt. Rainier, displays animals native to the Pacific Northwest and is dedicated to their protection and propagation.

Naturalist-guided, 90-passenger trams take visitors on a 5.5-mile, 50 minute tour through the mixed-species, prey animal habitat while paved pathways lead through the core area where predators inhabit large, naturalized exhibits. In addition, five miles of nature trails offer access to a natural woodland at the Park.

## VISITOR INFORMATION

**Directions:** From I-5 between Tacoma and Seattle, take Exit #142-B and head south on State Route 161. The Park is on S.R. 161, 17 miles south of Puyallup.

*Naturalist-guided trams take visitors through a 435-acre preserve
where elk, deer, bison, moose and other prey species roam free.
(photo courtesy Northwest Trek Wildlife Park)*

**Open to the Public:**  Opens 9:30 AM daily, March through October; open Fri.-Sun. and selected holidays the remainder of the year; closing time varies with the season. Trams run on the hour, from 10 AM to closing.

**Closed:**  Monday-Thursday, November through February, except selected holidays; closed Thanksgiving and Christmas.

**Admission (1993):**  Adult: $7.50    Child (3-4): $3.00 (5-17): $5.00    Senior: $6.50

**Parking Fee:** None

**Children's Zoo:** No (however, on-site Discovery Center)

**Annual Membership:** Individual: $30    Family: $50    Senior: $22.50

**Programs & Tours:**  A variety of educational programs and exhibits are offered at the Cheney Discovery Center and at the Forest Theater. Tram tours are guided by a naturalist.

**AAZPA Member:** Yes

## COLLECTIONS & EXHIBITS

**Collection:** The Park's current collection includes the following number of species:

| | | |
|---|---|---|
| Mammals: 30 | Birds: 16 | Reptiles: 2 |
| Amphibians: 5 | Fish: 1 | Invertebrates: 2 |

**Special Exhibits** at the Northwest Trek Wildlife Park include:

Free-roaming area - 435 acres of lake, forest and meadow habitats, inhabited by elk, deer, bison, bighorn sheep, moose, pronghorns and other prey animals; accessed by the naturalist-guided trams.

Cheney Discovery Center - this 1000 square-foot building is devoted to children with many "hands-on" displays and educational activities.

Core Area - paved walkways lead past large, naturalized habitats for predators: cougars, lynx, bobcats, tundra wolves, fishers, wolverines, bears, owls, eagles and other species.

**Future Plans:** A Grizzly and Black Bear Complex will open in 1993. Each exhibit will cover .75 acre and will be landscaped with natural vegetation.

## CAPTIVE BREEDING & RESEARCH

Northwest Trek Wildlife Park has had special **breeding** success with the following species:

| | |
|---|---|
| Woodland caribou | Mountain goat |
| Bison | Lynx |
| Elk | Fisher |
| Bighorn sheep | |

**Research projects** based at the Wildlife Park include:
- Captive breeding of wolverines and fishers

## SEASONAL FESTIVALS & PROGRAMS

Kids & Critters Naturefest - Martin Luther King Holiday weekend
National Wildlife Week - third week of April
Conservation Carnival - Summer
Hayrides - Autumn and selected holidays
Halloween Hoot 'n Howl - October

## FOR MORE INFORMATION

Northwest Trek Wildlife Park, 11610 Trek Drive East, Eatonville, Washington 98328; 206-832-6117; Info line: 800-433-TREK in Washington and Oregon; Director: Gary Geddes

# 136 WALK IN THE WILD ZOO
### Spokane, Washington

This 85-acre Zoo, founded in 1972, is but part of a 240-acre parkland, characterized by a botanical garden, meadows and natural woodlands. Many wild species inhabit the site, including deer, badgers, weasels, marmots, prairie dogs, hawks and great horned owls. A network of nature trails provides access to undeveloped areas of the park.

The Zoo, home to over 150 animals from five continents, is operated by the Inland Northwest Zoological Society, a non-profit organization.

## VISITOR INFORMATION

**Directions:** The Walk in the Wild Zoo is 10 miles east of downtown Spokane. Take I-90 East to the Pines Road Exit. Turn north and drive 1.5 miles. Turn right on Euclid which will take you to the Zoo entrance.

**Open to the Public:** 10 AM-6 PM Spring through Fall; 10 AM-4 PM Winter

**Closed:** Thanksgiving and Christmas Day

**Admission (1993):** Adult: $3.50 Child: $2.00 (under 3 free)
Senior: $3.00 ($2.50 on Mondays)

**Parking Fee:** None

**Children's Zoo:** Yes **Separate Admission:** No

**Annual Membership:** Keepers Club: $25 (up to 4 persons per visit)
Curators Club: $35 (up to 6 persons per visit)
Directors Club: $50 (up to 6 persons per visit + sponsorship of animal care)

**AAZPA Member:** No

## COLLECTIONS & EXHIBITS

**Collection:** The Zoo's current collection includes the following number of specimens:
Mammals: 65 Birds: 60 Reptiles: 15

**Special Exhibits** at Walk in the Wild Zoo include:
Moose Exhibit - one of only a few U.S. zoos that display this species
New 7-Acre Bison/Elk Exhibit
New Alaskan Brown Bear Exhibit

**Future Plans:** Eight Birds of Prey exhibits will be completed by summer, 1993. Completion of the Bison/Elk enclosure is also scheduled for 1993. A new Education Complex, an Information Booth and a project to completely pave the Zoo's walkways to improve handicapped access are all planned.

*This tiger and other species enjoy the Zoo's natural woodlands and open meadows.*
*(photo by Homer Bright; courtesy Walk in the Wild Zoo)*

### CAPTIVE BREEDING & RESEARCH

**Research** at the Zoo includes:
- Nutritional studies of the Alaskan brown bear
- The study of antler growth in elk

### SEASONAL FESTIVALS & PROGRAMS

Egg Hunt/Delta Day - Easter Season
Outdoor Concerts - Summer
Summer Camp for Children
Annual Golf Tournament - June
Country Western Day - July
Food & Brew at the Zoo - early October
Boo at the Zoo - late October
Cross Country Skiing - Winter & early Spring

### FOR MORE INFORMATION

Walk in the Wild Zoo, P.O. Box 14258, Spokane, Washington 99214; 509-924-7221;
Director: James L. Bousquet

# 137 METRO WASHINGTON PARK ZOO
## Portland, Oregon

Founded in 1959, the Metro Washington Park Zoo is home to the largest breeding herd of elephants of any zoo in the world. The 64-acre Park also boasts a fine collection of sculpture and other art work, both indoor and outdoor; an art gallery is located on the grounds.

## VISITOR INFORMATION

**Directions:** The Zoo is two miles west of downtown Portland on Highway 26.

**Open to the Public:** Daily; 9:30 AM-6 PM Summer; closes 5 PM Spring and Fall; closes 4 PM Winter

**Closed:** Christmas Day

**Admission (1993):** Adult: $5.00    Child: $3.00    Senior: $3.50

**Parking Fee:** None

**Children's Zoo:** No (except petting zoo in summer)

**Annual Membership:** Individual: $29    Family: $39

**AAZPA Member:** Yes

## COLLECTIONS & EXHIBITS

**Collection:** The Zoo's current collection includes the following number of species:
    Mammals: 51         Birds: 84         Reptiles: 25
    Amphibians: 9       Fish: 53          Insects: 52

**Special Exhibits** at the Metro Washington Park include the following:
    African Rainforest & Savannah Exhibits
    Underwater Polar Bear Viewing
    Cascades Exhibit - native species of the Pacific Northwest
    Alaskan Tundra Exhibit
    Penguinarium
    Elephant Museum and the largest breeding herd of elephants of any zoo in the world
    Insect Zoo (seasonal)
    Kongo Ranger Station

**Future Plans:** The Elk Meadow Exhibit (Roosevelt's Elk) and the Center for Species Survival are scheduled to open in 1993. The Oregon Exhibit will be completed in 1997.

## CAPTIVE BREEDING & RESEARCH

The Metro Washington Park Zoo has had special **breeding** success with the
following species:

| | | |
|---|---|---|
| Humboldt penguins | Francois langurs | Red pandas |
| Asian elephants | Orangutans | |
| Snow leopards | White-cheeked gibbons | |

**Research projects** based at the Zoo include:
- The study of environmental factors affecting reproductive success
- The study or reproductive biology in elephants
- Environmental enrichment program
- Behavioral biology studies involving endangered species

*The Metro
Washington Park
Zoo is home to the
largest breeding
herd of elephants
of any zoo in the
world.*
*(photo by Jesse Karr;
courtesy Metro
Washington Park Zoo)*

## SEASONAL FESTIVALS & PROGRAMS

Zoobloom Festival - mid April to mid May
Concerts at the Zoo - late June through mid August
Summer Programs - living history program, kongo rangers, Asian naturalist,
sidewalk zoologist (petting area), birds of prey shows
Zooboo (& Halloween train) - last three weeks in October
Zoolights Festival - December

## FOR MORE INFORMATION

The Metro Washington park Zoo, 4001 S.W. Canyon Road, Portland, Oregon 97221;
503-226-1561; Director: Y. Sherry Sheng

# 138 OREGON COAST AQUARIUM INC.
### Newport, Oregon

The Oregon Coast Aquarium, a non-profit educational facility, is dedicated to the display of Oregon's aquatic resources, from the Coast Range forest to the open Pacific Ocean. Phase One, which opened in May, 1992, focuses on coastal and off-shore habitats. Emphasis is placed on the natural history and fragility of these ecosystems.

## VISITOR INFORMATION

**Directions:** The Aquarium is located south of Newport on Yaquina Bay. From Newport, head south across the Yaquina Bay Bridge on Highway 101. Take the first right south of the bridge, crossing back under the highway to the Aquarium.

**Open to the Public:** 9 AM-6 PM, May 15 to October 15; 10 AM-4:30 PM, October 16 to May 14

**Closed:** Christmas Day

**Admission (1993):** Adult: $7.00    Child: $3.00 (4-12)      Senior: $5.00
$5.00 (13-18)
Under 4 Free

**Parking Fee:** None

**Annual Membership:** Individual: $25    Family: $45    Grandparent: $45

**AAZPA Member:** No (new facility)

## COLLECTIONS & EXHIBITS

**Collection:** The Aquarium's current collection includes the following number of species:
Mammals: 3    Birds: 4      Fish: 64
Invertebrates: 100

**Special Exhibits** at the Oregon Coast Aquarium include:

Outdoor Exhibits - 2.5 acres of replicated Oregon coast habitats including rocky pools, cliffs, caves, dunes and tidal pools; these habitats feature sea lions, seals, Alaskan sea otters, giant Pacific octopus and the largest seabird aviary in North America. The sea otters, now extinct in Oregon, were rescued from the Exxon Valdez oil spill. All other species in these exhibits are native to Oregon and can still be found along the Oregon coast.

Indoor Exhibits - within the Aquarium Building are an Introductory Exhibit, a Sandy Shores Habitat, a Rocky Shores Exhibit, a Coastal Waters Exhibit (including a deep-water reef) and a Coastal Wetlands Habitat. The New Currents Exhibit offers changing, hands-on displays. The U.S. West Whale Theater introduces the visitor to the annual migration of gray whales along the Oregon Coast.

**Future Plans:** A second jellyfish exhibit will open in the Coastal Waters Gallery in May, 1993. Future development of the facility is still in the planning stage but will be oriented toward Oregon's inland, freshwater habitats.

## CAPTIVE BREEDING & RESEARCH

Since the facility just opened in 1992, a **breeding** record has not yet been established. However, the Aquarium intends to breed the following species:

Alaskan sea otters                Pigeon Guillemots
Tufted puffins                    Common Murres
Rhinoceros Auklets

The facility will conduct **research** on the captive breeding of seabirds and on other husbandry issues related to the care of aquatic species.

## SEASONAL FESTIVALS AND PROGRAMS

On-site festivities are planned for Memorial Day, the Fourth of July, Labor Day and Halloween.

## FOR MORE INFORMATION

Oregon Coast Aquarium Inc., 2820 S.E. Ferry Slip Road, P.O. Box 2000, Newport, Oregon 97365; 503-867-3123; business office 503-867-3474; Executive Director: Phyllis A. Bell

*Outdoor habitats include rocky cliffs, caves, dunes and tidal pools.*
*(photo courtesy Oregon Coast Aquarium)*

# 139

## WILDLIFE SAFARI
### Winston, Oregon

Located 180 miles south of Portland in a broad, forested valley, Wildlife Safari is the only drive-through wild animal park in Oregon. Its 600 acres are home to 600 animals, representing 100 species, all of which live in natural herds. Nineteen of these species are either endangered or threatened in the wild.

Founded in 1972, Wildlife Safari leads the Western Hemisphere in the captive propagation of cheetahs.

## VISITOR INFORMATION

**Directions:**   From Interstate 5, six miles south of Roseburg, take Exit 119 and head west on Highway 42 toward Winston. Proceed 3 miles and turn right on Lookingglass Road, then right on Safari Road.

**Open to the Public:**   Open 365 days per year; open 8:30 AM in summer, 9 AM fall through spring; closing hours vary from 8 PM in summer to 4 PM in winter; call ahead for current hours.

**Admission (1993):** Adult: $8.95    Child: $5.75    Senior: $7.50
($1.00 charge per vehicle)

**Parking Fee:** None

**Children's Zoo:** Yes    **Separate Admission:** No

**Annual Membership:** Individual: $25    Family: $25

*Visitors drive among free-roaming wildlife; this motorist encounters ostriches and a southern white rhino.*
*(photo courtesy Wildlife Safari)*

**Programs & Tours:** Wildlife Safari sponsors an extensive outreach program, "Zoo-to-You," which brings educational animal demonstrations to schools throughout the State.

**AAZPA Member:** Yes

## COLLECTIONS & EXHIBITS

**Collection:** The Park's current collection includes the following number of species:
Mammals: 62        Birds: 30        Reptiles: 6

**Special Exhibits:** All animals at Wildlife Safari live in natural herds and interact with other species.

**Future Plans:** A new African Elephant/Giraffe Barn was completed in 1992 and the Park plans to add giraffes to its collection in 1993. A new Cougar Exhibit will also open in 1993.

## CAPTIVE BREEDING & RESEARCH

Wildlife Safari leads the Western Hemisphere in the captive **breeding** of cheetahs.

**Research projects** based at Wildlife Safari include:
- Studies on feline reproduction, immunology and pathology
- Research on cheetah genetics
- Behavioral studies of primates, ungulates and felines

## SEASONAL FESTIVALS & PROGRAMS

Spring Celebration - March
Spring Members' Weekend - April
Safari-Pepsi "Run For Their Lives" - early May
Elderhostel - May
Day of Discovery - May; event for disabled visitors
Zoo & Aquarium Month - June
Conservation Day - June
Animalversary Weekend - early October
Elderhostel - October
Boo at the Zoo - late October
Thanksgiving Day Celebration
Wildlights Celebration - December

## FOR MORE INFORMATION

Wildlife Safari, P.O. Box 1600, Winston, Oregon 97496; 503-679-6761; Director: Frank R. Hart

# 140

## ZOO BOISE
### Boise, Idaho

Located on the Boise River in Julia Davis Park, Zoo Boise was founded in 1916. This 10-acre facility places emphasis on the display of North American species and is one of only five American zoos to exhibit moose.

## VISITOR INFORMATION

**Directions:** From I-84, take the Vista Avenue Exit. Head north into Boise. Vista Avenue feeds into Capitol Blvd., which angles to the northeast. Cross the Boise River and turn right on Myrtle Street to the Zoo entrance; the Zoo is in Julia Davis Park.

**Open to the Public:** Daily, 10 AM-5 PM

**Closed:** Thanksgiving, Christmas and New Years Day

**Admission (1993):** Adult: $3.00    Child: $1.50    Senior: $1.75

**Parking Fee:** None

**Children's Zoo:** Yes    **Separate Admission:** No

**Annual Membership** (to Idaho Zoological Society):
Individual: $15    Family: $25    Senior: $7.50

**Programs & Tours:** Group tours are offered; advanced registration is required.

**AAZPA Member:** No

## COLLECTIONS & EXHIBITS

**Collection:** The Zoo's current collection includes the following number of species:
Mammals: 36          Birds: 32          Reptiles: 29
Amphibians: 4         Insect: 1

**Special Exhibits** at Zoo Boise include:
Moose Exhibit - one of only five American zoos to display moose
Otter Exhibit
Birds of Prey Aviary
Wolf Grottos

**Future Plans:** A Gift Shop and Education Center are planned for 1994.

## CAPTIVE BREEDING & RESEARCH

**Research projects** based at Zoo Boise include:
- Windmills and Birds of Prey; a cooperative study with Boise State University

## SEASONAL FESTIVALS & PROGRAMS

Zoo Days - third weekend in May
Feast for the Beast - mid August
Boo at the Zoo - Saturday before or on Halloween
Claus & Paws - Sunday before Christmas

## FOR MORE INFORMATION

Zoo Boise, 1104 Royal Blvd., Boise, Idaho 83706; 208-384-4230; Director: David Wayne

# 141 TAUTPHAUS PARK ZOO
## Idaho Falls, Idaho

Proclaimed "the best little zoo in the West," the Tautphaus Park Zoo was established in the 1920s. The 15-acre facility supported by the Tautphaus Park Zoological Society, plans to open three new exhibits in 1993.

## VISITOR INFORMATION

**Directions:** The Zoo is located in south-central Idaho Falls. From Yellowstone Avenue, turn east on 17th St. and then south on Boulevard to Tautphaus Park.

**Open to the Public:** 9 AM-7:30 PM Memorial Day to Labor Day; 9 AM-4:30 PM mid April to Memorial Day and Labor Day to mid October.

**Closed:** mid October to mid April

**Admission (1993):** Adult: $1.00    Child: $.25 (4-12)   $.50 (13-17)

**Parking Fee:** None

**Children's Zoo:** Yes    **Separate Admission:** No

**Annual Membership:** Individual: $25    Family: $40    Senior: $15

**AAZPA Member:** No

## COLLECTIONS & EXHIBITS

**Collection:** The Zoo's current collection includes the following number of species:
Mammals: 23          Birds: 27          Reptiles: 3

**Special Exhibits** at the Tautphaus Park Zoo include:
Giant Aldabra Tortoise Exhibit - new in 1992
Little Asia - home to Muntjac deer, Demoiselle cranes and Mandarin ducks
African Plains Exhibit
Bonneville Civitans Club Children's Zoo - features zebu cattle, pot-bellied pigs and karakul sheep
Idaho Pond Exhibit - native waterfowl and plants
Rain Forest Aviary - includes keel-billed toucans

**Future Plans:** Phase 1 of the Primate Center (Ring-tailed lemurs), a Spectacled Bear Exhibit and a Serval Exhibit are all scheduled to open in 1993. Phase 2 of the Primate Center (Gibbons) is slated for completion in 1994.

## SEASONAL FESTIVALS & PROGRAMS

Dr. Doolittle Days - late June
Fall Free Appreciation Day - late September

## FOR MORE INFORMATION

Tautphaus Park Zoo, P.O. Box 50220, 2725 Carnival Way, Idaho Falls, Idaho 83405; 208-529-1470; Director: William Gersonde

# 142

## ZOO MONTANA, INC.
### Billings, Montana

This 70-acre zoological park, scheduled to open in 1993, will be the newest zoo in the country. The zoo will feature Northern Hemisphere species, displayed in naturalized exhibits.

## VISITOR INFORMATION

**Directions:**  From Interstate 90, take Exit 446. Proceed west on King Avenue and then south on Shiloh Road to the Zoo.

**Open to the Public:** Daily, hours pending

**Closed:** Thanksgiving and Christmas Day

**Admission:** Fees not yet determined

**Parking Fee:** None

**Children's Zoo:** Yes

**Annual Membership:** Individual: $15     Family: $25

**AAZPA Member:** No (new facility)

## COLLECTIONS & EXHIBITS

**Initial Exhibits** at Zoo Montana will include:
Otter/Waterfowl Exhibit
Siberian Tiger Exhibit
Homestead House
Sensory Garden

## SEASONAL FESTIVALS & PROGRAMS

Christmas Tree Mulch - January
ZooGrass Festival - June
Boo at the Zoo - October 31

## FOR MORE INFORMATION

Zoo Montana Inc., 2100 South Shiloh Road, Billings, Montana 59106; 406-652-8100; Director: Dr. Bill Torgerson

# 143

## HONOLULU ZOO
### Honolulu, Hawaii

Blessed with a year-round tropical climate, the Honolulu Zoo is but a short distance from the surf of Waikiki. Covering 42 acres, the park was founded in 1947.

## VISITOR INFORMATION

**Directions:** Take the H-1 Freeway east to Exit 25-A (King St.); stay in the second lane from the right (Harding Ave.) and turn right at Kapahulu Avenue. Drive approximately 1.4 miles and turn left into the metered lot just before Kalakaua Avenue and the beach.

**Open to the Public:** Daily; 8:30 AM-4:00 PM

**Closed:** Christmas and New Years Day

**Admission (1993):** Adult: $3.00    Child: Free with adult

**Parking Fee:** Metered lot, $.25/hour

**Children's Zoo:** Yes    **Separate Admission:** No

**Annual Membership:** Individual: $20    Family: $30    Senior: $15

**AAZPA Member:** Yes

## COLLECTIONS & EXHIBITS

**Collection:** The Zoo's current collection includes the following number of species:
   Mammals: 44        Birds: 141        Reptiles: 63
   Amphibians: 7      Fish: 4

**Special Exhibits** at the Honolulu Zoo include:
   Hawaiian Forest Bird Display
   Galapagos Tortoise Display
   Bird of Paradise Exhibit

**Future Plans:** Phase II of the African Savannah Exhibit will open in 1993. Phase I of a tropical forest exhibit will be completed in 1994 with Phase II scheduled in 1995. Phase I of the Islands Exhibit is slated for 1996.

## CAPTIVE BREEDING & RESEARCH

The Honolulu Zoo has had special **breeding** success with the following species:
   Golden lion tamarins            African spur-thighed tortoises
   Superb bird of paradise         Blue-tongued skinks
   Tawny frogmouths                Prehensile tail skinks

**Research programs** at the Honolulu Zoo include:
- Artificial insemination of Asian elephants
- Hawaiian forest bird breeding program

## SEASONAL FESTIVALS & PROGRAMS

Zoo & Aquarium Month - June; special presentations

## FOR MORE INFORMATION

The Honolulu Zoo, 151 Kapahulu Avenue, Honolulu, Hawaii 96816; 808-971-7171; Director: Don G. Davis

# 144     WAIKIKI AQUARIUM
## Honolulu, Hawaii

Administered by the University of Hawaii's School of Ocean and Earth Sciences and Technology, the Waikiki Aquarium, established in 1904, is the third oldest aquarium in the United States. The facility is home to over 260 species of marine life and its exhibits depict the natural history of the mid-Pacific region.

## VISITOR INFORMATION

**Directions:** The Waikiki Aquarium is located on the Pacific Ocean in Waikiki's Kapiolani Park. From downtown Honolulu or from the Honolulu International Airport, take the H-1 Freeway East. Exit at King Street to Kapahulu Avenue. Follow Kapahulu to the beach, turn left and the Aquarium will be ¼ mile ahead, on the ocean side of Kalakaua Avenue.

**Open to the Public:** Daily, 9 AM-5 PM

**Closed:** Thanksgiving and Christmas Day

**Admission (1993):** Adult: $4.50    Child: Under 12 Free    Senior: $3.50

**Parking Fee:** None (limited parking on-site)

**Annual Membership:** Individual: $35    Family: $35    Senior/Student: $20

**Programs & Tours:** The Aquarium offers a wide variety of educational programs for children, adults and families. Members of the "Friends of the Waikiki Aquarium" receive advance notice of these programs through bulletins and the Aquarium's bimonthly newsletter, *Kilo i'a*.

**AAZPA Member:** Yes

*The Hawaiian
Monk Seal is an
endangered species.*
*(photo by Thomas Kelly;
courtesy of
Waikiki Aquarium)*

## COLLECTIONS & EXHIBITS

**Collection:** The Aquarium's current collection includes the following number of species:

| | | |
|---|---|---|
| Mammals: 1 | Reptiles: 2 | Fish: 177 |
| Mollusks: 15 | Other Invertebrates: 80 | |

Live exhibit galleries at the Waikiki Aquarium relate the natural history of the mid-Pacific region: Hawaiian Waters and Man, Hawaiian Marine Habitats, Hunters of the Reef, Diversity and Adaptations and South Pacific Marine Life.

**Special Exhibits** include:

Edge of the Reef - a living coral reef ecosystem; visitors are invited to touch sea creatures

Coastal Gardens - a collection of rare and endangered Hawaiian coastal plants

Tapestry of Life in the Sea - an introduction to marine ecology with emphasis on Hawaiian plants and animals

The Reef Machine - recreation of a living coral reef

Chambered Nautilus and Nautilus Nursery

Mahimahi Hatchery - a working aquaculture research exhibit where these oceanic fish are raised

Micronesian Reef Builders Exhibit

Giant Clams Exhibit

Hawaiian Monk Seals - an exhibit of this endangered species

SeaVision Theatre

**Future Plans:**   The Waikiki Aquarium was closed for six months, beginning in October, 1992, in order to complete an extensive, $2.5 million renovation.

New exhibits, all scheduled to open in June, 1993, include a Hawaiian Monk Seal Habitat, Hawaiian Marine Communities, Evolutionary Journey of Hawaii's Marine Life, Diversity and Adaptation of Hawaii's Marine Life, South Pacific Communities, Hawaiian Fisheries and Conservation and the Cephalopod Gallery.

## CAPTIVE BREEDING & RESEARCH

The Waikiki Aquarium has had special **breeding** success with the following species:
Chambered Nautilus
Mahimahi (also known as dorado or dolphinfish)
Harlequin shrimp

**Research projects** based at the Aquarium include:
- Studies on Indo-Pacific reef building, coral husbandry and propagation
- Research on Chambered Nautilus husbandry and propagation
- Mahimahi husbandry and propagation; aquaculture and stock enhancement

## SEASONAL FESTIVALS & PROGRAMS

Seasonal classes, workshops and field trips (year round)
Annual Natural History Lecture Series - February to April

## FOR MORE INFORMATION

Waikiki Aquarium, 2777 Kalakaua Avenue, Honolulu, Hawaii 96815; 808-923-9741;
Director: Dr. Bruce A. Carlson

# 145     SEA LIFE PARK HAWAII
### Waimanalo, Hawaii

Located at the eastern tip of Oahu, this 60-acre facility, founded in 1964, participates in several conservation programs. Its new Monk Seal Care Center, opened in cooperation with the National Marine Fisheries, takes in stranded, injured or orphaned monk seals, eventually returning these endangered animals to their native, Hawaiian habitat.

Waimea Falls Park, on Oahu's North Shore, is a "sister attraction" of Sea Life Park Hawaii. The Park features 1800 acres of tropical gardens, historical sites and cultural displays.

## VISITOR INFORMATION

**Directions:**   From Honolulu, follow Highway H-1 east. Continue east on the Kanalianaole Highway (Route 72) to Makapuu Point at the eastern-most tip of Oahu.

**Open to the Public:** 365 days per year; 9:30 AM-5 PM; open until 10 PM on Fridays
**Admission (1993):** Adult: $14.95 + tax    Child: $2.95 + tax (4-5) $7.95 + tax (6-12)
Senior: $10.95 + tax
**Parking Fee:** None
**Annual Membership:** Not available
**Programs & Tours:** Behind-the-Scenes tours, mini-lectures and animal shows are offered daily. An on-site Pacific Whaling Museum is free to visitors.
**AAZPA Member:** Yes

## COLLECTIONS & EXHIBITS

**Collection:** The Park's current collection includes the following number of species:
Mammals: 7          Birds: 2          Reptiles: 3
Fish: 145          Invertebrates: 95
**Special Exhibits** at Sea Life Park Hawaii include:
Hawaiian Reef Tank - this 300,000 gallon aquarium is home to 4000 specimens of marine life, including sharks, rays and moray eels
Sea Lion Feeding Pool - visitors are permitted to feed herring to this colony of sea lions
Bird Sanctuary - features oceanic birds of Hawaii, including red-footed and brown boobies, gooney birds and iwa birds
Turtle Lagoon - includes several species of sea turtles; over 1000 eggs have hatched here and the young turtles have been released into the wild
Rocky Shores - a recreation of the intertidal zone; dynamic wave action simulates the coastal habitat
Hawaiian Monk Seal Care Center - home to this endangered seal
Penguin Habitat - a breeding colony of Humboldt penguins native to South America
Touch Pool - a "hands-on" exhibit

## CAPTIVE BREEDING & RESEARCH

Sea Life Park Hawaii has had special **breeding** success with the following species:
California sea lions
Humboldt penguins
Pacific & Atlantic bottlenose dolphins
As mentioned above, the Hawaiian Monk Seal Care Center, a cooperative effort with the National Marine Fisheries, is located at the Park. The Sea Life Park also participates in Earthtrust, the coordinating agency for DriftNetwork; this project monitors and exposes the use of driftnets, a practice outlawed by the United Nations.

## SEASONAL FESTIVALS & PROGRAMS

A variety of special events are held at Sea Life Park Hawaii throughout the year. "Kamaaina Night," every Friday, is a celebration of Hawaiian music; performances begin at 8:30 PM at the Sea Lion Cafe and are free to Park visitors.

## FOR MORE INFORMATION

Sea Life Park Hawaii; Makapuu Point, Waimanalo, Hawaii 96795-1897; 808-259-7933; General Manager: Robert L. Moore
Waimea Falls Park, Waimea Bay; 808-923-8448 or 808-638-8511.

146. **Sequoia Park Zoo** (Eureka, California)
147. **Sacramento Zoo** (Sacramento, California)
148. **Marine World Africa USA** (Vallejo, California)
149. **Micke Grove Zoo** (Lodi, California)
150. **Steinhart Aquarium** (San Francisco, California)
151. **San Francisco Zoological Gardens**
     (San Francisco, California)
152. **The Oakland Zoo in Knowland Park**
     (Oakland, California)
153. **Applegate Park Zoo** (Merced, California)
154. **Monterey Bay Aquarium** (Monterey, California)
155. **Chaffee Zoological Gardens of Fresno** (Fresno, California)
156. **Charles Paddock Zoo** (Atascadero, California)
157. **Santa Barbara Zoological Gardens**
     (Santa Barbara, California)
158. **Los Angeles Zoo** (Los Angeles, California)
159. **Santa Ana Zoo** (Santa Ana, California)
160. **The Living Desert** (Palm Desert, California)
161. **San Diego Wild Animal Park** (Escondido, California)
162. **San Diego Zoo** (San Diego, California)
163. **Sea World of California** (San Diego, California)
164. **Tracy Aviary** (Salt Lake City, Utah)
165. **Utah's Hogle Zoo** (Salt Lake City, Utah)
166. **Denver Zoological Gardens** (Denver, Colorado)
167. **Cheyenne Mountain Zoo** (Colorado Springs, Colorado)
168. **Pueblo Zoo** (Pueblo, Colorado)
169. **Navajo Nation Zoological & Botanical Park**
     (Window Rock, Arizona)
170. **Wildlife World Zoo** (Litchfield Park, Arizona)
171. **Phoenix Zoo** (Phoenix, Arizona)
172. **Arizona-Sonora Desert Museum** (Tucson, Arizona)
173. **Reid Park Zoo** (Tucson, Arizona)

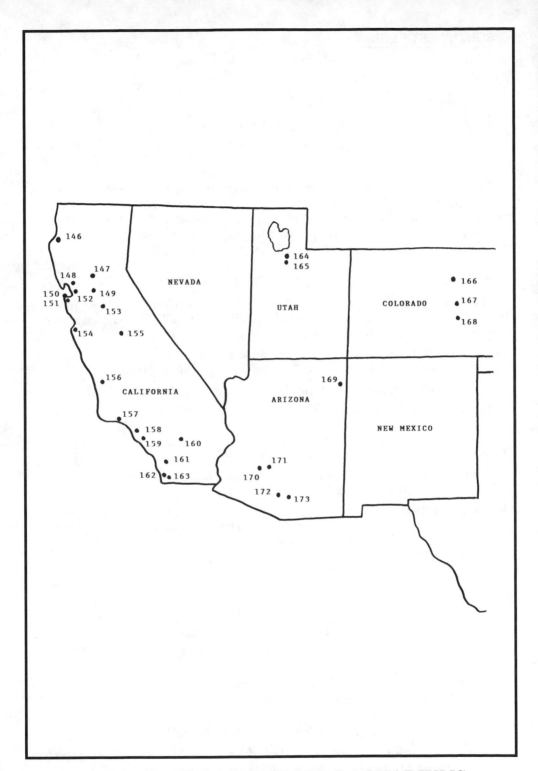

# SOUTHWEST REGION ZOOS & AQUARIUMS

# 146

## SEQUOIA PARK ZOO
### Eureka, California

Graced by tall redwoods, the Sequoia Park Zoo enjoys one of the most picturesque settings in America. This facility, founded in 1907 and operated by the City of Eureka, places emphasis on visitor education. The Sequoia Park Zoological Society, established in 1983, funds construction, renovation and maintenance of the Zoo's naturalistic exhibits.

## VISITOR INFORMATION

**Directions:** From U.S. 101, turn east on Harris St. (or south on H Street and then east on Harris). Proceed east on Harris St. to W Street and turn right; the Zoo will be a short distance, on your right.

**Open to the Public:** 10 AM-7 PM, Tues.-Sun., June to August;
10 AM-5 PM, Tues.-Sun., September to May.

**Closed:** Mondays; however, if a holiday falls on a Monday, the Zoo is open.

**Admission Fee:** Donations accepted

**Parking Fee:** None

**Children's Zoo:** Yes (mid June to September)

**Annual Membership** (to Sequoia Park Zoological Society):
Individual: $10      Family: $15

**Programs & Tours:** The Zoo offers a variety of educational programs, including guided tours, adult and youth classes, outreach programs and a curriculum book for school field trips.

**AAZPA Member:** No

## COLLECTIONS & EXHIBITS

**Collection:** The Zoo's current collection includes the following number of species:
Mammals: 40        Birds: 25        Reptiles: 4
Amphibians: 5       Invertebrates: 2

**Special Exhibits** at the Sequoia Park Zoo include:
Nancy Hilfiker Aviary - a walk-through aviary
Columbian brown-headed spider monkey (breeding colony)

## CAPTIVE BREEDING & RESEARCH

The Sequoia Park Zoo has had special **breeding** success with the following species:
Columbian brown-headed spider monkey

The Zoo is a member of the Zoo Conservation Outreach Group which helps to support Central American zoos by raising funds, providing information and participating in exchange programs. The Sequoia Park Zoological Society is also providing support for Dr. Richard Tenaza's work on the Mentawai Islands, off Sumatra. This project is an effort to protect rainforest habitat, home to several endangered primates.

### SEASONAL FESTIVALS & PROGRAMS
Whale Watching Celebration - early spring
Travel Adventures - periodic expeditions sponsored by the Sequoia Park Zoological Society

### FOR MORE INFORMATION
Sequoia Park Zoo, 3414 W Street, Eureka, California 95503; 707-442-6552; Superintendent: Jack Bellinger

# 147 SACRAMENTO ZOO
### Sacramento, California

Set among 200-year-old oak trees, the Sacramento Zoo was established in 1927. This 15-acre facility, part of a 230-acre Park, takes part in 18 Species Survival Plans. Its Chimpanzee Exhibit was hailed by Jane Goodall as one of the best in the country and the Zoo is one of only 14 U.S. zoos to participate in her Chimpanzoo Project.

### VISITOR INFORMATION
**Directions:** The Zoo is located 3 miles south of downtown Sacramento in William Land Park. From Interstate 5, take the Sutterville Road Exit. The Zoo is ¼ mile east of the Interstate.

**Open to the Public:** Daily, 10 AM-4 PM

**Closed:** Christmas Day

**Admission (1993):** Add $.50 on weekends and holidays.
     Adult: $3.50     Child: $2.00     Senior: Discount with local senior card

**Parking Fee:** None

**Children's Zoo:** The Zoo manages "Fairytale Town" across from the Zoo. Nursery Rhyme sets feature endangered domestic stock (among other animals).
Adult: $2.50 weekend / $2.25 weekday
Child: $2.00 weekend / $1.75 weekday

**Annual Membership:** Individual + Guest: $33     Family: $39     Grandparents: $33

**Programs & Tours:** The Zoo offers a variety of educational programs including tours, lectures, workshops and outreach programs.

**AAZPA Member:** Yes

## COLLECTIONS & EXHIBITS

**Collection:** The Zoo's current collection includes the following number of species:

    Mammals: 40          Birds: 36          Reptiles: 40

    Amphibians: 6       Invertebrates: 2

**Special Exhibits** at the Sacramento Zoo include:

    Rare Feline Complex - houses endangered South American cats; also home to birds and primates

    Reptile House - one of the finest in the country

    Sumatran Orangutan Exhibit

    Chimpanzee Exhibit - hailed as one of the finest in the U.S.

**Future Plans:** A Lake Victoria Exhibit, a Gift Shop, and Exhibits for the Titi Monkey and Two-toed Sloth are all scheduled for completion in 1993. A Madagascar Complex (to include a Lemur Exhibit) will open in 1995.

*Sumatran Orangutan*
*(photo by Carol Lofton, Distinctive Images Photography,*
*Sacramento, California, Sacramento Zoo Photographer)*

## CAPTIVE BREEDING & RESEARCH

The Sacramento Zoo has had special **breeding** success with the following species:

| | |
|---|---|
| Grevy's zebra | River otters |
| Sumatran orangutans | Siberian tigers |
| Francoi's monkeys | San Francisco garter snakes |
| Golden-bellied mangabeys | Arabian oryx |
| Thick-billed parrots | American flamingos |
| White-handed gibbons | Ne Ne geese |
| Wallaroos | Dumeril's ground boas |

**Research projects** based at the Sacramento Zoo include:
- Participation in 18 Species Survival Plans of the AAZPA
- Coordinates SSP for the endangered thick-billed parrot
- Studbook keeper for mangabeys
- Participation in Chimpanzoo (administered by Jane Goodall Institute)

## SEASONAL FESTIVALS & PROGRAMS

King of Feasts (gourmet food & wine tasting) - last weekend in June
Ice Cream Safari - last weekend in July
Conservation Celebration - September
Zoo Zoom (5K & 10K Run) - October

## FOR MORE INFORMATION

Sacramento Zoo, 3930 W. Land Park Drive, Sacramento, California 95822; 916-264-5166; Director: Maria Baker

# 148 MARINE WORLD AFRICA USA
### Vallejo, California

Marine World Africa USA is the only combination wildlife park and oceanarium in the country. Founded in 1968 and operated by the nonprofit Marine World Foundation, the Park moved to its current 160-acre site in 1986. Designed to promote understanding and appreciation of the natural world, the Park uses animal shows, educational exhibits and "close encounter" attractions to introduce visitors to a fantastic variety of wildlife, from sharks to butterflies.

## VISITOR INFORMATION

**Directions:** The Park is located 30 miles northeast of San Francisco, just off Interstate 80. Follow I-80 to Highway 37 (Marine World Parkway).

Alternatively, catch the Red & White Fleet's high-speed catamaran ferry at Pier 41 in San Francisco for a 1-hour excursion to the Park.

*Trainer Steve Johnson introduces visitors to Judy, a 25-year-old Asian elephant at Marine World Africa USA's "Elephant Encounter."*
*(photo courtesy Marine World Africa USA)*

**Open to the Public:** Daily, 9:30 AM-6 PM during the Summer; open Wednesday to Sunday, 9:30 AM-5 PM the remainder of the year.

**Closed:** Monday & Tuesday, Fall through Spring; also closed Thanksgiving and Christmas Day

**Admission (1993):** Adult: $21.95    Child: $15.95    Senior: $18.95

**Parking Fee:** $3.00

**Children's Zoo:** Yes    **Separate Admission:** No

**Annual Membership:** Adult: $49    Child: $40    Senior: $45

**Programs & Tours:** Seven major animal shows are presented. "Elephant Encounter" and a giraffe feeding area permit close encounters with these large mammals. The Park also sponsors lectures, workshops, field trips and outreach programs.

**AAZPA Member:** Yes

## COLLECTIONS & EXHIBITS

**Collection:** The Park's current collection includes the following number of species:

| | | |
|---|---|---|
| Mammals: 52 | Birds: 125 | Reptiles: 37 |
| Amphibians: 3 | Fish: 141 | Insects: 800 |
| Mollusks: 12 | Other Invertebrates: 71 | |

**Special Exhibits** at Marine World Africa USA include:

Butterfly World - the only free-flight butterfly habitat west of the Mississippi; includes species from around the world.

Lorikeet Aviary - visitors who venture into this walk-through exhibit are permitted to feed those colorful birds and often become temporary perches for the gregarious residents.

Tiger Island - home to Bengal tigers

Shark Experience - a moving walkway takes visitors through a clear, acrylic tunnel, introducing them to residents of a coral reef habitat; this 300,000 gallon exhibit opened in May, 1992.

**Future Plans:** "World of Dinosaurs" will be at the Park from April through October, 1993.

## CAPTIVE BREEDING & RESEARCH

Marine World Africa USA has had special **breeding** success with the following species:

| | |
|---|---|
| Bottle-nosed dolphins | Bengal tigers |
| Cuttlefish | Bactrian camels |
| Chimpanzees | |

**Research projects** based at Marine World Africa USA include:
- Analysis of diet in river otters; part of conservation program
- Auditory studies in dolphins and whales
- Killer whale research conducted by Dr. David Bain
- Artificial insemination of dolphins

## SEASONAL FESTIVALS & PROGRAMS

President's Day Celebration - February
Boy Scout Days - March
Camp Fire Days - April
Spring Break Celebration - April
Girl Scout Days - May
Annual Budweiser Intl. Water Ski Championship - June
Pepsi Fourth of July Celebration
Seniors/Grandparents Days - September & October
Safeway Snow World - mid December to early January

## FOR MORE INFORMATION

Marine World Africa USA, Marine World Parkway, Vallejo, California 94589; 707-644-4000, Info: 707-643-ORCA; President: Michael B. Demetrios

# 149

## MICKE GROVE ZOO
### Lodi, California

Located in a picturesque regional park and shaded by large oak trees, the Micke Grove Zoo was established in 1957. The Zoo shares the site with a Japanese garden, an historical museum and a small amusement park.

## VISITOR INFORMATION

**Directions:** Take the Armstrong Road Exit from Highway 99 and follow signs to the Zoo.

**Open to the Public:** Daily, 10 AM-5 PM; open until 7 PM on Saturday and Sunday during summer months.

**Closed:** Christmas Day

**Admission (1993):** Adult: $1.00    Child: $.25    Teens/Seniors: $.50

**Parking Fee:** $2 weekdays, $3 weekends

**Children's Zoo:** No

**Annual Membership:** Individual: $20    Family: $40    Senior: $15

**Programs & Tours:** The Zoo offers a wide variety of community educational programs.

**AAZPA Member:** Yes

## COLLECTIONS & EXHIBITS

**Collection:** The Zoo's current collection includes the following number of species:

| | | |
|---|---|---|
| Mammals: 31 | Birds: 37 | Reptiles: 13 |
| Amphibians: 1 | Insects: 1 | Fish: 1 |
| Other Invertebrates: 1 | | |

**Special Exhibits** at the Micke Grove Zoo include:

Island Lost in Time - focuses on the fauna and flora of Madagascar; features ruffed lemurs.

Mediterranean Waystations Aviary - exhibits birds native to the Mediterranean region and those that migrate through the area.

Sea Lion Exhibit - most of the sea lions in this colony were born at the Micke Grove Zoo.

**Future Plans:** A Mountain Lion Habitat, to open in 1993, is part of the Zoo's master-plan for development.

## CAPTIVE BREEDING & RESEARCH

The Micke Grove Zoo has had special **breeding** success with the following species:

| | |
|---|---|
| Snow leopard | Ruffed lemur |
| Cotton-top tamarin | Bali mynah |
| Sea lion | Green-winged macaw |
| White-handed gibbon | Prevost squirrel |

*A black & white lemur from the Zoo's "Island Lost in Time" Exhibit
which features flora and fauna native to Madagascar.
(photo courtesy Micke Grove Zoo)*

**Research** based at the Micke Grove Zoo includes:
- Cracid management and conservation

## SEASONAL FESTIVALS & PROGRAMS

Seal Day - March
Easter Eggsperience/Bunny Run - March/April
Senior Awareness Day - May
Conservation Day - June
"Groovin' in the Grove" - August
Howl-o-Ween at the Zoo - October
Winterfest at the Zoo - December

## FOR MORE INFORMATION

Micke Grove Zoo, 11793 N. Micke Grove Road, Lodi, California 95240; 209-953-8840,
209-331-7270; Director: Ken Nieland

# 150

## STEINHART AQUARIUM
### San Francisco, California

Established in 1923, the Steinhart Aquarium is located in Golden Gate Park. The four-acre facility is known for its research on the breeding behavior of endangered penguins and for its collection of bioluminescent fish.

## VISITOR INFORMATION

**Directions:** The Aquarium is located in Golden Gate Park, in northwest San Francisco. Route 1 crosses the park; follow signs to the Aquarium.

**Open to the Public:** Every day of the year; 10 AM-7 PM Summer; 10 AM-5 PM remainder of the year

**Admission (1993):** Adult: $6.00    Child: $1.50    Senior: $3.00

**Parking Fee:** None

**Annual Membership:** Individual: $35    Family: $45    Senior: $25

**AAZPA Member:** No

## COLLECTIONS & EXHIBITS

**Collection:** The Aquarium's current collection includes the following number of species:

| | | |
|---|---|---|
| Mammals: 2 | Birds: 1 | Reptiles: 180 |
| Amphibians: 60 | Mollusks: 10 | Fish: 350 |
| Other Invertebrates: 100 | | |

**Special Exhibits** at the Steinhart Aquarium include:
  A Roundabout Pelagic Tank
  A Touch Tidepool
  Living Coral Reef
  Reptile & Amphibian Swamp - as is evident in the species listing, the Steinhart
    Aquarium houses a large number of reptiles and Amphibians
  Penguin Environment
  Bioluminescent Fish Displays

**Future Plans:** A sequential renovation of the entire facility is currently underway; completion is anticipated by 1996-1997.

## CAPTIVE BREEDING & RESEARCH

The Steinhart Aquarium has had special **breeding** success with the following species:
    Black-footed penguins
    African & New World cichlids

**Research** at the facility includes:
    - Study of breeding behavior of endangered penguins and fish
    - Study of behavior of bioluminescent fishes

## SEASONAL FESTIVALS & PROGRAMS
Gary Larson 5K/10K "Run to the Far Side" - the Sunday after Thanksgiving

## FOR MORE INFORMATION
The Steinhart Aquarium, Golden Gate Park, San Francisco, California 94118; 415-750-7247; Director: Dr. John E. McCosker

*Face to face with a Pacific white-sided dolphin at Steinhart Aquarium*
*(photo by Susan Middleton, © California Academy of Science, 1984)*

# 151 SAN FRANCISCO ZOOLOGICAL GARDENS
### San Francisco, California

Established in 1929, the San Francisco Zoological Gardens welcomes over 1 million visitors each year. Covering 125 acres, 65 of which are developed, the Zoo harbors one of only six Insectariums in the U.S. and is home to the most successful breeding colony of captive Magellanic penguins in the world. The Zoo also boasts one of the oldest wooden carousels in the country.

## VISITOR INFORMATION
**Directions:** From I-280, take the Westlake Exit West. Turn right on Skyline and then left on Sloat.

**Open to the Public:** 365 days per year, 10 AM-5 PM

**Admission (1993):** Adult: $6.50   Child: $1.00 (3-11) / $3.00 (12-15)   Senior: $3.00

**Parking Fee:** None

**Children's Zoo:** Yes     **Separate Admission:** $1.00

**Annual Membership** (to San Francisco Zoological Society):
   Individual: $35      Family: $45

**Programs & Tours:** The Education Department offers a variety of programs including guided tours, wildlife demonstrations, summer school classes, outreach programs (Zoomobile) and on-site exhibits.

**AAZPA Member:** Yes

## COLLECTIONS & EXHIBITS

**Collection:** The Zoo's current collection includes the following number of species (38 of which are threatened or endangered in the wild).

|                          |              |
| ------------------------ | ------------ |
| Mammals: 103             | Birds: 150   |
| Reptiles & Amphibians: 31 | Insects: 67 |

**Special Exhibits** at the San Francisco Zoological Gardens include:
   Koala Crossing - this open habitat, landscaped with eucalyptus trees, opened in 1985
   Gorilla World - one of the largest naturalistic gorilla exhibits in the world
   Thelma & Henry Doelger Primate Discovery Center - exhibits 15 rare and endangered species of monkeys and prosimians in naturalized settings; also home to the Phoebe Hearst Discovery Hall which features 23 interactive exhibits.
   Penguin Island - designed to mimic the Patagonian coast, this exhibit houses the world's most successful breeding colony of captive Magellanic penguins
   Musk Ox Meadow - this 2.6 acre habitat features a herd of rare white-fronted musk oxen
   Greater One-Horned Rhinoceros Exhibit - home to a pair of these endangered rhinos from Nepal
   Children's Zoo - this 5-acre park features The Insect Zoo (one of only 6 Insectariums in the country), a Barnyard (petting zoo), the Animal Nursery, the Nature Trail and displays of Native American Animals.

**Future Plans:** The San Francisco Zoological Gardens has initiated a ZOO 2000 Plan which will emphasize naturalistic exhibits, visitor education and wildlife conservation. Exhibits will be grouped into 5 zoogeographic regions and will be designed to permit visitors to observe behind-the-scenes animal care. "Animal survival strategies" will be the unifying theme for future development.

   Phase I of the ZOO 2000 Plan will include 22 renovation projects, a Feline Breeding Center for small cats, a Leopards of Asia Exhibit, an Orangutan Field Station and development of the Zoo's first expansion area: the African Savanna.

## CAPTIVE BREEDING & RESEARCH

The San Francisco Zoological Gardens has had special **breeding** success with the following species:

Black & White casqued hornbills - first American zoo to breed these endangered birds

Magellanic penguins - most successful captive colony in the world; 100th chick hatched in 1991

Black rhinoceros - home to longest lived and most prolific pair in captivity (until male died in 1991)

Snow leopards - most successful captive breeding program in the world

African wild dogs

Primate species

White-fronted musk oxen - first captive births of this species

The Zoo participates in 16 Species Survival Plans, administered by the AAZPA. The Avian Conservation Center has raised and released more than 100 birds of prey and cooperates in the Pacific Bald Eagle Recovery Plan. The Ecosystem Survival Plan, a joint effort with the Nature Conservancy, promotes global conservation efforts through acquisition of threatened habitat; this program is partly funded by the "Conservation Parking Meter" located at the lion grottos.

## SEASONAL FESTIVALS & PROGRAMS

ZooFest - Spring
Summer Programs - a wide variety of activities
ZooRun - January

## FOR MORE INFORMATION

San Francisco Zoological Gardens, Sloat Blvd. at 45th Ave., San Francisco, California 94132; 415-753-7080; Director: David Anderson

# 152 THE OAKLAND ZOO IN KNOWLAND PARK
## Oakland, California

The Oakland Zoo, founded in 1922, is located in Knowland Park, a hilly, wooded preserve on the eastern edge of the City. The Zoo has embarked on an ambitious, 15-year renovation and expansion project. New development will group exhibits into three areas: Rainforests of the World, the African Savanna and California 1820; the latter will feature species native to the State.

## VISITOR INFORMATION

**Directions:** The Zoo is located in Knowland Park along the southeastern edge of the City. From Highway 580, take the Golf Links/98th Avenue Exit. Follow Golf Links Road to the Zoo.

**Open to the Public:** Daily, 10 AM-4 PM; hours extended on weekends and holidays in summer.

**Closed:** Thanksgiving and Christmas

**Admission (1993):** Adult: $4.50    Child: $2.00    Senior: $2.00

**Parking Fee:** $3.00/car, $7.50/bus

**Children's Zoo:** Yes    **Separate Admission:** No

**Annual Membership:** Individual: $30    Family: $40

**Programs & Tours:** The Zoo offers guided tours, educational classes, Zoo Camp and a Zoomobile outreach program.

**AAZPA Member:** Yes

## COLLECTIONS & EXHIBITS

**Collection:** The Zoo's current collection includes the following number of species:
    Mammals: 32            Birds: 20            Reptiles: 8

**Special Exhibits** at the Oakland Zoo include:
    Mahali Pa Tembo (African Elephant Exhibit) - a naturalized 1-acre exhibit
    African Lion Exhibit - cover 1.5 acres
    African Veldt - this large, natural habitat features 12 species native to Africa
    Hamadryas Baboon Cliff Habitat
    Chimpanzee Rainforest Exhibit

**Future Plans:** The Zoo's 15-year renovation and expansion program will group exhibits into three areas: Rainforests of the World, the African Savanna and California 1820. A California Interpretive Center and an Environmental Education Center are also planned.
    Siamang Island will open in 1993; 1994 will bring a Black Rhino Exhibit, Impala Exhibit and Farican Village. A Breeding Conservation Center will be completed in 1996.

*"Mahali Pa Tembo," the Oakland Zoo's African Elephant Exhibit.*
*(courtesy the Oakland Zoo)*

## CAPTIVE BREEDING & RESEARCH

The Oakland Zoo has had special **breeding** success with the following species:

| | |
|---|---|
| Reticulated giraffe | Chimpanzee |
| Dromedary camel | Tule elk |

The Oakland Zoo participates in Chimpanzoo, administered by the Jane Goodall Institute.

## SEASONAL FESTIVALS & PROGRAMS

Zoo Valentines - February 14
Easter at the Zoo - March/April
World Conservation Day - early June
Native American Pow Wow - August
Boo! at the Zoo - October 31

## FOR MORE INFORMATION

The Oakland Zoo in Knowland Park, 9777 Golf Li .ks Road, Oakland, California 94605; 510-632-9525; Director: Dr. Joel Parrott

# 153 APPLEGATE PARK ZOO
## Merced, California

Donated to the City of Merced by Lewis H. Applegate, Applegate Park became the site of a growing animal menagerie by the 1950s. To provide better homes for these animals the Applegate Park Zoo was constructed in 1961-62. Since that time the Zoo has focused on the display of species native to the Central San Joaquin Valley and nearby Sierra Nevada Mountains.

The Merced Zoological Society was established in 1983 to support Zoo improvements and to provide education programs relating to wildlife conservation.

## VISITOR INFORMATION

**Directions:** From Highway 99, exit onto R Street and drive north; proceed 12 blocks to the Zoo.

**Open to the Public:** Daily, 10 AM-5 PM

**Closed:** Thanksgiving, Christmas and New Years Day

**Admission (1993):** Free; donations accepted.

**Parking Fee:** None

**Children's Zoo:** Yes    **Separate Admission:** $.25/person

**Annual Membership** (to Merced Zoological Society):
Individual: $7.00    Family: $15.00    Student/Senior: $5.00

**Programs & Tours:** The Zoo offers guided tours, summer camp, classroom presentations and mobile zoo outreach programs.

**AAZPA Member:** No

## COLLECTIONS & EXHIBITS

**Collection:** The Zoo's current collection includes the following number of species:
Mammals: 16          Birds: 19          Reptiles: 1

**Special Exhibits** at the Applegate Park Zoo include:
California Species - the Zoo focuses on the display of animals native to the Central San Joaquin Valley and the nearby Sierra Nevada Mountains. Essentially all animals on exhibit are either "non-releasable" specimens raised by humans or surplus animals from other zoos. Further development of the Zoo will ensure that resident animals are displayed in natural habitats.
Petting Zoo - open on weekends, weather permitting

**Future Plans:** A Pacific Flyway/Wetlands Exhibit, a new Red Fox Exhibit, a Songbird Aviary and a Mink Exhibit are planned.

## SEASONAL FESTIVALS & PROGRAMS
Zoo Camp - mid July

## FOR MORE INFORMATION
Applegate Park Zoo, 25th & R Streets, Merced, California 95340; 209-385-6840; Director: Mr. Curtis Royer, Parks & Recreation, Merced

# 154 MONTEREY BAY AQUARIUM
## Monterey, California

Located on historic Cannery Row, the Monterey Bay Aquarium opened in 1978. The 2.2. acre facility serves as the interpretive center for the Monterey Bay National Marine Sanctuary, the 11th federally protected area in the United States. This Sanctuary, centered on Monterey Bay, covers 5300 square miles and contains North America's largest underwater canyon.

The Aquarium is dedicated to stimulating interest, increasing knowledge and promoting stewardship of Monterey Bay and other ocean habitats through public education and scientific research. Commanding a spectacular view of the Bay, the Aquarium acts as its living extension, piping up to 2000 gallons of raw seawater into the exhibit tanks each minute.

## VISITOR INFORMATION
**Directions:** The Aquarium is located on historic Cannery Row, on the northern coast of the Monterey Peninsula. From Highway 1, exit onto Del Monte Avenue and head west; follow the brown directional signs to Cannery Row and the Aquarium.

During Summer and holiday seasons, Waterfront Area Visitor Express shuttles link downtown hotels with the waterfront attractions.

**Open to the Public:** 10 AM-6 PM, daily; opens at 9:30 AM in summer and on holidays

**Closed:** Christmas Day

**Admission (1993):** Adult: $10.50    Child: $4.75    Senior: $7.75

**Parking Fee:** Public lots service the Aquarium and Cannery Row.

**Annual Membership:** Individual: $39    Family: $55    Senior: $29

**Programs & Tours:** Educational programs include tours, classroom and auditorium presentations, workshops, teacher seminars, field trips, curriculum materials and outreach programs (via the Aquaravan).

**AAZPA Member:** Yes

*The Great Tide Pool*
*(© 1990, Monterey Bay Aquarium)*

*The Kelp Forest exhibit is the tallest aquarium exhibit in the world.*
*(© 1992, Monterey Bay Aquarium)*

## COLLECTIONS & EXHIBITS

**Collection:** The Aquarium's current collection includes the following number of species:

Mammals: 1     Birds: 20     Reptiles: 2
Amphibians: 4    Fish: 150     Invertebrates: 233

**Special Exhibits** at the Monterey Bay Aquarium include:

The Kelp Forest - this 3-story kelp forest habitat is the tallest aquarium exhibit in the world.

Monterey Bay Habitats - a collection of Bay habitats from deep granite reefs to encrusted wharf pilings.

Sea Otter Exhibit - this 55,000 gallon habitat has just undergone a six month renovation; otters on exhibit here were either abandoned or injured in the wild.

The Great Tide Pool - blends the Aquarium with the intertidal zone of Monterey Bay; features a variety of fish and tide pool creatures; often visited by sea otters, harbor seals and sea lions.

The Sandy Shore - this walk-through aviary features coastal bird species

Touch Pools - "hands-on" exhibits for young and old alike

**Future Plans:** The "Planet of the Jellies" Exhibit will be at the Aquarium through early September, 1993. A special exhibition on marine life reproduction is scheduled for 1994-1995. A new exhibit wing will open in 1996, expanding the total exhibit space by almost 50%; its main exhibit will be a 1 million gallon, Open Ocean habitat, featuring blue and thresher sharks, ocean sunfish and schooling ocean fish.

## CAPTIVE BREEDING & RESEARCH

The Aquarium has had special **breeding** success with the following species:

Killdeer            Cuttlefish
Ruddy ducks       Surfperches

**Research projects** based at the Monterey Bay Aquarium include:

- the Monterey Bay Aquarium Research Institute studies deep-sea and open ocean systems using the Bay as a living laboratory
- Field studies of kelp forest development
- Research on sea otter behavior
- Research on physiology and husbandry of open ocean and deep-sea animals
- the Aquarium's Sea Otter Rescue & Care Program develops techniques for the care of injured and orphaned sea otters
- Studies on shark growth, aging and nutrition

## FOR MORE INFORMATION

Monterey Bay Aquarium, 886 Cannery Row, Monterey, California 93940; 408-648-4800; Director: Julie Packard

# 155 CHAFFEE ZOOLOGICAL GARDENS OF FRESNO
### Fresno, California

Established in 1920, Chaffee Zoological Gardens is owned and managed by the City of Fresno. This 18-acre Park is beautifully landscaped, interweaving animal habitats and botanical gardens.

## VISITOR INFORMATION

**Directions:** From Highway 99, take either the Belmont Avenue or Olive Avenue Exit. The Zoo is located in Roeding Park, east of Highway 99, between Belmont and Olive Avenues.

**Open to the Public:** 365 days per year; 10 AM-6:30 PM; closes at 5 PM in winter.

**Admission (1993):** Adult: $4.50    Child: $2.00    Senior: $3.00

**Parking Fee:** $1.00

**Children's Zoo:** No

**Annual Membership:** Individual: $20    Family: $35    Senior: $15

**AAZPA Member:** Yes

## COLLECTIONS & EXHIBITS

**Collection:** The Zoo's current collection includes the following number of species:
    Mammals: 49            Birds: 81
    Reptiles: 53           Amphibians: 12

**Special Exhibits** at the Chaffee Zoological Gardens of Fresno include:
    Butterfly/Hummingbird House
    Asian Elephant Breeding Center
    Reptile House - features individual, computer-controlled chambers
    Tropical Rain Forest Habitat

## CAPTIVE BREEDING & RESEARCH

The Chaffee Zoological Gardens of Fresno has had special **breeding** success with the following species:
    Azure poison dart frogs            Flamingos
    Madagascar geckos                  Egrets

The Zoo conducts a variety of **research** on reptiles.

## SEASONAL FESTIVALS & PROGRAMS

Breakfast with the Animals - April
Safari Night - third Saturday in June
Ice Cream ZooFari
Christmas at the Zoo - held in November

## FOR MORE INFORMATION

Chaffee Zoological Gardens of Fresno, 894 West Belmont Ave., Fresno, California 93728-2891; 209-498-4692; Director: Ralph E. Waterhouse

# 156      CHARLES PADDOCK ZOO
## Atascadero, California

Owned by the City of Atascadero and supported by the Zoological Society of San Luis Obispo County, the Charles Paddock Zoo was founded in 1956. The 5-acre Zoo is located in Atascadero Lake Park, a peaceful oasis shaded by groves of oak, sycamore and redwood. Nature lovers can explore the Park on a mile-long trail that circles the Lake and will find over 20 species of birds inhabiting its meadows, woods and wetlands.

## VISITOR INFORMATION

**Directions:** From Highway 1, take the Atascadero/Highway 41 exit in Morro Bay and drive east for 17 miles. The Park and Zoo will be on your right, shortly after entering the city limits.

From Highway 101, take the Morro Bay/Highway 41 exit and drive west for 1.5 miles. The Park and Zoo will be on your left.

**Open to the Public:** Daily, 10 AM-4 PM; remains open until 5 PM from Memorial Day to Labor Day

**Closed:** Thanksgiving, Christmas and New Years Day

**Admission (1993):** Adult: $2.00     Child: $1.00     Senior: $1.25

**Parking Fee:** None

**Children's Zoo:** Yes     **Separate Admission:** No

**Annual Membership:** Contact the Zoological Society of San Luis Obispo County at 805-461-5083.

**Programs & Tours:** The Zoo offers guided tours, educational classes, special presentations and outreach programs.

**AAZPA Member:** Yes

## COLLECTIONS & EXHIBITS

**Collection:** The Zoo's current collection includes the following number of species:
Mammals: 19      Birds: 20
Reptiles: 8       Fish: 3

**Special Exhibits** at the Charles Paddock Zoo include:
Bengal Tiger Habitat
Meerkat Island Exhibit
Children's Zoo - allows close contact with a variety of domestic animals

## CAPTIVE BREEDING & RESEARCH

The Charles Paddock Zoo has had special **breeding** success with the following species:
Arabian oryx
Golden-bellied mangabeys
Bennett's wallabies

**Research** based at the Charles Paddock Zoo includes:
- Research on jaguar species
- Participation in captive breeding and re-introduction of the endangered Arabian oryx

## SEASONAL FESTIVALS & PROGRAMS

Seniors Night - June
Zoo & Aquarium Month - June
Summer Camp
Open House Zoo Jamboree - July
Christmas Caroling - December

## FOR MORE INFORMATION

Charles Paddock Zoo; 9305 Pismo Street, Atascadero, California 93422; 805-461-5080; Director: Alan Metzler

# 157 SANTA BARBARA ZOOLOGICAL GARDENS
## Santa Barbara, California

The Santa Barbara Zoological Gardens, established in 1963, harbors over 10 acres of tropical and succulent gardens, including a superb collection of palms, corals, bananas and cacti; the entire complex spreads across 30 acres.

## VISITOR INFORMATION

**Directions:** Exit U.S. 101 at Cabrillo Blvd. Turn toward the ocean and follow Cabrillo Blvd. around the bird refuge. Ninos Drive will be on your right, at the Sheraton Inn.

**Open to the Public:** Daily; 9 AM-6 PM mid June to Labor Day;
10 AM-5 PM remainder of the year

**Closed:** Thanksgiving Day, Christmas Day

**Admission (1993):** Adult: $5.00     Child: $3.00     Senior: $3.00

**Parking Fee:** None

**Children's Zoo:** Yes     **Separate Admission:** No

**Annual Membership:** Individual: $20     Family: $40

**AAZPA Member:** Yes

## COLLECTIONS & EXHIBITS

**Collection:** The Zoo's current collection includes the following number of species:

| | | |
|---|---|---|
| Mammals: 39 | Birds: 58 | Reptiles: 35 |
| Amphibians: 5 | Fish: 3 | Invertebrates: 2 |

**Special Exhibits** at the Santa Barbara Zoological Gardens include:
Gibbon Island - one of the finest gibbon exhibits in the U.S.
The Nocturnal Hall
African Veldt
Discovery Area
Asian Elephant Exhibit
California Coastal Habitat

**Future Plans:** A North American Habitat is scheduled to open in 1993.

## CAPTIVE BREEDING & RESEARCH

The Santa Barbara Zoological Gardens has had special **breeding** success with the following species:

Giant anteater                     Chilean flamingo
African hedgehog                   Two-toed sloth
Roseate spoonbill

Current **research** at the Santa Barbara Zoological Gardens includes:
- Artificial insemination, Asian elephant
- African hedgehog reproduction

## SEASONAL FESTIVALS & PROGRAMS

Members' Night - mid April
Zoofeast - mid May
Conservation Day - first Saturday in June
Summer Evening Concert Series (planned)
Ice Cream Sunday - Fourth of July
Zoo B Que - September
Zoofari Ball - early October
Free Day - December

## FOR MORE INFORMATION

Santa Barbara Zoological Gardens, 500 Ninos Drive, Santa Barbara, California 93103; 805-962-5339; Director: Ted McToldridge

# 158

## LOS ANGELES ZOO
### Los Angeles, California

Established in 1966, the Los Angeles Zoo is home to 46 endangered species. The exhibits at this 80-acre Zoo are grouped into Continents, placing emphasis on the native habitats of the animals.

The Los Angeles Zoo, in cooperation with the San Diego Zoo & Wild Animal Park, has been instrumental in rescuing the California condor from the brink of extinction. Through a program of captive hatching and rearing, the condor population has increased from 28 to 64 individuals; reintroduction of the species was initiated in January, 1992.

## VISITOR INFORMATION

**Directions:** The Los Angeles Zoo is located at the junction of Interstate 5 (Golden Gate Freeway) and California 134 (Ventura Freeway) in the northern part of Los Angeles. Watch for directional signs.

**Open to the Public:** Daily, 10 AM-5 PM

**Closed:** Christmas Day

**Admission (1993):** Adult: $7.00    Child: $3.00 (under 2 free)    Senior: $5.00

**Parking Fee:** None

**Children's Zoo:** Yes    **Separate Admission:** No

**Annual Membership:** Individual: $35    Family: $45

**Programs & Tours:** The Education Department offers a wide variety of on-site and off-site programs. School Safari brings an educational slide show to regional schools. Other programs include Tours with Topics, World of Birds, Wild in the City, Animals & You, Biomes of the Earth, educational videos and live animal demonstrations.

**AAZPA Member:** Yes

## COLLECTIONS & EXHIBITS

**Collection:** The Los Angeles Zoo is home to 1500 specimens representing 400 species. As noted above, 46 of these species are endangered.

**Special Exhibits** at the Zoo include:

Adventure Island - the Children's Zoo exhibits animals in five habitats (mountain, meadow, cave, shoreline and desert); the facility also includes a nursery and the Pepsi Zoorific Theater.

Monkey Island - home to endangered woolly monkeys

Australia - features koalas, yellow-footed rock wallabies, great grey kangaroos and tasmanian devils

South America - home to golden lion and golded-headed tamarins, spectacled bears, mountain tapirs, jaguars, ocelots, pudu deer, maned wolves, scarlet macaws and Galapagos tortoises

Eurasia - includes siamangs, Indian rhinoceros, orangutans, white-cheeked gibbons, sloth bears and gaurs

Africa - features gorillas, black rhinos, Jentink's duikers, crowned and ruffed lemurs, chimpanzees, sifakas and drills

**Future Plans:** A renovated Tiger Exhibit will open in 1993. Phase 1 of the redevelopment masterplan will include an Education Visitor Village and renovation of the polar bear and penguin exhibits (target dates pending).

## CAPTIVE BREEDING & RESEARCH

The Los Angeles Zoo has had special **breeding** success with the following species:

Arabian oryx - the captive herd has increased from 3 in 1967 to over 100 today

Verreaux's sifaka - first birth of this lemur outside its native Madagascar

Drill - first birth of this baboon in U.S. in a decade

Mountain tapir - first birth of this species in captivity

Golden lion tamarin - the Zoo boasts an active, sustaining population of this endangered species

The Curatorial staff at the Los Angeles Zoo serve as coordinator of the Species Survival Plans for Andean & California condors, drills, Indian rhinoceros and chimpanzees.

**Research** at the Zoo includes on-going behavior studies on California condors, gorillas, drills and giant elands.

*Entrance to Adventure Island*
*(photo courtesy of Los Angeles Zoo)*

## SEASONAL FESTIVALS & PROGRAMS

Big Bunny Event - Easter
Music in the Zoo - evenings in July
Beastly Ball - major fundraiser in September
Twilight Trek for Members - Fall
Beastly Feast - November
Present for Primates - December

## FOR MORE INFORMATION

Los Angeles Zoo, 5333 Zoo Drive, Los Angeles, California 90027; 213-666-4650; Director: Mark Goldstein, D.V.M.

# 159     SANTA ANA ZOO
## Santa Ana, California

The Santa Ana Zoo, established in 1952, now covers 20 acres. Future development of the Zoo will be in accordance with a South American theme.

## VISITOR INFORMATION

**Directions:** The Zoo is adjacent to Interstate 5, between First Street and Chestnut Avenue in Santa Ana.

**Open to the Public:** 10 AM-6 PM, Memorial Day through Labor Day;
10 AM-5 PM remainder of the year

**Closed:** Christmas Day

**Admission (1993):** Adult: $2.00    Child: $.75    Senior: $.75

**Parking Fee:** None

**Children's Zoo:** Yes    **Separate Admission:** No

**Annual Membership:** Individual: $20    Family: $35

**AAZPA Member:** Yes

## COLLECTIONS & EXHIBITS

**Collection:** The Zoo's current collection includes the following number of species:

| | | |
|---|---|---|
| Mammals: 34 | Birds: 33 | Reptiles: 4 |
| Amphibians: 4 | Fish: 2 | Invertebrates: 2 |

**Special Exhibits** at the Santa Ana Zoo include:
Primate Collection
Children's Zoo
South American Display

**Future Plans:** "Amazon's Edge," to include black howler monkeys and capybaras, and a walk-through aviary will both open in 1993. A Patagonian Desert Shoreline, to include Magellan penguins, will be completed in 1995. As mentioned above, future development of the Zoo will be accordance with a South American theme.

## CAPTIVE BREEDING & RESEARCH

The Santa Ana Zoo has had special **breeding** success with the following species:

Celebes crested macaque — Red-handed tamarin
Black-capped capuchins — Blue & yellow macaw
Cotton-topped tamarin

## SEASONAL FESTIVALS & PROGRAMS

Sheep Shearing - April
Conservation Day - June
Zoo Camp - July & August
Boo at the Zoo - late October
Christmas Program - mid December
Member Events - throughout the year

## FOR MORE INFORMATION

The Santa Ana Zoo, 1801 E. Chestnut Avenue, Santa Ana, California 92701; 714-836-4000; Director: Ronald J. Glazier

# 160 THE LIVING DESERT
## Palm Desert, California

The Living Desert, established in 1970, exhibits desert animals from across the globe, many of which are rare and endangered. The 1200-acre facility also displays a tremendous variety of desert plants, representing ten distinct regions of the North American Desert.

## VISITOR INFORMATION

**Directions:** From Palm Springs, follow Highway 111 southeast to Palm Desert. Turn south on Portola Avenue and drive 1.5 miles to the entrance, on your left.

**Open to the Public:** 9 AM-5 PM, September 1 through June 15

**Closed:** June 16 through August 31; also closed Christmas Day

**Admission (1993):** Adult: $7.00    Child: $4.00    Senior: $6.00

**Parking Fee:** None

**Children's Zoo:** No

**Annual Membership:** Individual: $30    Family: $40

**Programs & Tours:** The Center offers a variety of educational programs, including guided tours, classes, workshops, and field trips.

**AAZPA Member:** Yes

## COLLECTIONS & EXHIBITS

**Collection:** The Living Desert's current collection includes the following number of species:

| | | |
|---|---|---|
| Mammals: 33 | Birds: 68 | Reptiles: 25 |
| Amphibians: 3 | Insects: 8 | Fish: 1 |
| Other Invertebrates: 2 | | |

**Special Exhibits** at The Living Desert include:

Desert Antelope & Gazelles

Small Desert Cats - many are endangered

Nocturnal Exhibit - features screech owls, snakes, bats and kangaroo rats

Nature Trails - this six-mile network introduces visitors to the local desert habitat; guide booklets enhance the experience

Botanical Gardens - interpret 10 distinct regions of the North American Desert

**Future Plans:** The Eagle Canyon Exhibit and a Palm Garden will be completed in 1993. Exhibits for the Abyssinian ground hornbill and the Addax antelope are also planned.

An East Africa Garden, a Madagascar Garden and a Bursera Garden are all slated to open in 1994.

## CAPTIVE BREEDING & RESEARCH

The Living Desert has had special **breeding** success with the following species:

| | |
|---|---|
| Arabian oryx | Kit fox |
| Cuvier's gazelle | Sandcat |
| Mhorr gazelle | Arabian wildcat |
| Slender-horned gazelle | |

**Research projects** based at The Living Desert include:

- Study of Upper Respiratory Tract Disease Syndrome in Desert Tortoises (cooperative research with the University of Florida)
- Survey and publication of "Flora of the Colorado Desert"

## SEASONAL FESTIVALS & PROGRAMS

Native American Events - mid February

Desert Plant Sale & Wildflower Programs - March

Earth Day Celebration - late April

Children's Summer Classes - late June to mid July

## FOR MORE INFORMATION

The Living Desert, 47-900 Portola Avenue, Palm Desert, California 92260; 619-346-5694; Director: Karen Sausman

# 161     SAN DIEGO WILD ANIMAL PARK
### Escondido, California

Seeking to expand the San Diego Zoo's breeding capabilities and to reduce its reliance on wild populations, Executive Director Dr. Charles Schroeder proposed the creation of a wild animal park in the rural countryside of San Diego County. A search for the site was initiated in 1959 and, in 1962, an 1800 acre parcel of land, owned by the City, was selected in the San Pasqual Valley.

Ground breaking ceremonies were held in 1969 and the Park was formally dedicated in May, 1972. Now home to a vast array of birds and mammals, the Wild Animal Park boasts 41 endangered species, 30 of which have been successfully bred at the facility. The Park has produced over 75 southern white rhinoceroses, more than any zoo or park outside of South Africa.

## VISITOR INFORMATION

**Directions:** The San Diego Wild Animal Park is located along California 78 between Escondido and Ramona, approximately 30 miles north of downtown San Diego. Follow Interstate 15 north from the city and watch for directional signs when nearing Escondido.

**Open to the Public:** 9 AM-5 PM June to August; 9 AM-4 PM September to May; extended hours for special events.

**Admission (1993):** Adult: $15.95     Child: $8.95     Senior: Discount Available

**Parking Fee:** None

**Annual Membership** (to Zoological Society of San Diego):
Adult: $45     Dual: $58     Child: $10

**Programs & Tours:** Photo Caravans (619-738-5022) and Behind-the-Scenes Tours (619-557-3966) can be arranged. School Safari field trips are also offered (619-738-5057). Educational animal demonstrations are scheduled daily at the Park.

**AAZPA Member:** Yes

## COLLECTIONS & EXHIBITS

**Collection:** The Wild Animal Park's current collection includes the following number of species:
Mammals: 125 (1500 specimens)
Birds: 325 (1500 specimens)

**Special Exhibits** at the San Diego Wild Animal Park include:

Wgasa Bushline Monorail - this 5-mile, 50 minute guided tour takes you past the Park's large, mixed-species habitats. Among the highlights are herds of African and Asian elephants, giraffes, gazelles, rhinos, antelope, tigers and flamingos.

Kilimanjaro Hiking Trail - this 1.75 mile path winds through botanical gardens and out past exhibits of African and Asian species (gorillas, cheetahs, lions, elephants and others).

Nairobi Village - covering 17 acres, the Village is a collection of shops, aviaries, ponds, waterfalls, small exhibits and botanical gardens

Hummingbird Pavilion - a walk-through, climate-controlled exhibit planted with lush vegetation and featuring a variety of hummingbirds.

Kupanda Falls Botanical Center - gardens and picnic area

## CAPTIVE BREEDING & RESEARCH

The San Diego Wild Animal Park has had special **breeding** success with the following species:

| | |
|---|---|
| Arabian oryx | Southern white rhinoceros |
| Slender-horned gazelle | South African cheetah |
| Przewalski's wild horse | California condor |
| Barashinga | Andean condor |
| Burmese thamin | Manchurian crane |
| Indian gaur | Rothschild's mynah |

The California Condor Recovery Program, a joint project of the U.S. Fish & Wildlife Service, the Zoological Society of San Diego and the Los Angeles Zoo, was established in the late 1970s. The Wild Animal Park constructed its 22,000 square-foot "condor-minium" in 1980; the world's first captive-conceived California condor was hatched at the Park in 1988. Continued breeding success allowed reintroduction of the first condor pair in January, 1992. Captive breeding will continue at the two zoos until two wild flocks, each numbering at least 100 birds and sustaining their populations, have been established.

## SEASONAL FESTIVALS & PROGRAMS

Arbor Day - first weekend in March; children admitted free for helping to plant a tree on the grounds

Special Species - spring & summer; evening monorail ride with an animal expert (call 619-557-3969)

Summer School Programs - summer (call 619-738-5057)

Running Wild - early fall; 10K run and fun walk (call 619-747-8702, Ext. 5140)

Beauty & the Beast Show - October; weekend botanical fair

Festival of Lights - December

## FOR MORE INFORMATION

San Diego Wild Animal Park, 15500 San Pasqual Valley Road, Escondido, California 92027-9614; 619-738-5065; Director: Douglas Myers; Zoological Society of San Diego: 619-231-0251

# 162

## SAN DIEGO ZOO
### San Diego, California

A mecca for zoo lovers, the San Diego Zoo was established in 1916. Today's 100 acre zoological and botanical garden actually originated as an animal menagerie, left behind after the Panama-California International Exposition of 1915-1916. Dr. Harry Wegeforth, a local physician, rescued the animals and founded the Zoological Society of San Diego. Incorporated in 1916, the Society has grown into the largest zoological membership association in the world.

Blessed with a mild climate and adorned with a superb collection of tropical and semi-tropical plants, the Zoo is home to 800 species of wildlife, many of which are endangered. Among other achievements, the San Diego Zoo boasts the largest collection of psittacine birds in the world.

## VISITOR INFORMATION

**Directions:** The Zoo is located in Balboa Park, just northeast of the downtown area. From the Cabrillo Freeway (California 163) exit on University Avenue, head east and turn south on Park Blvd. The entrance is on Zoo Drive.

From the Harbor area, follow Laurel St. east to Balboa Park; turn right on President's Way and then left on Park Blvd. to Zoo Drive.

**Open to the Public:** 365 days per year; opens at 9 AM; closing time varies with seasons.

**Admission (1993):** Adult: $12    Child: $4 (under 3 free)

**Children's Zoo:** Yes    **Separate Admission:** No

**Annual Membership** (to Zoological Society of San Diego):
Single: $45    Dual: $58    Child: $10

**Programs & Tours:** A Bus Tour of the Zoo is available at an additional charge. The Zoo's Education Department offers a wide range of programs geared to all age groups and works closely with regional schools and colleges.

**AAZPA Member:** Yes

## COLLECTIONS & EXHIBITS

**Collection:** The San Diego Zoo is home to 3800 animals, representing 800 species.

**Special Exhibits** at the Zoo include:
Children's Zoo - remodeled in 1979, this popular area features a nursery, walk-through aviaries, a petting zoo and small animal exhibits.
African Rock Kopje - home to klipspringers and pancake tortoises
Koala Exhibit - includes one of only two albino koalas in the world
Psittacine Birds - largest collection in the world

African Treehouse - sunny decks offer sweeping views of the Zoo; includes a cafe, a restaurant and a gift shop

Gorilla Tropics - planted with bamboo, fig and banana trees, this 2.5 acre habitat is home to the Zoo's gorilla family; the exhibit also includes four aviaries which house 200 African birds; 96 hidden speakers broadcast sounds recorded in African rain forests

Sun Bear Forest - this 1.5 acre habitat features Malayan sun bears, lion-tailed macaques and tropical birds

Tiger River: Kroc Family Tropical Rain Forest - home to tropical birds, mouse deer, Burmese pythons, tapirs and Sumatran tigers; an elaborate fogging system counteracts the dry, San Diego climate

Bonobo Exhibit - pygmy chimpanzees from the forest of Zaire

**Future Plans:** The San Diego Zoo is in the midst of a 20-year, $200 million renovation project which will reorganize the Zoo into ten bioclimatic zones. An Australasia Aviary complex is scheduled for completion in 1993.

*Spacious, naturalized exhibits characterize the San Diego Zoo.*
*(photo by Robert Folzenlogen)*

## CAPTIVE BREEDING & RESEARCH

Captive **breeding** efforts at the San Diego Zoo are divided between the Zoo and the Wild Animal Park. These facilities have successfully bred a wide range of species, many of which are endangered. Among those not mentioned in the Wild Animal Park listing:

Mhorr gazelle - one of few Western Hemisphere zoos to breed this species
Meyer's lorikeet - first to breed this bird in North America
Kiwi - only the second American zoo to hatch this New Zealand species

Laysan teal
Lory species
Bali mynah
Golden conures
Green-winged macaws
Scarlet macaws
Red-tailed black cockatoos

Gray-winged trumpeters
Eurasian bison
Siberian tigers
Sumatran tigers
Polar bears
Lemur species

The Center for Reproduction of Endangered Species, based at the San Diego Zoo, administers **research projects** on five continents; a new CRES Research Center is planned for the Wild Animal Park. The Center maintains Studbooks for Arabian oryxes, slender-horned gazelles and golden conures; it also leads an international effort to preserve the lion-tailed macaque and to eventually return this species to its native range.

Among many **CRES projects** based at the Zoo and Wild Animal Park are:

- Embryo implantation research
- Study of reproductive behavior and development in green iguanas
- Molecular genetics studies on California condors
- Cytogenetics lab with frozen cell collections from over 300 mammal species
- Study of viral illnesses in animals
- Research on immune response in cheetahs and black rhinos

## SEASONAL FESTIVALS & PROGRAMS

The San Diego Zoo and the San Diego Wild Animal Park host a variety of seasonal events throughout the year. Some of these are mentioned in the Wild Animal Park listing.

Zoo members can keep abreast of upcoming events by checking the ZOO LOG newsletter, published by the Zoological Society of San Diego. For information, call 619-231-0251.

## FOR MORE INFORMATION

The San Diego Zoo, P.O. Box 551, San Diego, California 92112; 619-234-3153 or 619-231-1515; Director: Douglas Myers; Zoological Society of San Diego: 619-231-0251.

# 163 SEA WORLD OF CALIFORNIA
### San Diego, California

Sea World of California, opened in 1964, is a 150-acre marine life park which seeks to balance family entertainment, research, education and wildlife conservation. Owned by Anheuser-Busch Companies, Inc., the Park offers five shows, more than 20 major exhibits and attractions, amusement rides and four aquariums.

## VISITOR INFORMATION

**Directions:** From the north or south, exit west from Interstate 5 onto Sea World Drive.

From the east, exit onto Mission Bay Drive from Interstate 8. Proceed to Sea World Drive.

**Open to the Public:** 365 days per year; hours vary with season; call 619-226-3901 for current hours.

**Admission (1993):** Subject to change
Adult: $25.95   Child: $19.95 (3-11; under 3 free)

**Parking Fee:** $4.00

**Children's Zoo:** No

**Annual Membership:** Subject to change.
Adult: $48   Child: $38   Senior: $38

**Programs & Tours:** Sea World of California offers four different tours. Education programs, including classes, workshops and field trips, are presented by the Education Department (call 619-226-3834).

**AAZPA Member:** Yes

## COLLECTIONS & EXHIBITS

**Collection:** The Park's current collection includes the following number of species:
Mammals: 14   Birds: 127   Reptiles: 8
Amphibians: 2   Fish: 300   Invertebrates: 90

**Special Exhibits** at Sea World of California include:
Penguin Encounter - six species of penguin inhabit this simulated Antarctic environment.
Shark Encounter - the world's largest collection of tropical sharks is viewed from an underwater, acrylic tunnel
California Sea Otter Exhibit
California Tide Pool - this exhibit re-creates the intertidal life zone, home to starfish, sea urchins, sea cucumbers, spiny lobsters and California moray eels
Forbidden Reef - includes bat rays and the world's largest group of moray eels
World of the Sea Aquarium - four 55,000 gallon tanks harbor kelp bed fishes, a coral reef, schooling ocean fish and large gamefish

*Commerson's dolphins:
Sea World of California
received the AAZPA's
Significant Breeding
Achievement Award in
1991 for its success
with breeding this
species.*

*Sea World of California is the only facility in the world to breed Emperor penguins
in captivity; they are seen here in Sea World's "Penguin Encounter."*

Freshwater Aquarium - 25 aquariums display aquatic life from freshwater
   habitats in Africa, Asia and South America
Avian Exhibits - populated by thousands of birds; the Avian Propagation Center
   conducts research, serves as a nursery and treats injured birds.
Botanical Gardens - adorned with over 3500 plant species
**Future Plans:**   Rocky Point Preserve is scheduled to open on Memorial Weekend,
                    1993; this marine mammal complex will feature bottlenose dolphins
                    and Alaskan sea otters; the latter are survivors of the Exxon Valdez
                    oil spill of 1989.

## CAPTIVE BREEDING & RESEARCH

Sea World of California has had special **breeding** success with the following species:
   Pacific blacktip shark - the only U.S. facility to breed this species
   Emperor penguins - only facility in the world to breed this species
   Killer whales
   Commerson's dolphins - first facility in the world to breed this species

Sea World of California has received numerous honors for achievements in
zoological research, breeding and husbandry, including the AAZPA's Significant
Breeding Achievement Award in 1991 for its success with breeding Commerson's
dolphins.

Sea World is affiliated with Hubbs-Sea World Research Institute. Among its
numerous **research projects** are:
   - Ocean Resources Enhancement & Hatchery Program; this program is dedicated
     to the propagation and release of self-sustaining populations of white seabass
   - Genetic fingerprinting of endangered loggerhead turtles to determine their
     nesting origin
   - Blackcod/Killer Whale study in Prince William Sound; this project is working to
     determine what sounds from long-line fishing boats are attracting killer
     whales (the whales are raiding the catch before it reaches the boat)

## SEASONAL FESTIVALS & PROGRAMS

Small Wonders - this annual event runs from March through mid June; exhibits and
   shows highlight successful breeding programs at Sea World
Summer Nights - evening entertainment and fireworks; mid June through Labor Day
Haunted Hallowen Cove - Halloween weekend; special shows, trick-or-treat stations,
   interactive displays and costume contests
Holiday Festivities - mid December through New Years Weekend; special shows,
   caroling, holiday decorations and lighting of the 320-foot "Skytower Christmas
   Tree."

## FOR MORE INFORMATION

Sea World of California, 1720 South Shores Road, San Diego, California 92109-7995;
619-226-3901; Executive Vice President & General Manager: Mike Cross

# 164        TRACY AVIARY
## Salt Lake City, Utah

Tracy Aviary, completed in 1938, is one of the oldest aviaries in the world and the only publicly owned and operated aviary in the western hemisphere. The entire facility covers 7.5 acres.

## VISITOR INFORMATION

**Directions:** From I-15, take the 9th South Exit. Enter the Park at 900 South, 600 East. Signs direct you to the Aviary.

**Open to the Public:** Daily; 9 AM-6 PM, Summer; 9 AM-4:30 PM, Winter

**Closed:** Christmas Day

**Admission (1993):** Adult: $1.50     Child: $.50     Senior: $.75

**Parking Fee:** None

**Annual Membership:** Individual: $10     Family: $20

**Programs & Tours:** Free-flying Bird Shows, displaying natural talents of more than 70 birds, are presented from March to November.

**AAZPA Member:** Yes

## COLLECTIONS & EXHIBITS

**Collection:** The Aviary is home to 220 species of birds.

**Special Exhibits** at Tracy Aviary include:
High Altitude Pheasantry
Waterfowl Collection
Free-flying Bird Show

**Future Plans:** New parrot exhibits are planned for 1993.

## CAPTIVE BREEDING & RESEARCH

Tracy Aviary has had special **breeding** success with the following species:

| | |
|---|---|
| Trumpeter swans | Asian turtledoves |
| Black-necked swans | Red-billed blue magpies |
| Bleeding-heart turtledoves | Finch-billed bulbuls |

## SEASONAL FESTIVALS & PROGRAMS

Summer Classes - June to August
Nature Fair - last weekend in August

## FOR MORE INFORMATION

Tracy Aviary, 589 E. 1300 S., Salt Lake City, Utah 84105; 801-596-5034; Director: O. Grenville Roles

# 165

## UTAH'S HOGLE ZOO
### Salt Lake City, Utah

Established in 1931, Utah's Hogle Zoo encompasses 52 acres.

## VISITOR INFORMATION

**Directions:** From I-15, take the 6th South/City Center Exit; proceed 2 blocks south to 8th South and then east to 2600 East.

**Open to the Public:** Daily; 9 AM-5 PM Fall & Spring; 9 AM-6 PM Summer; 9 AM-4:30 PM Winter

**Closed:** Christmas and New Years Day

**Admission (1993):** Adult: $4.00    Child: $2.00    Senior: $2.00

**Parking Fee:** None

**Children's Zoo:** No

**Annual Membership:** Individual: $30    Family: $50

**AAZPA Member:** Yes

## COLLECTIONS & EXHIBITS

**Collection:** The Zoo's current collection includes the following number of species:
Mammals: 109          Birds: 131          Reptiles: 76
Amphibians: 8         Fish: 2            Insects: 6
Other Invertebrates: 6

**Special Exhibits** at Utah's Hogle Zoo include:
Desert Canyon - displays flora and fauna of the world's deserts and explores man's impact on these species
Discovery Land - a unique area of interactive educational exhibits with habitat themed animal displays (forest, woodland edge, marsh, desert)
Climate Zoned Building for Small Animals - desert, temperate and tropical zones with representative mammals, birds, reptiles and amphibians on display

**Future Plans:** Complete renovation of the Zoo's central area is planned, including Monkey Island, waterfowl ponds, pheasantry, harbor seal display and otter exhibit; the Zoo's goal is to complete a new exhibit yearly.

*The Desert Canyon exhibit displays flora and fauna of the world's deserts
and highlights man's impact on these species.*
*(photo by Bill Lloyd; courtesy Utah's Hogle Zoo)*

## CAPTIVE BREEDING & RESEARCH

Utah's Hogle Zoo has had special **breeding** success with the following species:

| | |
|---|---|
| Orangutans | Pygmy hippo |
| Polar bears | Spiny agama |
| African lion | Rhea |
| Jaguar | Tommy gazelle |
| Bactrian camel | Suni antelope |

**Research projects** at the Zoo includes:
- Venom research in collaboration with the Veterans Hospital

## FOR MORE INFORMATION

Utah's Hogle Zoo, P.O. Box 58475, Salt Lake City, Utah 84158-0475; 801-582-1632;
Director: Lamar Farnsworth

# 166 DENVER ZOOLOGICAL GARDENS
## Denver, Colorado

The Denver Zoological Gardens originated as an animal menagerie on the north side of City Park in 1896. Construction of Bear Mountain in 1918 and the addition of Monkey Island (a WPA project) in 1936 hastened development of the Zoo which now covers 76 acres.

Renowned for its collection of hoofed mammals, the Denver Zoo has placed emphasis on large, naturalized exhibits. Renovation of the Zoo's Cat House was recently completed and Tropical Discovery, a complex of indoor, climate-controlled habitats, is scheduled to open in 1993.

## VISITOR INFORMATION

**Directions:** The Zoo is located in City Park, 1.5 miles east of the downtown area. From the State Capitol Building, drive east on Colfax Avenue; proceed 1.5 miles and turn left (north) on Josephine St. Drive another 8 blocks and turn right (east) on 23rd Avenue; the Zoo will be .5 mile ahead, on your right.

Alternatively, from I-70, east of I-25, take the Colorado Blvd. Exit and head south to 23rd Avenue. Turn right (west) and proceed to the Zoo entrance, on your left.

**Open to the Public:** 365 days per year; 10 AM-6 PM Summer; 10 AM-5 PM the remainder of the year

**Admission (1993):** Adult: $6.00    Child: $3.00 (under 4 free)    Senior: $3.00

**Parking Fee:** None

**Children's Zoo:** Yes    **Separate Admission:** No

**Annual Membership:** Individual: $25    Family: $40

**Programs & Tours:** The Zoo offers a wide variety of educational programs including guided tours, classes for children and adults, workshops, field trips and outreach programs.

**AAZPA Member:** Yes

## COLLECTIONS & EXHIBITS

**Collection:** The Zoo's current collection includes the following number of species:

| | | |
|---|---|---|
| Mammals: 118 | Birds: 172 | Reptiles: 80 |
| Amphibians: 19 | Fish: 109 | Invertebrates: 57 |

*Sea Lion Pool at the Denver Zoo's Northern Shores exhibit.*
*(photo by Robert Folzenlogen)*

*The wart hog exhibit is a recent addition to the Denver Zoo.*
*(photo by Robert Folzenlogen)*

**Special Exhibits** at the Denver Zoological Gardens include:

Northern Shores - a collection of naturalized, arctic habitats, featuring polar bears, sea lions, otters, arctic fox, waterfowl, harbor seals and wolves. This exhibit, which opened in 1987, includes underwater viewing of polar bears and sea lions.

Bird World - a series of walk-through, indoor aviaries simulating rainforest, coastal, swamp and treetop habitats; includes a hummingbird display and an outdoor penguin colony.

Cat House - recently renovated with use of artificial rocks, logs, caves and canyons; background dioramas depict natural habitats of the feline residents.

Wolf Pack Woods - a large, natural habitat for the Zoo's arctic wolf pack; shaded by a grove of ponderosa pines, the habitat also features a rock outcropping from which the wolves survey their territory.

Bear Mountain - renovated with new pools, waterfalls and rockwork in 1989.

**Future Plans:** Tropical Discovery will open in late 1993, housing a variety of tropical creatures in naturalized climate-controlled habitats. Primate Panorama is scheduled for completion in 1995.

## CAPTIVE BREEDING & RESEARCH

The Denver Zoological Gardens has had special **breeding** success with the following species:

| | |
|---|---|
| Eastern black rhino | Scimitar-horned oryx |
| Amur leopard | Bali mynah |
| Grevy's zebra | Pere David's deer |
| Przewalski's horse | Reticulated giraffe |

**Research projects** based at the Denver Zoo include:
- Participation in Species Survival Plans of the AAZPA
- Taxonomic Advisory Groups
- Brazilian Fauna Interest Group
- Vitamin E deficiency research

## SEASONAL FESTIVALS & PROGRAMS

Conservation Day - early June
Zoofest Concert Series - June through August
Native American Pow Wow - late August
Senior Citizens Day - mid September
Run for the Zoo - mid October
Boo at the Zoo - late October
Wildlights - December

## FOR MORE INFORMATION

Denver Zoological Gardens, City Park, Denver, Colorado 80205; 303-331-4110; Director: Clayton F. Freiheit

# 167 CHEYENNE MOUNTAIN ZOO
## Colorado Springs, Colorado

Stretching across the east face of Cheyenne Mountain, this 40-acre Zoo, established in 1926, offers spectacular views of Colorado Springs, backed by the High Plains of eastern Colorado. Indeed, with an elevation of 7000 feet, this is the highest zoo in the country.

Ironically, the Cheyenne Mountain Zoo, perched on the edge of the Rockies, has produced more giraffes than any zoo in the world.

## VISITOR INFORMATION

**Directions:** Take I-25 to Exit 138 (Circle Drive); this Exit is south of the downtown area. Head west to the Broadmoor Hotel. Turn left at the stoplight (in front of the Hotel) and follow the signs upward and southwestward to the Zoo.

**Open to the Public:** Daily; 9 AM-6 PM Summer; 9 AM-5 PM remainder of the year. Open 365 days per year.

**Admission (1993):** Adult: $5.50    Child: $3.00    Senior: $4.50

**Parking Fee:** None

**Children's Zoo:** Yes    **Separate Admission:** No

**Annual Membership:** Individual: $20    Family: $40

**AAZPA Member:** Yes

## COLLECTIONS & EXHIBITS

**Collection:** The Zoo's current collection includes the following number of species:
Mammals: 63          Birds: 39          Reptiles: 25
Amphibians: 10        Fish: 2

**Special Exhibits** at the Cheyenne Mountain Zoo include:
Primate World - recognized as one of the finest primate exhibits in the country, this facility opened in 1991; the indoor/outdoor habitats feature gorillas, orangutans and a variety of small primates.
Vulture Aviary

**Future Plans:** A Bat Cave and a Naked Mole Rat Exhibit will both open in 1993. Asian Highlands (beginning with outdoor enclosures for Siberian tigers and Snow leopards) is scheduled for 1994.

*Kodiak bears enjoy the cool climate of America's highest zoo.*
*(photo by Robert Folzenlogen)*

## CAPTIVE BREEDING & RESEARCH

The Cheyenne Mountain Zoo has had special **breeding** success with the following species:

Giraffe - largest number of captive births in the world
Snow leopards
Bongos
Siberian tigers
Primate species
Reptile species

The Zoo participates in 21 Species Survival Plans. **Research projects** based at the Cheyenne Mountain Zoo include:

- Studies on the captive breeding of black-footed ferrets
- Research on high-altitude amphibians
- Participates in reintroduction programs for golden lion tamarins, Andean condors, Virgin Island boa constrictors and black-footed ferrets

## SEASONAL FESTIVALS & PROGRAMS

Conservation Day - June
Zoobilee - June
Wildest Ride in Town - July

Teddy Bear Days - July
Feline Fiesta - August
Wildest Race in Town - August

## FOR MORE INFORMATION

Cheyenne Mountain Zoo, 4250 Cheyenne Mountain Zoo Road, Colorado Springs, Colorado 80906; 719-633-9925; Director: Ms. Susan Engfer

# 168

## PUEBLO ZOO
### Pueblo, Colorado

Founded in the 1930s, the Pueblo Zoo was granted accreditation by the American Association of Zoological Parks & Aquariums in 1992. This 25-acre facility is currently the only zoo in Colorado which offers underwater viewing of penguins.

## VISITOR INFORMATION

**Directions:** Take Highway 50 West to Pueblo Blvd. South; turn left on Goodnight; circle around the Park (the Zoo is on the south side).

**Open to the Public:** Daily; 10 AM-5 PM Summer; 9 AM-4 PM Winter

**Closed:** Thanksgiving, Christmas, New Years Day

**Admission:** Adult: $2.00    Child: $.50    Senior: $2.00

**Parking Fee:** None

**Children's Zoo:** Yes    **Separate Admission:** No

**Annual Membership:** Individual: $10-$15    Family: $15-$50    Senior: $8

**AAZPA Member:** Yes

## COLLECTIONS & EXHIBITS

**Collection:** The Zoo's current collection includes the following number of species:
　　Mammals: 40　　　Birds: 31　　　Reptiles: 20
　　Amphibians: 4　　Fish: 5　　　　Insects: 2
　　Other Invertebrates: 5

**Special Exhibits** at the Pueblo Zoo include:
　　The Ecocenter - contains two ecosystems: a tropical rainforest and a temperate, South American coast exhibit (which includes black-footed penguins)
　　Happy Time Ranch - a petting farm for children
　　Cold-Blooded Creatures Herpetarium - houses reptiles, amphibians and insects

**Future Plans:** Reconstruction of the entry gate and completion of a new 2,000 square-foot classroom facility are scheduled for 1993. A new African Lion Exhibit will open in 1994 and an Asian Mountain Habitat will be completed in 1996.

## CAPTIVE BREEDING & RESEARCH

The Pueblo Zoo has had special **breeding** success with the following species:
　　Hoofed Mammals
　　Tamarins

## SEASONAL FESTIVALS & PROGRAMS
Educational Speakers Program - early April
Zoo B Que - early May
Feast with Father - June
Seniors' Day - August
Zoofair - August to September
Harvest Event - October
Enchanted Holiday Zoobilee - December

## FOR MORE INFORMATION
The Pueblo Zoo, 3455 Nuckolls Avenue, Pueblo, Colorado 81005; 719-561-8686; Director: Jounene McFarland

# 169 NAVAJO NATION ZOOLOGICAL & BOTANICAL PARK
### Window Rock, Arizona

Dedicated on July 4, 1977, the Navajo Nation Zoological & Botanical Park exhibits plants and animals that have played a role in the history and culture of the Navajo people. The 8-acre Park, located in the semi-arid, high plateau region of northeastern Arizona, is adorned with native flora and displays both wild and domestic animal species.

Set beneath towering sandstone "haystacks," the facility also exhibits fork-stick and crib-log architecture, typical of early Navajo dwellings. The Park is a program of the Navajo Tribal Parks System and is funded by the Navajo Tribal Government and private donations. In 1982, the NNZBP became the only Tribally operated zoo in the U.S. to be licensed as an exhibitor by the United States Department of Agriculture.

## VISITOR INFORMATION
**Directions:** The Zoo is located in Tse Bonito Tribal Park. This Park is on the north side of Highway 264, ¼ mile west of the Arizona-New Mexico line and ¼ mile east of the Arizona 264/Indian Route 12 North intersection.

**Open to the Public:** Daily, 8 AM-5 PM

**Closed:** Christmas and New Years Day

**Admission (1993):** Free

**Parking Fee:** None

**Children's Zoo:** No

**Annual Membership:** Not available

**AAZPA Member:** No

*The Park is set beneath towering sandstone "haystacks."*
(photo courtesy of the Navajo Nation Zoological & Botanical Park)

## COLLECTIONS & EXHIBITS

**Collection:** The Zoo's current collection includes the following number of species:

| | | |
|---|---|---|
| Mammals: 22 | Birds: 13 | Reptiles: 7 |
| Amphibians: 1 | Fish: 3 | Invertebrates: 1 |

**Special Exhibits** at the Navajo Nation Zoological & Botanical Park include:

Navajo-Churro Sheep - introduced to the Southwest by Spanish explorers more than 400 years ago; this species has a double fleece with long (9-12") fibers in its outer coat which were used by early Navajo weavers.

Mexican Wolf - this endangered species has been exhibited at the Park for over a decade.

Native Flora - includes junipers, Indian rice grass, Navajo tea, Rocky Mountain bee plant, lupine, asters, penstamons and other species adapted to this semiarid environment.

## SEASONAL FESTIVALS & PROGRAMS

Navajo Nation Fair - Wednesday through Sunday following Labor Day weekend

## FOR MORE INFORMATION

Navajo Nation Zoological & Botanical Park, P.O. Box 308, Window Rock, Arizona 86515-0308; 602-871-6573; Director: Loline Hathaway, Ph.D.

# 170

## WILDLIFE WORLD ZOO
### Litchfield Park, Arizona

Established in 1974 as a breeding farm for rare and endangered species, this 45-acre facility opened to the public in October, 1984. Twice honored by the AAZPA for its breeding achievements, Wildlife World Zoo has been supplying animals to other zoos for almost two decades, thereby decreasing pressure on wild populations.

## VISITOR INFORMATION

**Directions:** Follow I-10 west to Cotton Lane and head north for 6 miles to Northern Avenue. Turn east and proceed .5 mile to the Zoo.

**Open to the Public:** 9 AM-5 PM daily, September 16 to July 15;
9 AM-5 PM weekends and holidays, 9 AM-3 PM weekdays, July 16 to September 15. Open 365 days per year.

**Admission (1993):** Adult: $6.75    Child: $3.00 (under 3 free)
Senior: $1.00 discount on Tuesdays

**Parking Fee:** None

**Children's Zoo:** No

**Annual Membership:** Individual: $40    Family: $50

**AAZPA Member:** Yes

## COLLECTIONS & EXHIBITS

**Collection:** The Zoo's current collection includes the following number of species:
Mammals: 80          Birds: 110          Reptiles: 50
Amphibians: 10          Insects: 20          Fish: 50

**Special Exhibits** at Wildlife World Zoo include:
Oryx Species - the Zoo exhibits 5 rare species of oryx
Tropics of the World - Arizona's only exotic reptile exhibit
Waters of the World - Arizona's first public tropical aquarium; features sharks and piranhas
Lory Parrot feeding exhibit - first of its kind in the world
White Bengal Tiger - the only exhibit of this species in Arizona
Exotic Bird Aviary - this walk-through exhibit is the largest exotic bird aviary in the Southwest and houses one of the finest collections in the country
Bird Collection - includes 8 species that are not displayed at any other U.S. zoo

**Future Plans:** An African Lion Habitat, an Education Building and Exhibits for the Andean Condor and King Vulture will all open in 1993.

## CAPTIVE BREEDING & RESEARCH

Wildlife World Zoo has had special **breeding** success with the following species:
South American birds - several "U.S. firsts" in the captive breeding of rare
South American birds
Kangaroo and Wallaby species
Dromedary camels
Gemsbok
Oryx species

Wildlife World Zoo conducts reproductive **research** on rare bird species.

## FOR MORE INFORMATION

Wildlife World Zoo, 16501 W. Northern Avenue, Litchfield Park, Arizona 85340;
602-935-WILD; Director: L. M. "Mickey" Ollson

# 171     PHOENIX ZOO
### Phoenix, Arizona

Founded in 1962, the 125-acre Phoenix Zoo is internationally credited with saving
the Arabian oryx from extinction.

## VISITOR INFORMATION

**Directions:** Located 3 miles east of Sky Harbor International Airport, at the intersection of McDowell Road and 64th St.

**Open to the Public:** 365 days per year; 7 AM-4 PM May through Labor Day;
9 AM-5 PM remainder of the year

**Admission (1993):** Adult: $6.00    Child: $3.00    Senior: $5.00

**Parking Fee:** None

**Children's Zoo:** Yes    **Separate Admission:** No

**Annual Membership:** Individual: $35    Family: $50

**AAZPA Member:** Yes

## COLLECTIONS & EXHIBITS

**Collection:** The Zoo's current collection includes the following number of species:
Mammals: 88      Birds: 154      Reptiles: 67
Amphibians: 9      Invertebrates: 23

**Special Exhibits** at the Phoenix Zoo include:
Tropical Rain Forest - 1 acre in area
African Savannah - covers 4 acres
Arizona Trail - species native to the American Southwest

**Future Plans:** A Spectacled Bear Exhibit is planned for 1994.

## CAPTIVE BREEDING & RESEARCH

The Phoenix Zoo has had special **breeding** success with the following species:
Arabian oryx - internationally credited with saving this species from extinction

| | |
|---|---|
| Sumatran tiger | Ocelot |
| Borneo orangutan | Indochinese leopard |
| White rhinocerous | Mandrill baboon |
| Grevy's zebra | South American tapir |
| Bali mynah | Galapagos tortoise |
| Nene | |

Current **research** at the Phoenix Zoo includes:
- Behavioral research of cheetahs and black-footed ferrets
- Study of color differentiation in elephants

*The new Tropical Flights exhibit.*
*(photo by Dick George; courtesy Phoenix Zoo)*

## SEASONAL FESTIVALS & PROGRAMS

"Wildest Ball in Town" - May 8
Zoofari - October 1
Boo! At The Zoo - late October
Zoolights - December

## FOR MORE INFORMATION

The Phoenix Zoo, 455 North Galvin Parkway, Papago Park, Phoenix, Arizona 85008-3431; 602-273-1341; Director: Warren Iliff

# 172 ARIZONA-SONORA DESERT MUSEUM
## Tucson, Arizona

Perhaps the most unique Zoo in the United States, the Arizona-Sonora Desert Museum was designed to introduce visitors to the natural history of the Sonoran Desert Region. Exhibits emphasize the interrelationships of land, water, plants and animals in this beautiful yet harsh environment. Visitors to the Museum will learn about the geology and flora of this ecosystem while being introduced to its native wildlife.

The Arizona-Sonora Desert Museum opened in 1952 and is operated by a private, non-profit organization. Development of the facility, which is now home to over 200 animal species and more than 1200 species of plants, is funded entirely through admissions, memberships and contributions.

## VISITOR INFORMATION

**Directions:** The Museum is in Tucson Mountain Park, 14 miles west of Tucson. From I-19, exit onto Ajo Way and head west, crossing Robles Pass. Angle to the northwest on Kinney Road which leads into the Park and to the Desert Museum.

**Open to the Public:** 365 days per year; 7:30 AM-6 PM, March through September; 8:30 AM-5 PM, October through February

**Admission (1993):** Adult: $7.95    Child: $1.50 (under 6 free)

**Parking Fee:** None

**Children's Zoo:** No

**Annual Membership:** Individual: $30    Family: $40

**Programs & Tours:** Museum volunteers offer on-site lectures and demonstrations daily. Educational workshops, field trips and outreach programs are also sponsored by the Desert Museum.

**AAZPA Member:** Yes

## COLLECTIONS & EXHIBITS

**Collection:** The Arizona-Sonora Desert Museum displays more than 200 animal species and harbors over 1200 plant species, all native to the Sonoran Desert Region.

**Special Exhibits** at the Desert Museum include:
Hummingbirds of the Sonoran Desert Region - a walk-through aviary; 7 species; completed 1988
Life Underground - view the dens of nocturnal creatures, from arthropods to mammals; completed 1989
Reptiles & Invertebrates - features chuckwallas, Gila monsters, tarantulas, scorpions and other desert species
Cave/Earth Sciences Complex - an introduction to the geology of the region

Mountain Habitat - represents the oak-pine woodlands between 4,000 and 7,000 feet; home to deer, Mexican wolves, black bears and mountain lions
Small Cat Grottos - feature bobcats, jaguarundis, ocelots and margays
Riparian Habitat - includes underwater viewing of otters and beaver
Desert Bighorn Sheep Exhibit
Cactus Garden - over 140 species of cactus and other desert plantlife
Demonstration Garden - introduces the visitor to the use of xeriscape plantings

**Future Plans:**   A Desert Grasslands Exhibit is scheduled to open in 1993. Arizona Uplands and Tropical Deciduous Forest Habitats are also in the planning stages.

## CAPTIVE BREEDING & RESEARCH

The Arizona-Sonora Desert Museum has had special **breeding** success with the following species:
Broad-billed hummingbird - an avicultural first
Grand Canyon rattlesnake - first captive birth in world (1989)

| | |
|---|---|
| Chuckwalla species | Harris' hawk |
| Kit fox | Desert tortoise |
| Ocelot | Montezuma quail |
| Burrowing owl | Redhead |
| Golden eagle | Thick-billed parrot (SSP) |

The Museum participates in captive breeding recovery programs for the endangered Mexican wolf and thick-billed parrot.

Some of the **research projects** based at the Desert Museum include:
- Study of animal remains in packrat middens
- Studies on the diets of Arizona chuckwalla and desert tortoise
- Survey of the flora of the Tucson Mountains
- Study of ancient flora via carbon dating of samples from packrat middens
- Floral studies to inventory ecological regions of the Sonoran Desert
- Research on genetic diversity of chuckwallas on the islands of the Gulf of California and studies on their nutritional needs

## SEASONAL FESTIVALS & PROGRAMS

Earth Day Celebration
Spring Plant & Mineral Sale
Saguaro Harvest - June
Nightstalkers - night tours in July

## FOR MORE INFORMATION

Arizona-Sonora Desert Museum, 2021 North Kinney Road, Tucson, Arizona 85743; 602-883-1380; Executive Director: David Hancocks

# 173 REID PARK ZOO
## Tucson, Arizona

The Reid Park Zoo, established in 1967, is owned by the City of Tucson and managed by its Parks & Recreation Department. The 17-acre facility harbors a fine collection of birds.

## VISITOR INFORMATION

**Directions:** The Zoo is southeast of the downtown area. From I-10, proceed east on 22nd Street; the Zoo is north of 22nd St. between Country Club and Alvernon Way.

**Open to the Public:** Daily, 9:30 AM-4:30 PM, September 15 to March 15; 8:30 AM-3:00 PM Mon.-Fri. and 8:30 AM-5:30 PM Sat.-Sun., March 15 to September 15 and holidays

**Closed:** Christmas Day

**Admission (1993):** Adult: $3.00     Child: $.75     Senior: $2.00

**Parking Fee:** None

**Children's Zoo:** No

**Annual Membership:** Individual: $15     Family: $25     Senior: $6

**AAZPA Member:** Yes

## COLLECTIONS & EXHIBITS

**Collection:** The Zoo's current collection includes the following number of species:

Mammals: 24          Birds: 106          Reptiles: 12
Amphibians: 1          Fish: 3          Invertebrates: 1

**Special Exhibits** at the Reid Park Zoo include:
Giant Anteater Exhibit
Bird Collection - one of the largest collections of any small zoo in the country; more than 300 specimens representing 106 species

**Future Plans:** A South American Area is planned.

## CAPTIVE BREEDING & RESEARCH

The Reid Park Zoo has had special **breeding** success with the following species:
Giant anteater               South American tapir
Siberian tiger               Trumpeter hornbill

**Research projects** based at the Reid Park Zoo include:
- Nutritional research (Vitamin E levels)

## SEASONAL FESTIVALS & PROGRAMS

Family Affair - Spring
Teacher's Day - early September
Festival of Lights - mid December

## FOR MORE INFORMATION

Reid Park Zoo, 1100 S. Randolph Way, Tucson, Arizona 85716; 602-791-3204; Director: J. Stephan McCusker

# APPENDIX

## Wildlife Conservation Organizations

The following is a **partial list** of organizations that are devoted to wildlife conservation and to the protection of natural habitats. Your active and/or financial support of their efforts will help to ensure the future welfare of endangered species and the preservation of vital wilderness areas.

**African Wildlife Foundation**, 1717 Massachusetts Ave., N.W., Washington, D.C. 20036; 202-265-8393

**American Association of Zoological Parks and Aquariums**, 7970-D Old Georgetown Rd., Bethesda, Maryland 20814; 301-907-7777

**American Museum of Natural History**, Central Park West at 79th St., New York, New York 10024; 800-234-5252

**Center for Marine Conservation**, 1725 DeSales St., N.W., Suite 500, Washington, D.C. 20036; 202-429-5609

**Cetacean Society International**, P.O. Box 290145, Wethersfield, Connecticut 06109-0145; 203-793-8400

**Defenders of Wildlife**, 1244 19th St., N.W., Washington, D.C. 20036; 202-659-9510

**Endangered Species Coalition**, 900 17th St., N.W., Washington, D.C. 20006-2596; 202-833-2300

**Environmental Defense Fund**, 257 Park Avenue S., New York, New York 10010

**Friends of the Earth**, 218 D St., S.E., Washington, D.C. 20003; 202-544-2600

**Greenpeace**, 1436 U St., N.W., Washington, D.C. 20009; 202-462-1177

**International Bird Rescue Research Center**, 699 Potter St., Berkeley, California 94710; 510-841-9086

**International Crane Foundation**, E-11376 Shady Lane Road, Baraboo, Wisconsin 53913-9778; 608-356-9462

**Izaak Walton League of America**, P.O. Box 824, Iowa City, Iowa 52244; 319-351-7073

**National Audubon Society**, Membership Data Center, P.O. Box 52529, Boulder, Colorado 80322; 800-274-4201

**National Geographic Society**, P.O. Box 2895, Washington, D.C. 20077-9960; 800-638-4077

**National Parks & Conservation Association**, 1776 Massachusetts Ave., N.W., Washington, D.C. 20036

**National Wildlife Federation**, Membership Services, 8925 Leesburg Pike, Vienna, Virginia 22184; 1400 16th St., N.W., 1st Floor, Washington, D.C. 20036; 202-797-5435

**National Wildlife Refuge Association,** 10824 Fox Hunt Ln., Potomac, Maryland 20854; 301-983-1238

**National Wildlife Rehabilitators Association,** Carpenter Nature Center, 12805 St. Croix Trail, Hastings, Minnesota 55033; 612-437-9194

**The Nature Conservancy,** 1815 N. Lynn St., Arlington, Virginia 22209; 703-841-5300

**Pacific Whale Foundation,** Kealia Beach Plaza, Suite 25, 101 N. Kihei Road, Kihei, Hawaii 96753; 808-879-8811

**Rainforest Action Network,** 301 Broadway, Suite A, San Francisco, California 94133; 415-398-4404

**Save the Whales,** P.O. Box 3650, Washington, D.C. 20007; 202-337-2332

**The Sierra Club,** 730 Polk St., San Francisco, California 94109; 415-776-2211

**Society for the Preservation of Birds of Prey,** P.O. Box 66070, Los Angeles, California 90066; 213-397-8216

**The Wild Dolphin Project,** 21 Hepburn Avenue, Suite 20, Jupiter, Florida 33458; 407-575-5660

**The Wilderness Society,** 900 Seventeenth St., N.W., Washington, D.C. 20006-2596; 202-833-2300

**Wildlife Conservation International,** c/o New York Zoological Society, Bronx, New York 10460; 212-220-5155

**World Wildlife Fund,** 1250 24th St., N.W., Washington, D.C. 20037; 202-293-4800

# BIBLIOGRAPHY

As mentioned in the Introduction, most of the information in this Guide was provided directly by the Zoos and Aquariums. In addition to responding to our questionnaire, many of the facilities also sent brochures and newsletters which illustrated unique features of their institution and related their activities in the areas of research, education and captive breeding.

Background information was also obtained from the sources listed below.

Bendiner, Robert, **The Fall of the Wild, The Rise of the Zoo,** E.P. Dutton, New York, 1981

Boyd, Linda J., Editor, **Zoological Parks & Aquariums in the Americas,** American Association of Zoological Parks and Aquariums, Bethesda, Maryland, 1992-1993

Lovett, Richard A., *"Window Opens on World Down Under,"* The Denver Post, Travel Section, June 14, 1992

Page, Jake and Franz Maier, **Zoo, The Modern Ark,** Facts on File Inc./Key Porter Books Limited, New York, 1990

Park, Edwards, *"A special treat awaits zoophiles in Washington,"* Smithsonian, February, 1993, pages 54-59

Rider, Alan, *"Excitement bubbles up beside the Mississippi,"* The Denver Post, Travel Section, June 14, 1992

Schlossberg, Dan, *"Aquarium portrays problems, solutions,"* The Denver Post, Travel Section, June 14, 1992

Shuttlesworth, Dorothy E., **Zoos in the Making,** E.P. Dutton, New York, 1977

Smith, Brad, *"Popular Oceanarium lets dolphins, whales thrive in Chicago,"* The Denver Post, Travel Section, June 14, 1992

Walls, Wuanda, *"Architecture makes Tennessee Aquarium stand out,"* The Denver Post, Travel Section, June 14, 1992

Zuckerman, Lord, Editor, **Great Zoos of the World, Their Origins and Significance,** George Weidenfeld & Nicolson Ltd., London, England, 1980; in U.S., published by Westview Press, Boulder, Colorado, 1980

# INDEX

Note: Animals included in this index are limited to those species that were highlighted by the Zoos & Aquariums with regard to captive breeding success, research projects or unique collections.